THE

Chicago Crime Commission

GANG BOOK

A detailed overview of street gangs in the Chicago metropolitan area.

chicago
crime
commission

C0-AQZ-499

Co-Editors:

James W. Wagner
President
Chicago Crime Commission

Kate Curran Kirby
Executive Vice President
Chicago Crime Commission

Principal Author & Researcher:

Kate Curran Kirby

Co-Authors:

Mars Eghigian, Jr.

Joseph Petrenko

A special thank you to Chicago Crime Commission Director of Operations Jeanette Callaway, General Counsel Jeannette Tamayo, Assistant Program Manager Valencia Lee and the Commission interns for their assistance in the development of this publication.

ISBN 0-9787471-0-0

ACKNOWLEDGEMENTS

The Chicago Crime Commission considers the development of this report to be an excellent example of the strong partnerships among law enforcement and others in the Chicago metropolitan area. The following persons and agencies have been especially valuable in providing information and their expertise for this report. Those interviewed in person are noted with an asterisk. Others have been interviewed through other means of communication or have reviewed the report before publication. Thank you to:

Bureau of Alcohol, Tobacco, Firearms & Explosives
Andrew L. Traver . . . . .Special Agent In Charge
Dana Nichols . . . . .Assistant Special Agent In Charge
* Michael G. Casey . . . . .Group Supervisor, Gangs North
Kevin McCann . . . . .Intelligence Group Supervisor

Chicago Police Department
* Philip J. Cline . . . . .Superintendent
Hiram Grau . . . . .Deputy Superintendent, Bureau of Investigative Services
* Michael Cronin . . . . . . .Deputy Chief, Narcotics and Gang Investigations
* John J. Risley . . . . .Deputy Superintendent, Bureau of Strategic Deployment
* Steve Caluris . . . . .Deputy Chief, Area 3 Patrol Division
* Steve Sesso . . . . .Sergeant, Deployment Operations Center
* Robert C. Buckley . . . . .Coordinator, Intergovernmental Affairs
* Robert Hargesheimer . . . . . . .Commander, Juvenile Advocacy Section
* John Kohles . . . . .Sergeant
* Rachel Johnston . . . . .Deputy Director, Research and Development
* Joe Kostuchowski . . . . .Sergeant
* Thomas Lemmer . . . . .Captain
Phil Williams . . . . .CHA Liaison
* David Franco . . . . .Drug and Gang House Enforcement Unit
* Eddie Yoshimura . . . . .Sergeant
* John Downes . . . . .Investigator, Asset Forfeiture Unit
Ken Boudreau . . . . .Commanding Officer, Asset Forfeiture Unit
Bee Cuello . . . . .Commander, 10th District
Steve Peterson . . . . .Commander, Area 4 Detective Division
Warren Richards . . . . .Sergeant, Area 4 Detective Division
Ray Kolasinski . . . . .Detective, Area 4

Chicago Public Schools
Arne Duncan . . . . .Chief Executive Officer
* Andres Durbak . . . . .Director, Safety and Security

Contributing Authors
Anne Keegan
Kenneth G. Kirby

Cook County Sheriff's Office
* Michael F. Sheahan . . . . .Cook County Sheriff
* Marjorie H. O'Dea . . . . .Chief of Police
* Thomas Kinsella . . . . .Deputy Chief
* Ellwood C. Egan (CCC Liaison) . . . . .Deputy Chief
* Joseph Vanacora . . . . .Commander
* Kevin Ruel . . . . .Lieutenant
* Andrew Douvris . . . . .Sergeant

Cook County State's Attorney's Office
Richard Devine . . . . .States Attorney
Brian Sexton . . . . .Supervisor, Gang Prosecution Unit

Drug Enforcement Administration, Chicago Field Division
* Richard W. Sanders .Special Agent in Charge
* Patrick J. O'Dea . . . . .Intelligence Group Supervisor
* Timothy J. Ogden . . . . .Associate Special Agent in Charge

DuPage County Sheriff's Office

Federal Bureau of Investigation National Intelligence
Matthew G. Kenyon

Federal Bureau of Investigation – Chicago Office
Robert D. Grant . . . . .Special Agent In Charge
* Denise Lecher . . . . .FBI Analyst
Lia Posada . . . . .Special Agent
Paul C. Bock . . . . .Acting Supervisory Special Agent, West Suburban Gang Task Force

HIDTA (High Intensity Drug Trafficking Area)
* Mary Kenny . . . . .Tactical Intelligence Coordinator
Lorena Butler . . . . .Intelligence Analyst

Illinois Attorney General's Office
Lisa Madigan . . . . .Illinois Attorney General

Illinois Criminal Justice Information Authority

Illinois Department of Corrections
Roger E. Walker Jr. . . . . .Director
Joseph Burke . . . . .Chief, Investigations and Intelligence
Manuel Acevedo . . . . .Commander of Intelligence
* Brad Curry . . . . .Deputy Commander – Central Intelligence Unit – Northern Region
Marvin Bateman . . . . .Officer, Gangster Disciple – Intelligence
Isidro Molina . . . . .Youth Supervisor II, Latin Folks
Jose Delgado . . . . .Officer, Latin King – Intelligence
Sean Furlow . . . . .Officer, White Supremists – Intelligence
Jason Bradley . . . . .Lieutenant, White Supremists – Intelligence
Bryan Kuder . . . . .Lieutenant, Bikers – Intelligence
Mike Magana . . . . .Officer, Black Gangster – Intelligence
Donald Enloe . . . . .Officer, Black P Stones – Intelligence
Lonn Howarter . . . . .Officer, Black Disciple – Intelligence
Brian Mumma . . . . .Officer, Vice Lord – Intelligence
Ken Hilgendorf . . . . .Officer, West Coast – Intelligence
Chris Marshall . . . . .Officer, Terrorism – Intelligence

Illinois State Police
* Kenneth A. Bouche . . . . .Deputy Director, Information and Technology
Tom Hiatt . . . . .Sergeant
Carl Anderson . . . . .Lieutenant, Zone 3
Mark Piccoli . . . . .Lieutenant, Zone 1

Kane County Sheriff's Office

Lake County Sheriff's Office

McHenry County Sheriff's Office

National Gang Crime Research Center
George Knox . . . . .Executive Director

Suburban Police Departments (82) That Returned The Gang Survey
See Section Three for Department Listing

Survey Analyst
John W. Binder

United States Attorney's Office, Northern District of Illinois
* David Hoffman . . . .(Former) Assistant U.S. Attorney
* David Weissman . . . . .Assistant U.S. Attorney

University of Chicago – Department of Sociology
Andrew V. Papachristos

University of Illinois – Chicago
Dr. John M. Hagedorn . . .Associate Professor, Dept. of Criminal Justice, College of Liberal Arts and Sciences, Great Cities Institute – University of Illinois at Chicago

chicago crime commission

79 West Monroe Street
Suite 801
Chicago, IL 60603-4906

Combating Crime in Metropolitan Chicago Since 1919

Dear Concerned Citizen:

This guide and training tool was developed to be of use to the most expert gang investigators, as well as to the parent, educator or business owner who may know little about Chicago metropolitan street gangs. It was designed to give the public the most complete and current information possible on the subject of gangs in a concise, easy-to-read manner.

The Chicago Crime Commission was able to produce this document due to the enthusiastic investment and strong partnership of numerous law enforcement and other sources. These sources, noted in the beginning of the book, provided the Commission with invaluable information and expert insight into the gang problems of today. We extend our sincere thanks to all of the individuals who helped us to bring you this invaluable resource.

There are an estimated 70 to 100 gangs in the Chicago metropolitan area with a membership of between 70,000 to 125,000. There are 10 to 20 gangs that are considered to be highly sophisticated. In Section One of this report, we will profile 56 street gangs, including *the largest Chicago area gangs* and *gangs to watch*. We will also discuss *suburban gangs,* providing new information based on a Crime Commission survey of over 80 suburban and county law enforcement departments and agencies.

In the City, the combined strategies of the Chicago Police and other law enforcement agencies have made great strides in effectively addressing gang crime. This success, however, has led to a concerning movement and growth of gangs in the suburbs.

While gangs continue to bring guns, drugs and violence into our communities, they are also making millions of dollars in fraudulent mortgage scams and by selling false identification. A few areas that law enforcement will need to monitor closely due to possible future gang interest include aiding terrorists, human trafficking and the expansion of dog fighting.

Gangs are active on many fronts, each of which has different levels of gang involvement and need different approaches for successful crime and violence reduction. Gangs are active on the streets, in the prisons, and in schools. They have infiltrated politics and criminal justice fields. This report discusses all of these areas.

It is also important for law enforcement and the public to understand how to recognize who and where the gang members are. Thus, the book includes gang maps, gang leader photos, gang colors, hand signs, graffiti, tattoos, and slang terms.

It is even more important to know when a gang member needs to be arrested and convicted and when he or she, instead, needs to be redirected into more positive life opportunities. It is the hope that this book will provide law enforcement with effective strategies for targeting the hardcore criminal, while at the same time providing the community, parents, teachers and youth with prevention and intervention assistance.

After extensive research and careful consideration, the Chicago Crime Commission has included a listing of *Recommended Strategies, Policies and Legislation on Gangs, Guns and Drugs.* We hope that you will find this book a useful tool in your work to make our city, our suburbs and most importantly, our children, safe from gang crime.

As a not-for-profit organization, we depend on your support to develop publications like this and to implement our many crime and violence reduction programs. If you would like to make a donation or learn more about the Chicago Crime Commission, please see Section Fourteen of this report or visit our website at www.chicagocrimecommission.org.

Sincerely,

J. R. Davis
Chairman of the Board
Chicago Crime Commission

James W. Wagner
President
Chicago Crime Commission

CHICAGO PUBLIC SCHOOLS

Office of Chief Executive Officer• 125 South Clark Street, 5th Floor • Chicago, Illinois 60603
Telephone 773/553-1500 • Fax 773/553-1501

Dear Concerned Citizen:

At the Chicago Public Schools, there is nothing more important to us than the safety of our students and staff. And we rely on the community and great partners like the Chicago Police Department, CAPS, and the Chicago Crime Commission for help in making our schools and the areas around them as safe as they can be.

We devote an unprecedented amount of security resources to our schools. And it's paid off, with fewer incidents and fewer weapons in and around our buildings. But one incident, one weapon is one too many. We need to keep getting better, and that means we need to stay on top of any threats to the safety of our schools and our students.

That's what makes the Chicago Crime Commission's "Gang Book" so valuable. Gangs and guns are the two biggest threats to our children. The more we know about their prevalence and allure, the better equipped we are to counteract their effect on our students.

Information is power, and the information in this book is critical for every school and every family in Chicago to have. We at the Chicago Public Schools are appreciative of the hard work of the Chicago Crime Commission, and we look forward to continuing to work with the Commission and all of our partners to make our schools and our communities safer.

Sincerely,

Arne Duncan
Chief Executive Officer

Richard M. Daley
Mayor

Department of Police • City of Chicago
3510 S. Michigan Avenue • Chicago, Illinois 60653

Philip J. Cline
Superintendent of Police

My Fellow Citizens,

It is my great honor to write this introduction to the Chicago Crime Commission's Gang Book.

As a career lawman I have spent almost four decades fighting crime in the City of Chicago. I have seen first hand the rampant devastation that gang crime carries with it. I have experienced the ruined lives, destroyed neighborhoods and demolished families that gang crime creates. I have seen the fear that street gangs bring, the decay they bring to the social fabric of our society, and the sad loss of life.

I know how deadly street gangs can be, how dangerous they are to innocent citizens and the most lethal in profitable organized crime enterprises in the history of the country.

The Chicago Crime Commission's publication "The Gang Book" is an essential, no-nonsense, factual encyclopedia that brings these criminal organizations out of the shadows and into the pages of a well organized, insightful, and articulate treatise that will be useful to crime fighters, parents, teachers and concerned citizens.

I had several thoughts as I read this remarkable book. Most books are written by writers. This one is written by the real experts in the field who give their best in the field. Their expertise comes not from reading but from doing it.

I am thankful to President James Wagner and Executive Vice President Kate Kirby for this fine piece of work. If knowledge is power, their work, and that of their collaborators, have given us in law enforcement, a very powerful tool.

On behalf of the Chicago Police Department I would like to thank the Chicago Crime Commission and pledge our continued support and partnership in the battle against gangs.

Sincerely,

Philip J. Cline
Superintendent of Police

Emergency: 9-1-1 • **Non-Emergency:** (Within City limits) 3-1-1 • **Non-Emergency:** (Outside City limits) 312-746-6000
TTY: 312-746-9715 • **E-mail:** police@ci.chi.il.us • **Website:** www.ci.chi.il.us/CAPS

5

TABLE OF CONTENTS

LAW ENFORCEMENT DEFINITION

A street gang is an organized group that participates in criminal, threatening or intimidating activity within the community. This anti-social group, usually of three or more individuals, evolves from within the community and has recognized leadership as well as a code of conduct. The group remains united during peaceful times as well as during times of conflict. A street gang is an organization that exhibits the following characteristics in varying degrees:

1. a gang name and recognizable symbols;

2. a definable hierarchy;

3. a geographic territory;

4. a regular meeting pattern;

5. a code of conduct; and

6. an organized, continuous course of criminal activity.

SCHOOL DEFINITION

Any ongoing organization or group of three or more persons having as one of its primary activities the commission of one or more criminal acts, which has an identifiable name or identifying sign or symbol, and whose members individually or collectively engage or have engaged in a pattern of criminal activity.

SECTION 1

Gang Profiles

The United States Attorney's Office — Northern District of Illinois estimates that there are 75-100 gangs in Chicago with a membership of approximately 70,000. There are 10-20 highly sophisticated gangs in Chicago.

In August 2005, CHRISC, (Chicago Police Criminal History Records Information System) identified approximately 70 street gangs with a membership of at least 25,000 in the greater Chicago metropolitan area. Other agencies such as the National Drug Intelligence Center (NDIC) and the Department of Justice (DOJ), in the past, have suggested the numbers to be higher. For instance, in October 2004, the DOJ estimated the Chicago membership of one gang alone to be 30,000. NDIC suggested the number of gangs as 125 with a projected membership of 125,000. The figures will always be somewhat fluid with small gangs coming and departing, membership numbers fluctuating, territories shifting and leadership roles changing. Yet, with this said, there are street gangs known to law enforcement as the "super" street gangs because of the dominance in both membership numbers and controlled territory. The largest street gangs in Chicago appear to be the Gangster Disciple Nation (GDN), Black Gangsters/New Breeds (BG), Latin Kings (LKs), the Black P Stone Nation, Vice Lords (VLs), the Four Corner Hustlers and the Maniac Latin Disciples (MLDs). These gangs account for more than 80% of gang membership locally.

Many of today's most powerful Chicago gangs tried to mask their illegal gang activity in the 1970s and appear as legitimate organizations wanting to serve their communities. They were quite effective in their efforts and received major dollar grants from private foundations and the federal government. Some experts believe that this funding enabled them to strengthen their gang recruitment and illegal activities, thus creating the foundation for their "super gang" status.

People, Folks and Independents

In the mid-1970s, Latin gangs, African American gangs and Caucasian gangs merged into two major groupings, the "People" and the "Folks." "Independents" refers to gangs not involved in these two alliances. These groups were formed in the penitentiary system by incarcerated gang members seeking protection through coalition building. The alliances were hammered out the same way that modern nations establish national boundaries and formalize peace treaties. Until recent years, these alliances were respectfully maintained on Chicago's streets and the People and Folks were strong rivals and enemies.

In past years more than today, gang members would "represent" or identify themselves as either People or Folks in many ways. The "People" gangs would represent to the left - wearing hats with visors to the left side; earrings in the left ear; the left shoe tied a certain way; the pant leg on the left side cuffed; the left pocket hanging out, etc. The "Folks" gangs would do the same, but they would represent to the right rather than the left. In the past, drive-by-shootings often occurred as a result of a "Folk" or a "People" being spotted in an enemy's territory.

Now, although street gangs still align themselves with the People or the Folks, law enforcement agencies all seem to agree that these alliances mean little. "People" gangs will not hesitate to make deals with "Folks" gangs if enough money can be gained. Today, it's all about the money.

THE SEVEN LARGEST GANGS

NOTE: Throughout this report, Chicago neighborhoods are referenced by name. To see the location of the neighborhoods, refer to the Chicago Neighborhoods Map on page 43.

GANGSTER DISCIPLE NATION (GDN) (GANGSTER DISCIPLES AND BLACK DISCIPLES) (Alliance – Folks)

The GDN was founded in the early 1960s when the Black Disciples (BDs), under the leadership of David Barksdale, united with the Gangster Nation led by Larry Hoover. Barksdale became supreme leader with Hoover second in command. Upon Barksdale's death in 1974, two factions developed within the GDN.

In 1973, Hoover was sentenced to 150-200 years in prison for murder and later received a life term for a federal narcotics conviction. While Hoover was still thought to be running the Gangster Disciple Nation from behind prison walls in Illinois, Jerome "Shorty" Freeman and several other GDN leaders severed ties and returned to the streets as the Black Disciples. After this split, Hoover continued to run the present day Gangster Disciples or GDs from prison. Out of the split also came a third group — the Black Gangsters street gang (see Black Gangsters or New Breeds for description). Eventually each gang developed their own particular culture, symbols and territories.

Gangster Disciples

Today, the GDs are considered one of the most structured and largest Chicago street gangs with CHRISC identifying at least 7,300 members locally and with some estimates running as high as 30,000. Since the federal indictments/ convictions of most of Hoover's board members, the hierarchical structure of the GDs is thought to be in some disarray.

Still, the Chicago Police Department (CPD) has recently identified at least 36 GD factions in the City. The GD's main gang rivals include the Latin Kings, Black Disciples, Black P Stones and the Vice Lords. Membership consists mostly of African American youths who operate in a vast domain including Englewood, Roseland, Morgan Park, Garfield Park, Lawndale, the Near West Side,

Bronzeville, Washington Park, Calumet Heights, Avalon Park, South Chicago, many Chicago suburbs and in an estimated 30 states across the country.

Many of the high-rise projects in which they operated such as the Robert Taylor Homes, Cabrini-Green, Stateway Gardens, Henry Horner Homes and Rockwell Gardens have been or will be demolished. This will likely upset some of their activities by forcing the gangs to relocate to different geographical locations — some of which may be controlled by rival gangs.

Principal criminal activities include narcotics trafficking, homicide, aggravated battery, armed robbery, arson, auto theft, theft, extortion (street taxes on independent drug dealers), kidnapping, money laundering, mortgage fraud and assault.

Gangster Disciples identifiers include: black and blue colors

Symbols: the six-point star, the numeral "6" or three "6" numerals in a triangle form, pitchforks, heart with wings, a tail and horns, a three-point crown, numerals "7 4" or "2 7 4" signifying letters "GD" or "BGD."

Current status of some reputed GD members:

- Larry Hoover, "Chairman of the Board" of the GDs, is serving a life term in ADX in Florence, Colorado.

- Gregory Shell, reputed second-in-command, is serving a life term in ADX in Florence, Colorado.

- Jimmy Gholson, third ranking GD under Hoover, is serving a life term in USP Marion, Illinois.

- Darryl Johnson, GD board of directors, is on death row in USP Terre Haute.

- Melvin Haywood, high-ranking leader, is on parole.

Black Disciples

In the early 1980s, the Black Disciples fought a bloody war with the GDs over street turf to sell narcotics. Then, in 1990, Freeman was sentenced to 28 years in prison following a narcotics conviction. Though incarcerated, Freeman was thought to still command his BD nation. However, according to recent federal court testimony, the BDs on the street are alleged to be under the leadership of Marvel "King" Thompson. Law enforcement

*Gangster Disciples honor a fallen member.
He was killed with an AK47 on April 25, 2006.*

shootings and assault are frequent means for the street gang to enforce their creed. Perhaps the most public BD episode occurred in 1994 when an 11-year old BD member was sent to kill a GD; instead, he only wounded him. In the process, however, he killed an innocent young female bystander. When news of the murder caused an uproar, the BDs had their own 11-year old assassin murdered.

Black Disciples identifiers include:
black with red and blue colors

Symbols: winged heart with combination of: crossed pitchforks, devils horns and/or tail, crossed pitchforks, letters "BD", or numbers "78" signifying the split with the GD Nation. The six-point star is used by the BDs and each point symbolizes love, life, loyalty, unity, knowledge and understanding.

Current status of some reputed BD members:

- In March 2005, Jerome "Shorty" Freeman was released on parole. Prior to release, he stated that he had stepped down as head of the BDs.

- Marvel Thompson, acting king of the BDs, is awaiting sentencing.

- Melvin Herbert, BD "Chairman of the Board", is awaiting sentencing.

- Arthur Robinson, reputed BD board member, is serving a term in USP McCreary until 2020.

- Albert Span, a reputed BD King, is serving a life sentence in federal prison.

- Donnell Jehan, aka "Scan" and reputed BD King, is a fugitive from justice.

---

sources state that because of the indictment and arrest of many GD leaders, the BDs under Thompson expanded their operations on the south side. However, on May 12, 2004, the FBI/CPD Joint Task Force on Gangs arrested Marvel Thompson. He and other top BD members/leaders were indicted in federal court on conspiracy, drug and money laundering charges as the result of a six-year federal investigation conducted by the FBI, Chicago Police and the Internal Revenue Service. With the arrest of Thompson, his reputed second in command and Chairman of the Board, Melvin Herbert, and nine other high-ranking members, the hierarchical structure of the BDs should be in some disarray. According to law enforcement sources, Freeman was released from prison in March 2005 on active parole and should be considered a "person of interest."

CHRISC estimates there are nearly 1,300 Black Disciple members. Gang members are primarily of African American origin. The BDs are active in 13 police districts within the City of Chicago with spheres of influence generally including many of the same areas and housing projects as the GDs with whom they are usually at battle.

Principal criminal activities include drug trafficking, the sale of illegal firearms, armed robbery, theft, extortion of independent drug dealers and gambling. The latter consists of operating large crap games and dog fighting. Murder, drive-by

BLACK GANGSTERS OR NEW BREEDS
(Alliance – Folks or Independent)

The Black Gangsters or New Breeds street gang takes its origin from within the Gangster Disciple Nation. In the 1960s, street gangs in Chicago were joining forces and becoming larger, structured organizations. The Black Gangster Disciple Nation was one of these groups and was led by David Barksdale and Larry Hoover. In 1972, Barksdale died from complications resulting from a gun shot wound. Hoover made Barksdale into a Martyr-type figure, preaching the teachings of "King David" (Barksdale) and making himself the supreme leader and king of the organization.

Following the death of Barksdale, leadership roles within the gang were challenged. The result was the splintering of the group into their original two nations, the Disciple Nation (Black Disciples) and the Gangster Nation (Gangster Disciples). During this period of transition, many members who vied for leadership roles in the organization formed splinter groups when they were unsuccessful. One of these members, George Davis, would eventually form the Black Gangsters.

George Davis, a.k.a. Boonie Black, was originally the leader of the Black Gangster Disciples on the west side of the city in the early 1970s. He was incarcerated in the Illinois Department of Corrections (IDOC) at the time. In 1987, Boonie Black was stabbed by members of the Black Souls street gang while in prison and one of his lieutenants was killed. The incident arose when one of his high ranking members left the gang to become a member of the Black Souls. Following the incidents, Boonie Black redirected his west side group, dropping "Disciples" from their name. It appears that Boonie Black either felt targeted or didn't receive support from his gang due to the close associations between the Black Souls and the Gangster Disciples. Boonie Black then began to call his west side group the Black Gangsters.

Early Black Gangster/LLL (Love, Life, Loyalty) leaders were fascinated with the Italian Mafia and lived near Little Italy. This fascination with organized crime shaped early Black Gangster/LLL thinking and leadership structures which are still utilized by the organization today. Black Gangster originators used history as a basis for shaping their literature. Some of their literature theories can be traced back to Hannibal, the King of Carthage, Africa. Hannibal married a Sicilian Princess during the second Punic war and led his people in a successful attempt to conquer Europe. During the war, Africans and Sicilians integrated, creating mixed children. History alleges that after betrayal by his own men, Hannibal decided to leave Sicily. However, he entrusted his son with the "Code of Silence" and laws to protect it. Black Gangster/LLL originators decided they would adopt this "Code of Silence" and adapt it to their own culture. It is similar to the Italian organized crime code of "Omerta", but conforms to their African American heritage.

Another Italian organized crime link created by early GDN leaders was the "Royal Family" concept. The original "Royal Family" was supposed to contain the leader for each major gang in Chicago. This concept was created to mirror the Italian organized crime concept of a "Commission" that acts as a governing body over all members of several different crime families. The "Royal Family" concept did not stick with other gangs. However, it remained intact within the Black Gangster/LLL gang. Black Gangster/LLL "Royal Family" members were the "top notch guys" under the six point star.

In the 1980s, the gang tried to further separate themselves from their old gang ties and changed their name to the "Triple L" or "Tre L." This was derived from part of their literature (Love, Life & Loyalty).

The "LLL" (Love, Life, Loyalty) concept was adopted by Maurice "Baldy" Jackson, Samuel "King Ram" Lawrence and George "Boonie Black" Davis. Allegedly, "Baldy" was represented by the first or "Love L", "King Ram" was represented by the second or "Life L", and "Boonie Black" was represented by the third or "Loyalty L" because he was the "LLL" architect.

It has been stated that members of the Black Disciples and Gangster Disciples street gangs joined the Triple L group because of the high street taxes being imposed by Larry Hoover and the lack of legal aid that their incarcerated members were receiving. In the early 1990s, Davis changed the name once more, calling the gang the "New Breeds." This is the name most often used by the gang today as it continues its attempt to control narcotic operations throughout the City.

The heart of the gang has been located within the A.B.L.A. homes along Roosevelt Road in the 12th Police District. The A.B.L.A. homes are a combination of four housing projects: Grace Abbott Homes, Robert Brooks Homes and Brooks Extensions, Loomis Courts and Jane Addams Homes. While the original housing projects are being demolished, the gang still continues to operate in the area. The gang also has a strong influence in Garfield Park, Lawndale and in the K-town area of Chicago's west side. The Black Gangsters, or New Breeds, are active in seven Police Districts within the City of Chicago and are growing every day.

Rank structure within the gang consists of Don, King, Prince, General, Field Marshall, Commander, Lieutenant and members. Boonie Black has been recently released from prison and is still recognized as the reputed leader of the New Breed street gang.

Their main income is derived from narcotic trafficking, but they are also involved in illegal firearms trafficking, homicide, extortion, armed robbery, theft and assault.

Black Gangsters (New Breeds) identifiers include: black and gray colors

Symbols: winged heart with combination of crossed pitchforks, devil's horns and/or tail, letters "LLL", Roman numeral III, sword, shotgun.

Current status of some reputed members:

■ Jeffrey Denson, a ranking member, is serving a prison term in Menard Correctional Center until at least 2022.

LATIN KINGS
(Alliance-People)

The Latin Kings (LKs), the oldest and largest Hispanic-led gang, is thought to have formed in the mid-1950s or 1960s in the Humboldt Park area of Chicago with the initial aim of defending Hispanics from encroaching African American gangs. CHRISC has identified at least 2,700 members. The gang is active in nearly every Hispanic neighborhood and has 70 or more street factions. Over the years, it has expanded nationally under a highly organized and structured leadership. Chapters exist in at least 33 other states, including New York, Indiana, Michigan, Florida and California. In the Chicagoland area, the LKs have two main groups: a southern faction and a northern/west side faction. Both have regional officers in charge and supervisors (Incas) in charge of specific territories.

The LK motto is "Once a King, always a King". Of the factions known to exist, the Mexican factions formerly were identified by a five-point crown symbol (representing honor, obedience, sacrifice, righteousness and love) with the colors black (symbolizing knowledge of superiors past and present), red (symbolizing blood of brothers lost defending the Almighty Latin King Nation [ALKN] and crown), and gold (symbolizing the sun shining on the ALKN crown). The Puerto Rican factions were represented by a three-point crown with similar attributes. Today, the only colors used are black and gold and the five point star is the primary symbol as differences (represented by the three point star) are no longer valid since the gang is so racially diverse.

In Chicagoland, Gustavo "Lord Gino" Colon is the reputed leader of the northern/west side LKs, while Raul "Baby King" Gonzalez allegedly runs the southern LKs. Even after arrest and confinement on a heroin charge, Gino Colon continued to command the gang from his prison cell. In 1997, he was charged with running a drug ring from state prison and is now serving a life sentence in the Florence, Colorado ADMAXX prison. And though several other leaders have been arrested, authorities believe they continue to possess the ability to coordinate the gang from their cells.

Police search a reputed Latin King member.

Gang membership consists primarily of Hispanics, but also includes Caucasians, African American and Middle Eastern individuals. Active in many parts of the City, the LKs retain great influence over the Hispanic populations on the southwest side of Chicago.

Criminal activities include the sale of narcotics (especially cocaine), identity theft, auto theft, robbery and extortion. Murder, drive-by shootings and intimidation are used as enforcement tools. They are allied with the Vice Lords (but have been in conflict with Vice Lords around Humboldt Park) while rivals include the Gangster Disciples and several smaller Latin gangs aligned with the Folks.

Latin King identifiers include:
black and gold colors

Symbols: the letters "L K", "A L K", or "A L K N", a five-point crown, lions, a five-point star or cross with five rays, the numeral "5."

A.L.M.I.G.H.T.Y. (A Love Measured In Great Harmony Towards Yahve.)

A.D.C. (Amor De Corona/King Love)

A.M.O.R. (Term used to show love and respect for one another and it is an acronym for Almighty Masters of Righteousness.)

Current status of some reputed members:

■ Gustavo Colon, Son of King for the Almighty Latin Kings Nation, is serving a life term in ADX in Florence, Colorado.

■ Jorge Martinez, Colon's second-in-command, is serving a term in USP Allenwood until 2027.

■ Raul Gonzalez, Son of King of the South Side Latin Kings, is serving a term in USP Pollack until 2007.

■ Macario Veizca, Gonzalaz's second-in-command, is serving a term in FCI Lexington until 2018.

■ William Cabrera, council member (now Corona), is serving a life term in Tamms.

■ Edward Rodriguez, council member (now Corona), is serving a prison term in Tamms until at least 2027.

■ Jorge Parades, council member, awaits deportation.

BLACK P STONE NATION
(Alliance-People)

In 1959, Eugene "Bull" Hairston, along with five other neighborhood friends, decided to form a neighborhood gang in the Woodlawn community on Chicago's south side in an attempt to defend themselves and other neighborhood youths from being intimidated by other gangs in the area. Hairston and his friends subsequently named the group the Blackstones, in reference to the geographical area that the group considered their territory (63rd-67th & Blackstone). Shortly thereafter, the group's name was expanded to the "Blackstone Rangers."

The first core group of the Blackstone Rangers consisted of Hairston, Charles Edwards-Bey, Wesley Brown, Ernest Vaughn, Charles Knox, Henry "Mickey" Cogwell and Jeff "Angel or Malik" Fort. At that time, Hairston, Fort and Cogwell were considered the overall leaders of the gang and by the mid-to-late 1960s they had turned the small neighborhood gang into a mini-organized crime syndicate absorbing numerous surrounding gangs.

As the gang continued to rapidly grow in numbers, Hairston, Fort and Cogwell decided to form the "Main 21", which consisted of 21 of the most highly respected Blackstones and would become the ruling body of the ever-growing Blackstone Rangers, with each member ultimately receiving their own branch or "set." Later, at a time when the "black revolution" was beginning to peak, leaders of the group renamed themselves the Black P Stone Nation. The letter P is said to represent People, Power, Prosperity, Peace, Potential and Progress.

In the 1960s, Jeff Fort applied for and received thousands of dollars in grants for inner-city development, promising to use the taxpayers' money for the education of children and expansion of jobs. Instead, the money helped finance organizational campaigns for gang recruitment, the purchase and sale of weapons and a terror campaign aimed at the small businessmen of Chicago's Woodlawn community. In 1972, Fort was sent to USP Leavenworth (KS) for misappropriation of federal funds.

While in prison Fort adopted an Islamic doctrine, modeled after that of the Moorish Science Temple, for his organization. During that time, Fort, along with leaders of the Latin Kings and Vice Lords, helped form the "People Alliance" in the prison system. Also, Fort began to use the moniker "Prince Imam Malik." Upon his release from federal prison, Fort, now the predominant leader of the gang, directed that the Black P Stone Nation would be named the El Rukns (Arabic for "The Stones"). This direction was not received as well as Fort was expecting as several Black P Stone leaders not only refused to become El Rukns but questioned Fort's declaration that he was the overall leader. Additionally, several of these leaders, including Mickey Cogwell, openly voiced their objections to Fort who, intent on demonstrating his seriousness and intolerance for insubordination, allegedly ordered Cogwell's murder.

During a federal investigation, it was learned that Fort ran his enterprise from a federal prison through the help of three-way calling and the use of a coded language. Federal agents listened in during the mid-to-late 1980s and found Fort planning to make money through the sale of cocaine and heroin, extortion, government fraud, real estate schemes and murder. In 1986, Fort, along with other high ranking El Rukns, was indicted for attempting to purchase high powered weapons from Libya to commit terrorist acts against the United States government. Jeff Fort was sentenced to an additional 80 years in federal prison. One of Fort's co-defendants in this case was another El Rukn named Melvin Mays. According to transcripts, Mays attempted to purchase an anti-tank weapon from a man who turned out to be an undercover FBI agent.

On the streets, the original name Black P Stone Rangers has resurfaced. In 1999, several other top BPS leaders were arrested during "Operation Mo-Down," a Chicago Police operation. Various BPS branches began to feud amongst themselves for positions of power and drug territory. To date, a few pocket groups of Black P Stones remain loyal to Bull Hairston and do not recognize Jeff Fort as their leader; however, the majority of the Black P Stones identify Jeff Fort (aka "Chief Malik") as the overall leader of their organization.

The Black P Stones are currently the second largest street gang in Chicago, next to the Gangster Disciples, and have an estimated membership of 20,000 on the streets of Chicago and over 3,000 in prison systems throughout the U.S. They control a large portion of the north Englewood and South Shore communities, and have strongholds along Halsted, Jeffrey, Cottage Grove, Stony Island, 87th street and 79th street in the Auburn-Gresham, Calumet, Woodlawn and Burnside communities within the City of Chicago. They have migrated throughout the state and have strongholds in the following communities: Alton, Alsip, Aurora, Bloomington-Normal, Bolingbrook, Calumet Park, Carbondale, Carpentersville, Champaign-Urbana, Crestwood, Decatur, Dolton, East St. Louis, Elgin, Evanston, Ford Heights, Galesburg, Harvey, Hanover Park, Hoffman Estates, Joliet, Justice, Kankakee, Markham, Maywood, North Chicago, Peoria, Quad City Area, Quincy, Robbins, Rockford and Schaumburg. The Gang membership is primarily African American.

Other affected Cities/States include, but are not limited to:

Little Rock, AR	Minneapolis, MN
Oak Forrest, AR	St. Paul, MN
Los Angeles, CA (Blood Stones)	Mississippi
Oakland, CA (Blood Stones)	St. Louis, MO
Sacramento, CA	Atlantic City, NJ
Florida	New York
Jacksonville, FL (Blood Stones)	Cleveland, OH
Atlanta, GA	Columbus, OH
Gary, IN	South Carolina
Hammond, IN	South Dakota
Indianapolis, IN	Tennessee
Michigan City, IN	Houston, TX
South Bend, IN	Beloit, WI
Burlington, IA	Kenosha, WI
Cedar Rapids, IA	Madison, WI
Kentucky	Milwaukee, WI
Massachusetts	Racine, WI
Detroit, MI	Virginia
Flint, MI	

Criminal activities consist of graffiti, assault, narcotics sales, drive-by shootings, extortion and murder.

The closest allies of this gang include the Latin Kings (Chicago based), Bloods (West Coast street gang), Black Guerilla Family *or Front* (prison gang) and the Melanics (Michigan based gang).

Black P Stone identifiers include:

Red – "Represents the blood shed by our forefathers from the time we were stolen from the shores of Africa to this very day. It represents the blood and lives that have been sacrificed and lost in the struggle for our nation by our brothers and sisters. It represents the blood that will be shed in the future as we engage in this struggle to put every block of the pyramid back in its proper place and order."

Black – "Represents the hue of that perfect seed that we descended from (but not our race or nationality). It represents the deaths and oppression that our people have suffered. It represents the soil of our motherland, Africa. It's symbolic of the condition that our African tribe is in, here in North America."

Green – "Represents the growth, prosperity and balance of our nation. It represents our children and unborn seeds that are the purity and future of our nation."

Symbols:

Five Point Star – Represents their affiliation to the "People" Alliance; the five points of this star also represents the "Five highest principles known to man: Life, Truth, Peace, Freedom and Justice."

Crescent Moon – Represents peace and unity.

"All seeing eye" – "360 degrees of pure wisdom, knowledge and understanding."

21 Stone Pyramid – Represents the "Main 21," or original governing body, and the 21 branches of the Black P Stone Nation.

Rising Sun – Represents "a Nation on the rise, a new day, a new era of time and the light that shows the way."

"Circle 7" – 7 surrounded by a circle broken into four parts representing Birth, Life, Mortality and Death; Seven is considered the perfect number known to man.

Aliases:

"BPSN" (Black P Stone Nation), "Blackstones," "El Rukns," "Stones" and "Mo's."

Current status of some reputed members:

- Jeff "Malik" Fort remains in federal custody in USP Marion and is not scheduled for parole until November 2038.

- Watkeeta "Keeta" Valenzuela, second-in-command, is serving a federal term in USP Leavenworth until at least January 2023.

- Randy "Black Ruben" Dillard, leader of the Rubenites faction, is currently on parole.

- Robert "Buttons" East, leader of the Titanic Stones faction, is currently on parole.

- Jakie "Jack Black" Kelly, leader of the Jet Black Stones faction, was released from parole.

VICE LORDS
(Alliance-People)

In 1958 in the St. Charles, Illinois reformatory for boys, several African American young men from an area known as North Lawndale formed a new "club." The club was given the title of "Vice Lords." The meaning of the word "Vice" was taken from a dictionary meaning "to have a tight hold" or "keeping it tight and not letting go." The newly formed club was led by an intelligent and ruthless individual identified as Edward "Pepalo" Perry. The Lawndale population was rapidly changing from a predominantly Caucasian neighborhood to an African American neighborhood and was considered a breeding ground for delinquent groups that were primarily organized for fighting. As this group was gradually released from custody, they returned to the Lawndale community, continued to "socialize" and fight and subsequently began to recruit other area African Americans. As a result, the Vice Lords quickly grew in numbers and were constantly involved in conflicts with other neighborhood "clubs." The Vice Lords were a formidable and feared adversary due to their violent behavior, use of intimidation and extortion tactics. These tactics placed fear in the citizens of the Lawndale community.

By 1964, the Vice Lords became a primary target for law enforcement due to their illegal activities, which included robberies, thefts, assaults, batteries, intimidation and extortion. As a result, the Vice Lord leadership saw an immediate need to change the public's perception of their organization. They added the word "Conservative" to the club's name in an effort to soften their image. (The Conservative Vice Lord faction of the Vice Lords is the foundation for the entire Vice Lord Nation or "VLN".) The Conservative Vice Lords also implemented new logos such as the top hat, gloves and a cane to advertise their new image. During this transition, the Conservative Vice Lords advertised themselves as a community outreach group and petitioned for a new chapter under the name "Conservative Vice Lord Incorporated (CVL, Inc.)."

The Conservative Vice Lord, Inc. and their leaders were initially successful in changing their public appearance and they began receiving positive notoriety from community leaders and politicians for their efforts. The Conservative Vice Lords even established a peace treaty with another rival gang, the Blackstone Rangers, and they worked jointly in repairing their image. CVL, Inc. established various recreational areas for neighborhood youth, such as teen centers, which were used as CVL meeting places after hours.

Around 1970, CVL, Inc. and two of their leaders, Alfonso Alfred and Bobby Gore, had successfully applied for and received $275,000 in grant money from the Rockefeller Foundation. The Rockefeller Foundation was unaware that this organization would grow into a powerful street gang. By 1970, the Vice Lords were also successful in converting all the neighborhood cliques (the Cherokees, the Morphines, the Commanchees, the Continental Pimps, the Imperial Chaplains, the Clovers, the Cobras and the Braves) in the Lawndale area under the Vice Lord Nation. Regardless of the perception that CVL Inc. attempted to convey to the public, it soon became apparent that they were, without a doubt, still a criminal element. The Lawndale residents were now witnessing the introduction of narcotics into their community, along with an increasing number of crimes and incidents involving intimidation, extortion and an occasional murder of a business owner who refused to pay for "protection." Lawndale citizens who witnessed crimes were also subjected to similar tactics. These activities brought negative publicity and a loud public outcry from the community. Due to public pressure, local leaders and politicians demanded a federal investigation into the apparent fraud/misuse of grant monies received by CVL Inc. from the

Rockefeller Foundation. As a result of their activities, several CVL leaders were subsequently arrested and incarcerated.

In the early 1980s, the overall leadership of the CVLs had changed. Eddie "Pepalo" Perry and Alphonso Alfred had passed away and Bobby Gore was incarcerated for murder. Samuel "Mahdi" Smith and a younger hard-core CVL Enforcer identified as Willie "Rieco" Johnson (the Minister of Justice) allegedly assumed control over the Conservative Vice Lord Nation.

In the 1990s, Johnson authored a new concept to mask the organization's ideology using the guidelines of Islamic religion. The concept was introduced as the "Almighty Lords of Islam" (L.O.I). The L.O.I. literature outlined and addressed new guidelines for the CVL Nation. A few of these include:

The Flag – The emblem and a symbol of knowledge relating to Black history and cultural position. The flag is also symbolic of the entire L.O.I. and consists of the following: 1. Circle 2. Fire 3. Darkness 4. Moons 5. Star 6. Pyramid Triangle 7. Sun 8. Hat 9. Cane 10. Gloves.

The Rules – There are 50 outlined rules under the L.O.I. literature.

Principles of Law – There are eight Principles of Law outlined under the L.O.I.

Code of Conduct – each code is outlined – 1. Respect 2. Discipline 3. Meetings 4. Dues 5. Horseplay 6. Fighting 7. Movement 8. Summary

Chain of Command – Chief Elite – Minister of Justice – Elites – Minister of Command – Lieutenant (assistant to the M.O.C.) – Minister

The Current Generation – Today the entire Vice Lord Nation recognizes the deceased national leader of the Conservative Vice Lords, Samuel "Mahdi" Smith, by celebrating his birthday on September 13th. Madhi was killed on November 8, 1993.

Willie Johnson (aka "Reico," "Ol' Man," "Rahim Justice El," "the Minister of Justice"), is currently incarcerated in Menard Correctional Center and is serving an indeterminate sentence for murder. Inmate Johnson legally changed his name to Rahim Justice El on September 30, 1992. Also at that time, he formally requested to change his religious denomination from Baptist to Sunni Muslim. Johnson is the reputed national level leader of the Conservative Vice Lords with major influence within the prison and on the streets.

The headquarters of the Conservative Vice Lord Nation is referred to as the "Holy City" and is located in the vicinity of 16th and Pulaski.

It is important to note that the Vice Lord Nation includes numerous gangs in addition to the original Conservative Vice Lord faction. Some of these include: Cicero Insane Vice Lords, Ebony Vice Lords, Executioner Vice Lords, Imperial Insane Vice Lords, Mafia Insane Vice Lords, Renegade Vice Lords, Traveler Vice Lords, Undertaker Vice Lords and the Unknown Vice Lords.

Today, CHRISC has identified at least 3,600 VLN members with other estimates as high as 30,000. Membership is predominantly African American. Their sphere of influence encompasses low income neighborhoods directly west of the Loop to as far north as Howard and as far south as Altgeld Gardens.

Primary criminal activities include the sale of narcotics, extortion (street tax on independent drug dealers), robbery, auto theft, theft and arson, with murder and assault as means of enforcing their territory. They have also become sophisticated in their activities and are very involved in mortgage fraud, credit card fraud and money laundering.

Vice Lord identifiers include:
black and red or black and gold colors

Symbols: a five-point star, crescent moons, a "playboy" bunny with bowtie, glove, cane, top hat, martini glass, dice, dollar signs or circle with fire.

Current status of some reputed members:

- Anthony Harris, leader of the Cicero Vice Lords, was released from IDOC on May 24, 2006.

- Willie Johnson, leader of the Conservative Vice Lords, is serving a term in MCC with his full term to expire in 2015.

- Arter Clay, a founding member of the Ebony Vice Lord faction, is eligible for parole in 2007.

- Roosevelt Clay, reputed gang leader of the Ebony Vice Lords, was sentenced on April 12, 2006 to a 23 year term in IDOC. He is currently in Stateville.

- Willie Jones, reputed leader of the Imperial Insane Vice Lords faction, was paroled in September 2005.

- Leonard Lofton, reputed gang leader of the Imperial Insane Vice Lords, is serving a prison term in Galesburg Correctional Center until at least 2006.

- Mather Williams, second-in-command of the Imperial Insane Vice Lords, was released in July 2002.

- Troy Martin, leader of the Mafia Insane Vice Lords is a pre-trial inmate in MCC Chicago.

- Donell Simons, reputed gang leader of the Mafia Insane Vice Lords, is in federal custody awaiting trial.

- Calvin Hunt, second-in-command of the Mafia Insane Vice Lords, was released from prison in August 1995.

- Henry Gaston, reputed gang leader of the Renegade Vice Lords, was released from prison in November 2000.

- John Taylor, an institutional leader of the Renegade Vice Lords, is serving a prison term in Western Correctional Center until at least 2010.

- Eddie Richardson, King for the Undertaker Vice Lords, is serving a life term in USP Terre Haute, Indiana.

- Carmen Tate, reputed gang leader for the Undertaker Vice Lords, is serving a life term in USP Terre Haute, Indiana.

- Kerry Dockery, high-ranking gang leader for the Undertaker Vice Lords, is serving a prison term in Jacksonville Correctional Center until at least 2006. As of this printing, he remains incarcerated.

- Willie Lloyd, Nation King for the Unknown Vice Lords, was released from a prison term in March 2005. Lloyd is a quadriplegic due to gun shot wounds.

- Tyrone Williams, reputed gang leader for the Unknown Vice Lords, is serving a prison term in Tamms until at least 2028.

- Andrew Paterson, national leader of the Traveling Vice Lords, is serving a life term in FCI Memphis.

- Terry Young, a former high-ranking Traveling Vice Lord, is serving a life term in MCC Chicago.

- Darren Jones, reputed gang leader of the Traveling Vice Lords, was paroled August 2005.

FOUR CORNER HUSTLERS
(Alliance – People)

The Four Corner Hustlers are one of the largest Chicago street gangs. "King" Walter Wheat ("Walt" or "Al-Bahdee Hodari"), Freddy Gage, Jr. ("Al-Malik Hodari"), Monroe Banks, Jr. ("Money" or "Al-Ghani") and Richard Goodwin ("Lefthand" or "Al-Mustafa") founded the Four Corner Hustlers on the west side during the early 1970s. Most Hustlers today recognize Walter Wheat as the national founder. Shortly after they were founded, the Hustlers allied themselves with the Vice Lords. As they began to operate in the Garfield Park and Austin areas, "Money" Banks rose to power and those Hustlers who identified with him differentiated themselves by adopting a black diamond in their logo.

By 1993, three Hustler leaders had died or were killed. One of the young Hustlers who emerged to leadership was Angelo Roberts. Under Roberts, the Hustler's relationship with the Vice Lords weakened significantly and the Hustlers began to undercut the amount of street taxes set by the Vice Lords.

Roberts also masterminded a plot in the 1990s to blow up the Chicago Police Department's Area 4 Headquarters at Harrison and Kedzie using a M72A2 LAWS rocket anti-tank weapon. Roberts declared all-out war on the Chicago Police because of a grudge he held against the police for cracking down on his drug operations and for numerous arrests. Several gang members were arrested in connection with the bomb plot. However, Roberts remained at large until January 1995, when his frozen body was found in the trunk of a car with his throat slashed. Roberts was believed to be involved in at least two murders, including the July 1994 slaying of Walter Wheat, the founder of the gang.

Ray Longstreet then assumed leadership of the Hustlers and re-affirmed ties to the Vice Lords, especially in correctional institutions. Since that time, he was arrested, served time on drug related charges, was released in 2004 and was recently arrested again in the federal investigation "Operation Street Sweeper."

In the past decade, the Hustlers have greatly expanded their membership and territory throughout the south side and the far south suburbs. The mostly African American membership has been identified in as many as 54 Chicago neighborhood "sets." Numerous others have been documented in Chicago's suburbs, in other Illinois cities and towns, in the neighboring states of Indiana and Wisconsin, and as far away as New York, Texas and Washington.

While maintaining a certain partiality towards independence, they still maintain strong ties to the Vice Lords. The Hustler membership prides itself on its money making capacity. Besides assault, murder and graffiti, crime activities include armed robbery, extortion, drug trafficking, renting out drug turf to independent dealers, prostitution, firearms sales and laundering money through businesses owned by the gang.

Four Corner Hustlers identifiers include: black and gold, black and red, or black and white color schemes.

Symbols: the numeral "4" with letters "C" and "H" combined with possibly a black diamond, a five-point star, cane, top hat, "playboy" bunny, dollar signs and dice.

Current status of some reputed members:

- Former chief of the Four Corner Hustlers Ray Longstreet was taken into custody on May 25, 2005 in "Operation Street Sweeper" and is awaiting trial.

- Shawn Betts, a "Prince", was released from Tamms in April 2006.

- Jerome Murray is awaiting trial.

MANIAC LATIN DISCIPLES
(Alliance – Folks)

The Maniac Latin Disciples (MLDs), aka Latin Disciples, are thought to have originated in the mid-1960s in the 14th Police District around Rockwell and Potomac. Led by Albert "Hitler" Hernandez, the distinguishing gang symbol became the backwards swastika. The gang joined the United Latin Organization (ULO), which also included smaller Latin gangs such as the Latin Eagles. The allegiance was formed to fight off the Latin Kings. Later they joined the Folk alliance of street gangs and then formed the "Maniac Family" to bond several smaller Hispanic gangs under their specific sphere of influence.

Of past MLD leaders, "Hitler" Hernandez was killed in 1970 and Fernando "Prince Ferne" Zayas was incarcerated on murder charges. Officials believe Zayas is running the gang from behind prison bars. In 1996, reputed second in command Johnny Almodovar was arrested on murder charges as well. Afterwards, MLD leadership seemed to splinter when a fellow MLD member gunned down street leader Enrique "Rick Dog" Garcia. During 1998-1999 and in 2004, authorities arrested several high-ranking members on drug charges. On the streets, it is believed that many previous MLD allies have skirmished with MLD over turf.

The MLD sphere of influence remains around the Humboldt Park area and in several parts of Chicago, Chicago suburbs, numerous outlying Illinois cities including Elgin, Joliet and Rockford as well as in several midwest and southern states. MLD has historically been a leader in the sale of illegal narcotics. Other primary criminal activities include armed robbery, auto theft, kidnapping and extortion. Murder, shootings and intimidation are a means of control.

Membership consists of a mix of Hispanic, Caucasian and African American individuals. Their primary rivals are the Latin Kings, who killed their original MLD leader.

Maniac Latin Disciples identifiers include:
black and light blue colors

Symbols: heart with horns and tail, pitchforks, monks and backwards swastikas.

Current status of some reputed members:

- Johnny "Loco D" Almovodar, reputed second-in-command, is serving a prison term in Tamms until at least 2036.

- Francisco Garcia, nation leader, is serving a prison term in Tamms until at least 2007.

- Fernando Zayas, nation prince, is serving a life term in Tamms.

OTHER GANGS

AMBROSE
(Alliance – Folks)

Primarily a Hispanic street gang, the Ambrose gang originated in the West Side Pilsen area during the 1960s. It is believed they allied with the Latin Counts and joined the Folk alliance in the early 1980s. As a result, they are constantly at odds with Hispanic gangs of the People alliance over south side and southwest side turf, especially the Party People, Satan Disciples and the La Raza gangs. In 1999, an Ambrose gang member killed a Chicago police officer. CPD and federal agents then implemented "Operation Blue Water," which resulted in the 2001 arrest of 17 high-ranking Ambrose members on drug charges. However, Ambrose still maintains a presence in several Chicago neighborhoods engaging in drug sales, aggravated battery, auto theft, armed robbery, arson and murder.

Ambrose identifiers include:
black and light blue clothing

Symbols: a knights helmet, spears and three dots.

Current status of some reputed members:

- Peter Guzman, founding member and leader, is serving a term in Tamms until at least 2019.

- Paulino Vollagomez, second-in-command, is serving a term in Tamms until 2006.

- Willie Perez, a high-ranking leader, was released on May 4, 2000.

- Hector Delgado is serving a life term for the murder of Police Officer Brian Strouse in Tamms Supermax prison facility.

ASHLAND VIKINGS
(Alliance – Folks)

The Ashland Vikings were established in the early 1960s around the East Village area of Ashland and Augusta Boulevard in opposition to the Latin Kings. Originally, they were members of the Insane Family under the Spanish Cobras. In the past, they often battled the Harrison Gents and the Satan Disciples over turf. These prolonged battles as well as police efforts have generally forced the Vikings out of their Ashland stronghold.

However, they still operate in the 13th Police District, with a faction operating in the 24th District near Clark and the 25th District near Greeenleaf. They have also been identified in the suburb of Cicero and in Milwaukee, Wisconsin.

Primary criminal activities include drug trafficking, auto theft, theft and arson. Members are mostly Hispanic.

> **Ashland Vikings identifiers include:** black and green clothing
>
> **Symbols:** a Viking helmet, eight-point star and diamonds.
>
> **Current status of some reputed members:**
> - Edwin "Youngblood" Perez, a prince, is serving a term in Tamms until at least 2006.

BISHOPS
(Alliance – People)

A founding member of the People alliance, the Bishops originated on 18th Street and Bishop Avenue in the early 1980s as an offshoot of the Latin Counts. Since then, they have spread west along 18th Street towards Damen. Though their name originates from Bishop Avenue and possesses no religious significance, they use the symbol of a church Bishop as their moniker. Since the early 1990s, they have been at odds with their former allies, the Latin Counts.

Though small in numbers, they are considered an extremely dangerous and violent group and have been suspected of moving their influence to the Quad Cities area of Illinois and Iowa. Their stronghold is currently in the suburbs. Their main activities include the sale of narcotics, theft, robbery, aggravated battery and graffiti.

> **Bishops identifiers include:** black and copper clothing
>
> **Symbols:** a Catholic cross, a bishop's cress and fedora, and a five-point star.
>
> **Current status of some reputed members:**
> - Jimmy Salinas, an institutional leader, was released from prison in September 1995.
> - Martin Silva, a leader, was paroled in March 2006.

BLACK SOULS
(Alliance – Folks)

The Black Souls formed near Madison and California streets due to an internal struggle within the BGDs in the late 1960s. Currently, they consist of six different factions each with its own leaders: the Gangster Black Souls and Mad Black Souls with about 300 members each, the New Life Black Souls and Cobra Black Souls with about 50 members each, the Outlaw Black Souls with about 30 members and the Impression Black Souls with about 25 members. The group has remained tight-knit and is primarily engaged in the sale of narcotics and illegal firearms in several west side neighborhoods as well as in a few suburbs. They also have a presence in Indiana, Wisconsin, Missouri and Ohio.

> **Black Souls identifiers include:** black and white clothing
>
> **Symbols:** the numbers "444", black diamond, heart with wings and a four-point star.
>
> **Current status of some reputed members:**
> - Willie Jones, leader of the Egyptian Cobra Souls faction, is serving a term in Stateville Correctional Center until 2026.
> - Sam McKay, leader of the Gangster Black Souls, is serving a term in Menard Correctional Center until 2051.

BOSS PIMPS
(Alliance – Folks, if any.)

Originally part of the Black Gangster Disciples, this faction splintered away in the 1980s adopting the BGD creed "Brothers of the Struggle" (BOS). When the group split for good, it added another "S" to differentiate itself and has since been battling factions of the Gangster Disciples, Black P Stones and Four Corner Hustlers for turf in the area of East 93rd Street and South Jeffrey. Principal criminal activities include drug trafficking (particularly marijuana and crack cocaine), illegal firearms sales, armed robbery, theft and assault. Boss Pimps are alleged to have a Folk alliance, though on the street they profess renegade status.

Boss Pimps identifiers include:
black, red and blue colors

Symbols: pitchforks, "playboy" bunny and dollar signs.

CITY KNIGHTS
(Alliance – Folks)

The City Knights are a smaller street gang of primarily Hispanic membership which has been identified in the 48th and Wood and 58th and Albany areas of Chicago as well as in Joliet, Elgin and Waukegan.

City Knights identifiers include:
black and gray colors

Symbols: the knight chess piece or a grim reaper with CKN or ICKN (Insane City Knights).

C-NOTES
(Alliance – Folks)

This street gang consists of primarily Caucasian and Hispanic youth. The origins for the group are thought to extend back to the 1950s. The gang has undergone a change of doctrines over the years as it evolved from its Italian origins to its 1970s white supremacist philosophy. It then broke away from that pursuit and remained independent through the 1980s, before finally joining the Folks alliance and the Insane Familia of the Spanish Cobras. Today, its primary concentration of operations is in the area of Ohio and Leavitt, and in Jefferson Park. Principal criminal activities include drug sales, armed robbery, auto theft, racketeering and assault.

C-Notes identifiers include:
black and green colors

Symbols: the dollar sign, a $100 bill, the diamond shape and a money bag.

CULLERTON DEUCES
(Alliance – People)

Originally established in the 1970s, the Cullerton Deuces first thrived and then waned in the 1980s with the arrests of several key members. In the 1990s, they re-emerged as a somewhat forceful street gang consisting primarily of Mexican with a few Puerto Rican members. They currently are active in the 10th Chicago Police District.

Cullerton Deuces identifiers include:
gray, black or white colors

Symbols: the letters "CD" with a spade from a deck of cards.

LA FAMILIA STONES
(Alliance – People)

Originally aligned with the Latin Kings, they formed in the late 1970s in the 14th District around Logan Square. La Familia Stones later broke away and established themselves around Kedzie and Lawrence. Another faction has been identified in the Belmont and Sheffield area since the 1980s. They have fought wars with the Simon City Royals, the Maniac Latin Disciples and Latin Eagles, and though they consider themselves members of the People alliance, they have fought wars over drug selling turf with members of the same alliance. Members are mostly Puerto Rican, but illustrate some racial diversity with the inclusion of some African American and Caucasian youths. Though not large in numbers, they are considered extremely vicious. Currently all factions of the Future Puerto Rican Stones and the Puerto Rican Stones refer to themselves as La Familia Stones as a show of unity. They exercise considerable power in the Albany Park area along Kedzie where they engage in drug sales, graffiti, assault, "ramming" (running a vehicle purposely into another vehicle/motorcycle) and murder.

Note: La Familia Stones are a faction of the Black P Stones.

La Familia Stones identifiers include:
black and orange clothing

Symbols: a pyramid with a diamond, five-point star, crescent moon and swords.

Current status of some reputed members:

- Robert Anderson, a leader, is in Cook County Jail awaiting trial on a murder charge.

Almighty Gaylords identifiers include:
black and gray or black and light blue clothing

Symbols: a Maltese cross surrounded by flames.

Current status of some reputed members:

- William Giles, an institutional leader, was paroled December 2005.

- Darryl Rowe, an institutional leader, was released from prison in May 2000.

GANGSTER STONES
(Alliance – Independent)

The Stones originated on the west side, probably in the 1960s or 1970s, though their exact affiliation is uncertain. During the 1980s, they aligned with the Vice Lord Nation, but have since split. Today, they are thought to remain unaffiliated with either the Folk or People alliances. The Henry Horner Homes area appears to be their principal area of operations. Criminal activities include drug trafficking, armed robbery, theft and assault.

Note: Gangster Stones are a faction of the Black P Stones.

Gangster Stones identifiers include:
black and red clothing

Symbols: a shotgun, the dollar sign and the letter "G" over a triangle with three dots.

ALMIGHTY GAYLORDS
(Alliance – People)

The Gaylords (Great American Youth Love Our Race Destroy Spics) are a Caucasian (originally racist) group originating on the north side. The gang is nearly non-existent today. Originally an Italian youth gang of the late 1950s, over the years it evolved into a supremacist group. They joined the People Alliance in the early 1980s and dropped their supremacist philosophy because of the diversity of the street gangs in the alliance. At that time, lack of recruitment and loss of leadership due to incarcerations greatly weakened this gang. They are still known to operate on a small scale in the Kilbourn Park and Sayre Park areas.

HARRISON GENTS
(Alliance – Folks)

The Gents were originally thought to have started in Harrison High School at Harrison and Western in the 1960s, but relocated to the East Village area during the 1970s, where they still maintain a presence. They have fought turf wars with the Ashland Vikings and more recently with the Satan Disciples. The latter resulted in intense police operations that significantly slowed their activities. However, some suspect their presence in the Rogers Park area, Cicero, Berwyn and in Kankakee, Illinois. Primary activities include drug sales, auto theft, armed robbery, theft, arson, assault, ramming and kidnapping. Mostly a Hispanic group, they are allied with the Folks.

Harrison Gents identifiers include:
black and purple clothing (purple was the original high school color)

Symbols: a cross with four slashes, skull, top hat, gloves and a cane with four dots.

Current status of some reputed members:

- Antwan Wells, a high-ranking leader, is serving a term and eligible for parole in August 2007.

- Luis Rivera, a high-ranking leader, was released from prison on August 6, 2004.

IMPERIAL GANGSTERS
(Alliance – Folks)

The Imperial Gangsters originated around the West Humboldt Park area of Palmer and Drake in the late 1960s, and since the 1970s, have continually fought the Latin Kings over territory. As a result of this feud, they allied with the Spanish Cobras and helped form the United Latino Organization. Today, as members of the Folk alliance, this gang is an inter-racial mix of Latino, African American and Caucasian youth.

Imperial Gangsters identifiers include:
black and pink clothing

Symbols: a panther (usually pink), shotguns and a gangster crown.

Current status of some reputed members:

- Ronald Carrasquillo, a gang leader, is serving a term in Danville Correctional Center until 2270.
- David Colon, a high-ranking leader, is serving a prison term in Hill Correctional Center until at least 2018.
- Geraldo Iglesias, a high-ranking leader, is serving a term in Dixon Correctional Center until at least 2010.
- Mario Navarro, a high-ranking leader, is serving a term in Danville Correctional Center until at least 2016.

Community residents talk about how to deal with graffiti.

INSANE DEUCES
(Alliance – Folks)

The Insane Deuces were the result of a merger of two north side street gangs in the 1960s. Through the years, they have controlled much of their original territory consisting of the Hamlin Park area and the Lathrop Homes. In doing so, they have had running battles with the Simon City Royals and the Latin Kings. The intense dispute with the LKs caused a switch of allegiance from the People to the Folks and an alliance within the "Insane Familia" of the Spanish Cobras. During the 1990s, the most intense battles with the LKs appear to have taken place around the Lathrop Homes and in Aurora. In 2001, gang members suffered numerous arrests on weapons charges as the result of "Operation Stacked Deck." That was followed by more arrests through "Operation Double Down." Still, they have increased their presence to include the Portage Park area and several Chicagoland suburbs. Gang membership is composed primarily of Hispanic and Caucasian youth.

Insane Deuces identifiers include:
black and green clothing

Symbols: a spade or dice with two dots or the Roman numeral "II."

INSANE DRAGONS
(Alliance – Folks)

A Hispanic gang established around the area of Augusta and Sacramento in the mid-1970s to protect youth from neighboring white gangs, they now frequent areas in the 23rd Police District around Francisco and Iowa Streets, and along Iowa Street between 2500 and 2800 West. In the 25th Police District, they can be found around Belden and Rutherford, Fullerton and Tripp, Kildare and Palmer, Rutherford-Sayre Park and the Brickyard Mall. They have no ties with the Latin Dragons of the 4th Police District.

Insane Dragons identifiers include:
gray and maroon clothing

Symbols: dragons breathing fire, torch and diamonds.

Current status of some reputed members:

- Jesus Fernando, reputed second-in-command, was released from prison in December 1997.

- Eduardo Delgado, an institutional leader, is serving a prison term in Menard Correctional Center until at least 2039.

- Luis Mejias, a reputed leader, was released from prison in July 2002.

- Billy Phillips, an institutional leader, is serving a prison term in the Big Muddy River Correctional Center until at least 2008.

INSANE UNKNOWNS
(Alliance – People)

The Insane Unknowns originated in the mid-1970s around Leavitt and Schiller, and aligned themselves with the Latin Kings in a war with the Maniac Latin Disciples. Their prestige diminished after their ranks were depleted in a war with the Spanish Cobras and the Simon City Royals. Over the last decade, gentrification of their old turf has also strained their activities. Today, though small in numbers, they continue to sell narcotics and firearms, as well as commit armed robberies, thefts and assaults. Their membership is mostly Hispanic. They currently operate in the 25th Police District near Division and Pulaski.

Insane Unknowns identifiers include:
black and white clothing

Symbols: ghosts with shotguns, five-point stars, candles and shields.

Current status of some reputed members:

- Keith Hoddenback, a reputed leader, is serving a prison term in Danville Correctional Center until at least 2039.

- Ruben Hernandez, an institutional leader, is serving a prison term in Pontiac Correctional Center until at least 2059.

- Edwin Suarez, an institutional leader, is serving a prison term in Menard Correctional Center until at least 2017.

KRAZY GET DOWN BOYS
(Alliance – Folks)

This street gang apparently emerged in the Marquette Park area in the early 1990s and quickly aligned with the Ambrose gang. From 71st and California, they moved into the Blue Island neighborhoods, and despite incarceration of a key leader, they also established operations along 61st Street around Troy and Lawndale, as well as in Calumet City, Kankakee and northwest Indiana. Membership is comprised mostly of Hispanic and Caucasian youth who consistently battle with the Satan Disciples, Latin Kings and La Raza. Primary criminal activities include drug trafficking, armed robbery, theft and assault.

Krazy Get Down Boys identifiers include:
purple and white colors

Symbols: a shield, sword and six dots.

LA RAZA
(Alliance – Folks)

La Raza was formed by Mexican immigrants moving into the Pilsen community in the early 1970s. La Raza, meaning "The Race", recruits only Mexican youth and is closely affiliated with the Party People street gang. Since the 1980s, La Raza is thought to have gained and controlled the 48th Street corridor between Ashland and Racine in the Back of the Yards area. Gang cohesion is tight; gang rules are strictly enforced. La Raza doesn't hesitate to use extreme violence to defend its turf.

La Raza identifiers include:
the colors of the Mexican flag: red, white, and green

Symbols: the Mexican flag, an eagle's head, cross or six-point star.

Current status of some reputed members:

- Jose Gutierrez, reputed gang leader, was released from prison in August 2002.

- Alberto Pacheco, a founding member of the gang, is serving a prison term in Danville Correctional Center until at least 2010.

- Benjamin Monteza, an institutional leader, is serving a prison term until 2012.

- Osvaldo Torres, an institutional leader, is serving a prison term in Danville Correctional Center until at least 2019.

LATIN BROTHERS
(Alliance – People)

Formed in the Austin district, probably in the late 1970s, the Latin Brothers are a tight-knit gang with a reputation for extreme violence, often battling the Spanish Cobras, Maniac Latin Disciples, Imperial Gangsters, and factions of the Four Corner Hustlers and Latin Kings for control of turf. After the Hispanic population of the Austin neighborhood relocated to other parts of the City, the Latin Brothers moved operations to the Belmont and North Cicero Avenues area. They are a small gang and primarily active in the 16th and 17th Police Districts. Historically, the Latin Brothers have allied with the Insane Unknowns. Primary criminal activities include drug trafficking and assault.

Latin Brothers identifiers include:
black and purple clothing

Symbols: a Trojan helmet, spear, five dots or a cross.

LATIN COUNTS
(Alliance – People)

The Latin Counts originated in the Pilsen community in the mid-1960s to protect themselves from gangs already in the neighborhood. They remain there and now have a faction on Commercial Avenue from 91st to 103rd streets. The Counts also have a reported presence in the suburbs of Cicero, Addison and Chicago Heights as well as strong ties in Detroit, Michigan. They have battled with Ambrose, Satan Disciples and La Raza for turf. Recently, because of a quarrel with the Latin Kings, the Counts may have allied themselves with the Vice Lords — particularly in the prison system. Primary criminal activities include drug trafficking, armed robbery, arson, assault and kidnapping.

Latin Counts identifiers include:
black and red clothing

Symbols: a knight helmet, a cross with five slashes or a five-point star.

Current status of some reputed members:
- Juan Castillos, reputed second-in-command, was paroled in July 2002.

- Manuel Rios, a high-ranking leader, was released from prison in November 2003.

LATIN DRAGONS
(Alliance – Folks)

Mostly Hispanic in membership, the Latin Dragons materialized on the south side during the early 1980s and originally associated themselves with the People alliance and the Latin Kings. During the 1990s, they split from the LKs, flipped alliance to the Folks, and have been battling the LKs, the Latin Counts and Spanish Gangster Disciples, among others, for turf on the south side. Accordingly, their reputation is one of extreme violence, which they use to maintain their territory from East 83rd to East 87th between Colfax and Commercial as well as select locations in Calumet City and over the state border in Whiting, Indiana. Primary criminal activities include drug sales, armed robbery and assault.

Latin Dragons identifiers include:
black and white clothing

Symbols: dragons, diamonds and six dots.

war with both groups, pledging allegiance to no one. They are concerned only for their own money-making businesses, which include the sale of narcotics, auto theft, armed robbery and theft. However, gentrification and police actions have slowed their operations and they have adopted a very low profile.

LATIN EAGLES
(Alliance – Folks)

Formed in the area of Addison and Halsted in the late 1960s as the result of the combination of two militant political clubs, the Latin Eagles transformed into a full-fledged street gang by the 1970s. They became part of the United Latino Organization with the Latin Disciples, Spanish Cobras and Imperial Gangsters. Eventually, they expanded to the Uptown and Kelvyn Park areas. However, because of urban development affecting their original turf around Wrigleyville, they have relocated to the area around Gill Park on Sheridan Road and Lake View High School at 4015 N. Ashland. They have since formed a faction near Armitage and Kostner. Primary criminal activities include drug sales, auto theft and armed robbery.

Latin Eagles identifiers include:
black and gray clothing

Symbols: an eagle, three dots or a six-pointed star.

Current status of some reputed members:

■ Thomas Jiminez, a high-ranking leader, is serving a prison term in Dixon Correctional Center until at least 2007.

LATIN JIVERS
(Alliance – Folks, if any.)

The Latin Jivers formed from a band of young organized criminals who left the Maniac Latin Disciples in the late 1980s to operate around the Rockwell and Potomac area. In the past, the Jivers attempted to merge with the Latin Kings, and later, with their enemies the Spanish Cobras. Disagreements have caused the Jivers to be at

Latin Jivers identifiers include:
black and brown clothing

Symbols: a skull with top hat and cane.

Current status of some reputed members:

■ Ramiro Rodriguez, an institutional leader, was released from prison in April 2004.

LATIN LOVERS
(Alliance – Folks)

The Latin Lovers were started by former members of the Spanish Cobras and the Maniac Latin Disciples in the mid-1970s around Palmer and Rockwell. The gang joined the Folk alliance, and in the early 1990s, they joined the "Maniac" alliance under the umbrella of the MLDs. Tension with the MLDs over drug turf caused the Lovers to break away from the "Maniac" alliance and join the "Insane" alliance with the Spanish Cobras. Currently, they are thought to center their criminal activities around Milwaukee and California Avenues. Primary criminal activities include drug trafficking and assaults.

Latin Lovers identifiers include:
red and yellow clothing

Symbols: a heart and universal symbol.

Current status of some reputed members:

■ Nelson Padilla, a reputed nation leader, is serving a term in USP Coleman, Florida until at least May 2016.

■ Mark Rosado, an institutional leader, was paroled on March 25, 2005.

LATIN PACHUCOS
(Alliance – People)

Originating in the Humboldt Park area during the early 1980s, the gang is thought to have based its image on the Lowrider Magazine character. Sometime in the 1990s, they established themselves in the Hanson Park area and eventually battled the Four Corner Hustlers, Spanish Cobras and Maniac Latin Disciples for turf. Currently, they are thought to have established themselves in the Kilbourn Park area as well as in Cicero. Primary criminal activities include drug trafficking, arson, assault and ramming.

Latin Pachucos identifiers include:
black colors

Symbols: a "lowrider" figure, cross with three rays and a five-point star

LATIN SAINTS
(Alliance – People)

Originating in the Back of the Yards community near 45th and Wood in the late 1960s, the membership of this gang shifted in composition to the present day mostly Hispanic membership. Throughout the years, the Saints have kept primarily to their original Back of the Yards territory between 43rd and 47th Streets from Winchester to Ashland, and the area around 60th and Homan. Known as one of the most reclusive groups among the gang world, the Saints have become one of the most aggressive and violent street gangs in the Chicago area. Once aligned with the Folks, they switched to the People alliance after a bitter rivalry with La Raza. Primary criminal activities include murder, assault, drug sales, armed robbery, auto theft, theft, arson and kidnapping.

Latin Saints identifiers include:
black and light blue clothing

Symbols: stickman with a halo and three slashes

Current status of some reputed members:

- Joe Krentokowski, a reputed gang leader, was released from prison in December 2000.

LATIN SOULS
(Alliance – Folks)

The Latin Souls were established as a Hispanic gang on the south side near 55th and Halsted in the early 1960s to protect themselves from the encroaching African American community. They relocated to the Back of the Yards area after the Hispanic population was eventually displaced. Though never big in numbers, they have fought a series of turf wars with the Latin Saints and have even become fierce enemies of fellow Folks gangs, La Raza and the Satan Disciples. During the 1990s, a war with Ambrose weakened the Souls, allowing the Party Players to take over much of their Marquette Park operation. They are affiliated with the Black Souls. They still maintain a presence along 49th Street between Wolcott and Marshfield and are expanding to: Alton, Illinois; St. Louis, Missouri; New Jersey; Florida; and Texas. Primary criminal activities include drug sales, armed robbery, theft and assault.

Latin Souls identifiers include:
black and maroon clothing

Symbols: Spanish cross with three dots on each end and a six-point star

LATIN STYLERS
(Affiliation – Folks)

The Latin Stylers cropped up in the late 1960s around the Logan Square area near Diversey and Kedzie. For years they have maintained a presence in the Hermosa neighborhood, and during the 1990s, expanded into the Blackhawk Park area. Members are primarily of Hispanic origin and, at one point, allied with the Spanish Cobras under the "Insane Familia" Folks group. However, after a bitter dispute with the Cobras, they joined with the Maniac Latin Disciples under the "Maniac Family." They are now active in the 17th Police District. Primary gang activities include graffiti, assault, armed robbery, auto theft, murder and drug trafficking.

Latin Stylers identifiers include:
maroon and gray clothing

Symbols: shields and/or the letters "LS"

Current status of some reputed members:

■ Johnny Rodriguez, an institutional leader, was released from prison in June 2004.

MICKEY COBRAS
(Alliance – People)

The Mickey Cobras originated in the mid-1950s on Chicago's West Side under the leadership of James Cogwell and were originally known as the Egyptian Cobras. Pushed out of their territory by the Vice Lords, they moved to the south side under the leadership of James Cogwell's younger brother, Mickey. They quickly established ties to the Black P Stones under Jeff Fort and began operating in the Robert Taylor Homes. Later they were known to control a portion of the Cabrini-Green housing project.

When Mickey Cogwell was killed in the late 1970s (allegedly by Jeff Fort), the gang renamed itself the Mickey Cobras in his honor and then slowly dissolved some of its ties to the Black P Stones. Since that time, reputed leader Theotis Clark has been in federal prison, Cabrini-Green was demolished and, in 2001, Cornell Green (who allegedly ran street level drug operations) was indicted — all crippling the Cobra operations to a degree.

Still, the Cobras maintain a presence in the Dearborn Homes, Fuller Park, South Shore, Woodlawn and Roseland areas. Membership is mostly African American. Primary criminal activities include drug trafficking (their specialty being heroin sales), armed robbery, auto theft, theft, kidnapping and assault.

Mickey Cobras identifiers include:
black, red and green clothing

Symbols: a five-point star, crescent moon, pyramid with 21 bricks and an eye, cobra snake, flail and whip

MILWAUKEE KINGS
(Alliance – Folks)

The Milwaukee Kings were established in the early 1980s near North Milwaukee and West Grand Avenues. By 1992, they launched their main operations from the East Village area and allied themselves with the Maniac Latin Disciples. Wars with rival gangs as well as police pressure forced a move of operations to Chicago's north side Mont Clare neighborhood. The Milwaukee Kings then broke away from the MLDs after the MLDs murdered a ranking figure in the Kings. Primary gang activities include graffiti, assaults, theft, robbery, kidnapping, murder and drug trafficking.

Milwaukee Kings identifiers include:
black and orange clothing

Symbols: a king's crown

Current status of some reputed members:

■ Joseph Matos, an institutional leader, was paroled October 2005.

■ Efrain Murales, reputed current gang leader, is serving a prison term in Tamms until at least 2041.

MORGAN BOYS
(Alliance – Folks)

A street gang of small numbers and of mostly Hispanic membership, the Morgan Boys appear to operate in the 16th and 18th Place and Morgan areas of the City and are also known in northwest Indiana.

Morgan Boys identifiers include:
blue and red clothing

Symbols: a cross with slashes, a six-point star and other representations of the numeral "6."

ORCHESTRA ALBANY
(Alliance – Folks)

When a Latin King killed a member of a salsa band on the north side, those associated with the band formed this group to fight the LK. The name of the gang derives from Orchestra meaning "band" in Spanish, and Albany, which reflects the street they occupied. They joined the Folk alliance and continue to fight the LKs today. Towards that end, they have formed a close alliance with the Spanish Cobras and helped found the Insane Family, which includes many Hispanic alliance groups. They currently occupy the area of Belden to Milwaukee and Kedzie to Sacramento.

Orchestra Albany identifiers include:
brown and gold clothing

Symbols: a letter "A" slightly inside a letter "O" and a diamond.

Current status of some reputed members:
- Vincent Reyna, an institutional leader, is serving a prison term in Tamms until at least 2023.

PARTY PEOPLE
(Alliance – Folks, if any.)

Party People are a mostly Hispanic street gang founded in the late 1970s in the Pilsen area to protect members from existing street gangs such as the La Raza, Ambrose, Bishops and Latin Counts. Consequently, they have entrenched themselves in the area of 18th and May and have extended operations to Gage Park and Marquette Park, frequently battling the Latin Kings, Black P Stones, Latin Souls and Two Six Nation. In the mid-1990s, gang member Geraldo Ferrer shot and wounded a member of the Chicago Police Department. He was later arrested and sentenced to eight years for attempted murder. Afterwards, and as the result of the murder of a young child by a Party People member, CPD initiated "Operation Just Cause." The operation has put a significant dent in gang operations. Primary criminal activities include drug sales, auto theft and assault. Originally thought to be of the Folk alliance, some members reportedly prefer a renegade street status.

Party People identifiers include:
black and white clothing

Symbols: a "playboy" bunny, cross with three slashes on top and a circle on the bottom

PARTY PLAYERS
(Alliance – People)

The roots of the Party Players apparently trace back to the Back of the Yards area in the late 1970s or early 1980s. Mostly Hispanic, the Players originally aligned with the Two Six street gang and adopted many of the same symbols. Both fought the Latin Saints. During the 1990s, the Players established contacts with the Latin Kings and expanded their presence from the Marquette Park area to include Chicago suburbs and Wisconsin. Primary criminal activities include the sale of narcotics and assault.

Party Players identifiers include:
white and maroon clothing

Symbols: a "playboy" bunny, five-point star, hatchet cross with three dots.

POPES
(Alliance – Folks on the Northside and People on the Southside)

In Chicago, there are north and south side Pope street gangs. Originally formed by Caucasian youth who sought to protect their turf from Hispanics in the early 1970s, the north side faction, or the Insane Popes, started in the Kolmar Park area, then moved factions further north into the 20th and 24th police districts. Subsequently, they allied with the Simon City Royals. Upon joining the Folk alliance, the gang recruited members of many nationalities, but was unable to maintain much of its former territory. Their primary base appears to be in the East Albany Park area where they are active in assaults, theft and drug sales.

Northside Popes identifiers include:
black and powder blue clothing

Northside Popes symbols: Pope fedora, cross with three slashes, monks and pitchforks.

Around the mid-1970s, another Pope street gang appeared on Chicago's south side in the area of Hoyne Park. While some believe this group is an off-shoot of the north side Popes, others disagree. Eventually the south side group took the name Almighty Popes and spread its influence through several areas. However, during the early 1990s, police pressure and internal disputes seriously disrupted gang activities forcing them out of much of their territory. Today, they are thought to be small in numbers, but still active in the Archer Heights area while edging into some east side neighborhoods. Main activities consist of drug sales, armed robbery, theft and assault. Unlike their north side counterparts, they are members of the People alliance.

Southside Popes identifiers include:
black and white clothing

Southside Popes Symbols: a Grim Reaper with a cross, a cross with two slashes, a half black-half white diamond, a top hat with canes and a five-point star.

Current status of some reputed members:
- Michael Hamilton, reputed Southside current gang leader, was released from prison in May 2001.

RACINE BOYS
(Alliance – Folks)

The Racine Boys street gang has only a few known members. However, graffiti has shown up in Dvorak Park and at the 18th Street and Sangamon intersection. They can also be found in Zion, Illinois.

Racine Boys identifiers include:
black and light blue colors

Symbols: a cross with curved middle, three dots and a knight's helmet with a spiked plume.

SATAN DISCIPLES
(Alliance – Folks)

Formed in the Pilsen district in the late 1960s, the Satan Disciples established themselves in the vicinity of West 24th Street and South California. During the 1980s, they remained strong in that area and quickly expanded into the East Village, Gage Park, Brighton Park and Bridgeport areas. Officials have also identified factions in the Illinois towns of Calumet City, Summit, Cicero, Berwyn, Bensenville, Joliet and Lockport and in Hammond, Indiana. The Satan Disciples are an exceptionally violent gang that is constantly at battle with gangs of the People alliance and are known to even battle gangs of their Folk alliance if necessary. Recently, it has been noted that a faction of Satan Disciples in the 10th District has attempted to splinter away and rename themselves as the Renegade Satan Disciples. Primary criminal activities include drug trafficking, armed robbery, theft, ramming, kidnapping and assault.

Satan Disciples identifiers include:
black and yellow clothing

Symbols: a baby devil, pitchforks, shields, a six-point star, a heart with wings, horns and tail.

Current status of some reputed members:
- Jose Trejo, a reputed gang leader, is serving a prison term in Hill Correctional Center until at least 2014.
- Elliott Montes, an institutional leader, is serving a prison term in Stateville Correctional Center until at least 2015.

SIMON CITY ROYALS
(Alliance – Folks)

The Simon City Royals are probably the oldest predominately Caucasian street gang in Chicago. The Royals originally formed in the 14th Police District around the Simon Park area in the late 1960s to fend off Hispanic gangs then moving into the area. When the ethnicity of the area changed drastically, they moved their activities north and west into the 17th and 25th police districts. Since the 1980s, however, they have suffered from discord in their ranks. They were further depleted by arrests and wars with rival gangs. It has been suspected for some time that the Royals within the prison system have aligned themselves with the BGDs for protection in exchange for firearms. The Royals still have strong ties with the BGDs, and though not as active as in the past, they continue to conduct their activities in the Albany Park area. Primary activities consist of narcotic and weapon sales, theft, armed robbery, extortion, kidnappings and obtaining businesses to launder money. The Royals were one of the founding members of the Folk alliance.

> **Simon City Royals identifiers include:**
> black and royal blue clothing
>
> **Symbols:** cross with three slashes, shotguns, swords, shields, bunnies with their right ear bent, a cane and a crest with lions
>
> **Current status of some reputed members:**
>
> - Brian Nelson, a gang leader, is serving a prison term in Tamms until at least 2015.
>
> - David Shilney, an institutional leader, is due for parole in 2007.

SIN CITY BOYS
(Alliance – Folks)

A street gang made up of mostly Caucasian and Hispanic members, the Sin City Boys are small in numbers, but have been identified in Cicero, Berwyn, Naperville, West Chicago and as far away as Texas.

> **Sin City Boys identifiers include:**
> black and navy blue colors
>
> **Symbols:** hooded bunny, sword with two lines and two dots, and a heart or club from a deck of cards.

INSANE SPANISH COBRAS
(Alliance – Folks)

A large Hispanic gang, the Cobras were formed in the early 1970s around the area of Division and Maplewood by Richard "King Cobra" Medina. This gang was originally part of the MLDs, but broke away after disagreements. Since then, they have joined the United Latino Organization, which includes the MLDs, in order to fight the Latin Kings, and helped found the Insane Familia association to organize several smaller gangs to help fight MLD influence within the Folk alliance. The Cobras have extended their gang influence to several parts of the City, including Logan Square, Kelvyn Park, Bucktown and Albany Park. They have also been identified in several outlying areas of Illinois as well as in Wisconsin, Indiana, and the eastern states of Ohio, New York and Connecticut. Primary criminal activities include the sale of narcotics and illegal firearms, murder, extortion, theft, armed robbery, assault, arson and kidnapping. They are allied with the Ashland Vikings, Harrison Gents, Insane Deuces, Insane Dragons and Latin Lovers.

> **Spanish Cobras identifiers include:**
> black and green clothing
>
> **Symbols:** a cobra snake and diamonds on a shaft with three dots
>
> **Current status of some reputed members:**
>
> - Annibal Santiago, a reputed gang leader, is serving a prison term in Tamms until at least 2018.
>
> - Melvin Santiago, an institutional leader, was released from prison in June 2005.
>
> - Luis Hernandez, an institutional leader, is in Cook County Jail.
>
> - John Guevara, an institutional leader, was paroled in April 2005.
>
> - Adam Rodriguez, an institutional leader, was released from prison in October 2004.
>
> - Adalberto Santiago is awaiting trial in the MCC on drug conspiracy charges. He is the reputed leader of a crew who would kidnap drug dealers for ransom, and was implicated in a kidnapping where the victim was tortured and shot to death. The victim's body parts were disposed of throughout the city.

SPANISH GANGSTER DISCIPLES
(Alliance – Folks)

The Spanish Gangster Disciples (SGDs) were formed in the early 1980s by a former member of the MLDs, Rudy Rios. While in prison, he helped form the "Spanish Growth and Development" group in order to settle any problems within Latino Folk gangs. Once released, he transformed this organization into the Spanish Gangster Disciples after receiving permission from the BGDs on the south side. They quickly earned a reputation for extreme violence. Initial territory included the Trumell Park Homes at 106th and Bensley. Their territory grew rapidly to include the area of 87th to 90th between Baltimore and Commercial Avenue on the east side (85th and Houston is the heart).

A north side and somewhat distinct sect of the Spanish Gangster Disciples appeared at about the same time that the Hispanic members of the GDs joined with the MLDs to adopt a combined GD and Spanish Growth and Development creed. They quickly gained recognition among fellow gangs as main suppliers of marijuana and have since been operating in the Rogers Park, Uptown and Albany Park areas.

Exact ties between the north and south groups remain somewhat vague, but over the years, the SGDs have fought several wars with other Hispanic gangs, including many of their former allies. As a result, in the past 20 years, four ranking members of the gang, including Rudy Rios, have been slain. Along with a visible lack of unity within the gang itself, their activity and membership has declined. They still, however, maintain a presence in the aforementioned areas of Chicago and a presence in certain outlying Illinois areas such as Calumet City, Lockport, Prospect Heights and Romeoville. Main rivals appear to be the Latin Kings, Latin Counts, Latin Dragons, Latin Eagles and Spanish Cobras. Primary criminal activities include drug trafficking, armed robbery, auto theft and assault.

Spanish Gangster Disciples identifiers include: black and light blue clothing by the North Side SGDs and black and blue clothing by the South Side SGDs

Symbols: a 6-point star, a heart with horns, wings and tail, a gangster crown and a Spanish cross.

Current status of some reputed members:

- Enrique Romero, a reputed gang leader, is serving a prison term in Lawrence Correctional Center until at least 2011.
- David Cruz, a reputed high-ranking leader, was released from prison in May 2004.

SPANISH LORDS
(Alliance – People)

The Lords originated around the Wicker Park area in the mid-1960s, and for years, as a predominately Hispanic gang, they have aligned closely with the Latin Kings. Due to the gentrification of their original territory, the Lords have operated primarily in the Bucktown area and their membership has remained fairly small in numbers. They maintain a fairly low profile, though they have been known to battle the Insane Unknowns and Maniac Latin Disciples, as well as other Folk gangs for turf. Primary criminal activities include drug trafficking, armed robbery and ramming.

Spanish Lords identifiers include: black and red clothing

Symbols: Spanish cross with a heart in the middle, ruby on staff, swords and 5-pointed stars.

STONED FREAKS
(Alliance – People)

A mostly Caucasian street gang that is small in numbers, they originated in the Kelvyn Park area as a punk, party group. By the late 1970s, they adopted their moniker and engaged mostly in petty thefts, then gravitated to narcotic sales, specializing in LSD and White Asian Heroin. They battled other white groups as well as Hispanic gangs, especially the Spanish Cobras, Latin Eagles and the Maniac Latin Disciples, who were then moving into the area as a result of changing demographics. Eventually, they were forced out of their original turf, and today, they are thought to have set up operations in the Edgewater and Portage Park vicinities as well as maintaining a presence around Jefferson Park. They are thought to have entered into an alliance with the Latin Kings. Primary criminal activities include the sale of narcotics (of which they prefer the drive-up delivery system), robbery, theft, illegal dog fighting and assault.

Stoned Freaks identifiers include:
black and red colors

Symbols: five-point star, skull with top hat, crossbones and a heart.

GANGSTER TWO SIX NATION
(Alliance – Folks)

The Gangster Two Six Nation name was derived from the street on which they first operated during the mid 1960s, 26th Street near Pulaski. Initially comprised of Caucasian and Hispanic members, the gang rapidly expanded, and today, is one of the largest predominately Mexican gangs in Chicago. When the Two Six Nation ventured into narcotics sales along 26th Street, they battled the Latin Kings, who remain their main enemies.

Although their reputed leader through the 1970s, David Ayala, has been serving a life term in federal prison since 1981 for murdering several Latin Kings, the gang is viewed as possessing well-structured leadership and has quickly developed into one of the most violent street gangs in Chicago. They expanded and maintained turf in South Lawndale, Marquette Park and Brighton Park. In recent years, they have also expanded operations into Cicero, Chicago suburbs, the outlying Illinois communities of Joliet, Rock Island and Kankakee, and neighboring states such as Indiana and Wisconsin. Primary criminal activities include drug sales, murder, drive-by shootings, thefts, robberies and assault.

Two Six identifiers include:
black and tan (beige) clothing

Symbols: a bunny with a bent right ear, six-point star, dice with two and six spots, heart, club or spade.

Current status of some reputed members:
- Franciso "Smoke" Sanchez, a reputed gang leader and IDOC Latin Folks Leader, is serving a prison term in Tamms Correctional Center until at least 2009.

YOUNG LATINO ORGANIZATION COBRAS (YLO COBRAS)
(Alliance – Folks)

The YLO Cobras are mainly an Hispanic street gang that operates mainly on the west side, mostly along Central Park and Tripp. They were an offshoot of the Young Latino Organization, a quasi-community youth group used to cover gang activity around the area of Yates School, and in the early 80s, splintered into the YLO Cobras and YLO Disciples. They coexisted peacefully within the Folk alliance, but became enemies when the Folks broke up into the Insane and Maniac sub-groups.

YLO Cobras identifiers include:
black and green colors

Symbols: cobra snake, staff with a diamond and three dots

Current status of some reputed members:
- Jimmy Diaz, an institutional leader, was paroled in June 2005.
- Efrain Torres, a reputed gang leader, is eligible for parole in 2006.

Note: The YLO Disciples gang is also active today. They operate in the 14th and 25th police districts.

TWO TWO BOYS
(Alliance – Folks)

Also known as the 22nd Street Boys, and named for 22nd Street in the Pilsen area, they emerged near the intersection of 22nd and California Avenue in the 1970s. The Two Two Boys maintain tight relations with the Ambrose street gang and constantly battle the Latin Kings for turf. Since their emergence, they extended their influence to Cicero, Brookfield, Bolingbrook and Franklin Park as well as Wisconsin, Kentucky, California and Florida. Membership is primarily Hispanic and Caucasian, and while arrests of several members somewhat diminished their influence in and around the suburbs, they are thought to be exerting their influence once again. Primary criminal activities include drug sales, auto theft, armed robbery and assault.

Two Two Boys identifiers include:
black and light blue clothing or brown and beige colors

Symbols: four-point crown, four dots, shields and the Roman numeral II.

GANGS TO WATCH

CASE EXAMPLE:

In March 2006, some 375 MS 13 gang members (or other gangs with immigrant criminal members) were arrested in 24 states through Operation Community Shield, which combined local law enforcement with federal immigration forces. Gang members were arrested in Illinois.

MS 13 or MARA SALVATRUCHA

MS 13 is a primarily El Salvadoran street gang that developed in the 1980s in the Los Angeles area, primarily to fend off predatory Mexican gangs. The gang members were part of the wave of refugees/immigrants who fled the Central American country during a civil war and had ties to the La Mara (a violent El Salvadoran street gang). Some had ties to the Farabundo Marti National Liberation Front (FMNL), a highly trained Salvadoran group of guerilla fighters. A few of the suburban police departments noted MS 13 in their areas, including Riverside, Westmont and Wheaton, however, the FBI Chicago office reports that after assessing the data from various law enforcement agencies and departments throughout Illinois, there is no credible documentation that places the MS 13 gang in the Chicago metropolitan area.

Since the 1980s, first generation Salvadoran-Americans have also joined and MS 13 has migrated east appearing in New York, Virginia, Maryland, and North Carolina, while still maintaining ties to the factions in El Salvador. Reports have them in Illinois and Michigan as well.

Unlike many street gangs, no single leader runs MS 13. Instead, the various cliques around the country of 10 to 80 members each take their cues from the principal gang in Los Angeles. MS 13 members also use no single signature identifier, but rather an assortment of gang tags or identifiers usually with "M" or "MS" with the numeral "13," or sometimes with the words "Salvadoran Pride." Members often wear the white or blue colors associated with the El Salvadoran flag with black.

Though gang enterprises include robberies, extortion and drug trafficking, weapons smuggling and carjackings appear to be primary activities. In the latter, vehicles are driven to El Salvador and traded for drugs. (One estimate has 80% of the cars driven in El Salvador as stolen from the U.S.) Also, from their home country, they have access to military weapons in abundance which they can trade elsewhere. However, the particular danger presented by this group appears to be its reputation for extreme violence and their fearless attitude towards law enforcement. Newsweek magazine published an article on the gang in March 2005, pronouncing them "the most dangerous gang in America." They have been suspected in the execution of three federal agents and numerous shootings of law officers around the country.

Their acute viciousness extends also to any member who cooperates with the law. In 2003, a seventeen year-old MS 13 member, sixteen weeks pregnant, was found nearly decapitated in Virginia after she was assumed to be giving information to authorities.

Additionally, MS 13 has increased its power by aligning with the Mexican Mafia, hence the numeral "13" in its name (M is the 13th letter in the U.S. alphabet and stands for Mexican Mafia). The Mexican Mafia is thought to guard or control much of the weapons, human and drug smuggling on the southern border with Mexico. According to CPD information, MS 13 is not likely to move into the City because the competition with long-established street gangs is too steep. If and when MS 13 moves into the Chicago area, it is more likely they will target suburban areas.

SURENO 13s

Often confused with MS 13, because they use similar identifiers, is the Sur 13 or Los Surenos street gang. Surenos (southerners) evolved in California as an umbrella group for prisoners there representing Hispanics of southern California origin (versus those of nortenos or northerners) and are comprised chiefly of individuals of Mexican nationality. Sur 13 gangs have now appeared as far away as the east coast, but the FBI believes that, unlike MS 13, Sur 13 street gangs outside California appear to be imitators with few connections to their west coast origins. However, Sur 13 has also associated itself with the Mexican Mafia, hence the "13" in the name.

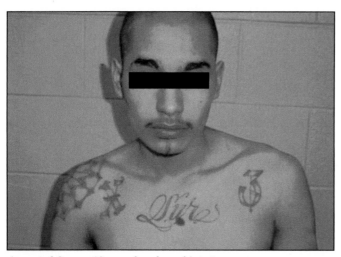

A reputed Sureno 13s member shows his tattoos.
Photo supplied by the West Chicago Police Department.

Unfortunately, Sur 13 street gangs have been in outlying Chicagoland areas since at least 1995 and are gradually pushing towards the City, filling voids around established core gang areas, especially in the suburbs. Criminal activities include drug sales, burglaries, robberies, and murders, but unlike most other Chicago area street gangs, they show little fear of law enforcement, and in March 2004, five teenage Sur 13 members were indicted for murder in Maine Township.

Both MS 13 and Sur 13 members are sometimes identified by tattoos with the number "13" or "trece." They will also use the word "sureno" to identify themselves. Thus, tattooing themselves with SUR (abbreviation for sureno) is common. Other tattoos common with the two, as well as other Hispanic gangs, are three dots, meaning "hospital, jail, death"; it can also represent "mi vida loca" or "my crazy life." Dots can be found on various parts of the body, including the web between fingers, corner of the eye, on the knuckles of the hand or around the top of any cross tattoo. In some parts of the United States, gang members refer to them as "chuke" dots.

The Sureno 13s have been reported as the most prominent emerging gang in Chicago's suburbs. They have been reported in Algonquin, Arlington Heights, Bensenville, Aurora, Cicero, Downers Grove, Elgin, Grayslake, Hanover Park, Harvard, Harwood Heights, Highland Park, Hodgkins, Hoffman Estates, Marengo, Melrose Park, Montgomery, Mt. Prospect, Mundelein, Naperville, Oak Lawn, Palatine, Park Ridge, Stickney, Streamwood, Waukegan, West Chicago, Westmont, Wheeling and Woodstock. Due to the fact that they have direct ties to the Mexican Mafia, law enforcement and affected communities should watch closely for increased drug distribution and the possibility of the Sureno 13s moving into human trafficking activities in the future.

18th STREET GANG

The 18th Street Gang was formed in the Rampart area of Los Angeles during the 1960s primarily by disenfranchised Hispanic youths unable to join the already established Clanton Street gang near 18th Street. Members of that gang had already entered its second generation, and generally, were thought to exclude non-citizen Hispanics then coming into the country. Authorities now suspect membership of the 18th Street gang in California alone to exceed 30,000 in about 30 different affiliates or cliques and now consider it one of the most violent street gangs in the country. Significantly, 18th Street set a precedent among California's Hispanic street gangs by becoming the first to break the racial barrier of recruitment to include not only Hispanics, but also Asians, African Americans and Caucasians. They were also thought to be the first California Hispanic street gang to recruit outside the state. As a result, 18th Street expanded recruitment during the 1990s to include many west and midwest states. Lately, law enforcement officers have encountered members in 14 states outside of California, including, unfortunately, Illinois.

Gang identifiers include tattoos and street graffiti comprising the numeral 18 or the Roman numeral version (XVIII). Even "666" tattoos show up occasionally. These body markings may appear anywhere, though the forehead area just above the eyebrows seems common. It is extremely important to point out though: lately, many members have gone to great lengths to conceal membership in the gang so as to make identification with the gang and prosecution more difficult. Graffiti, however, will often mark their turf and thus alert the community of their presence.

Authorities have observed a wide range of clothing identifiers (depending on gang cliques), including sports team paraphernalia. However, the most common clothing associated with the gang appears to be brown or black pants coupled with a simple white t-shirt.

18th Street gang crime consists mainly of carjackings, drive-by shootings, street taxes, arms trafficking and drug trafficking. Their drug networks and sales are believed to be international with connections to both the Mexican and Colombian drug cartels and national with connections to many African American gangs. Their main drug commerce is believed to consist of the sale of "crack" cocaine, marijuana, tar heroin and Methamphetamine or Meth. Authorities believe, as the popularity of Meth

sales increase, the 18th Street gang will grow to fill that demand.

Tax collecting from legitimate neighborhood shop owners or illegitimate street businesses seems to be a considerable source of revenue for the gang. Those who do not pay are usually met with extreme violence, including death. In 1994 alone, the L.A. District Attorney's office prosecuted 30 murders attributed to 18th Street tax collectors. Interestingly, those tax crews may consist of local street gang affiliates brought into the fold, but only with a prerequisite reputation for extreme violence. They then become enforcers, tax collectors and the like for the 18th Street.

18th Street has also extended its commerce to fraudulent immigration cards and identification papers, credit cards and even counterfeit food stamps.

Arms trafficking has allowed the gang to access a great variety of automatic weapons to reinforce their fierce reputation. So far these have included Tech 9s, Mac 10s, Mac 11s and AK 47s. Common gang firearms include .25 and .380 caliber handguns.

Finally, Chicagoland should be aware, this gang is regarded as highly sophisticated and organized. 18th Street is known to favor early recruitment of members who often come from elementary or middle-school and is thus known in some circles as the "Children's Army." They are then strongly indoctrinated in gang rules, the final of which is that leaving the gang will result in the death of the individual, or possibly even his or her family. As one gang member in California commented to investigators, "There is only one way out, and that's in a body bag." They have been reported to be in the suburb of Wheaton.

GIRLS IN GANGS

(Source: Chicago Crime Commission's *Girls Behind The Boys: Girls In Gangs* report)

Unfortunately, biases, misconceptions and a general lack of awareness in the past led to what we believe to be a vast misreporting and underreporting of female crime connected to street gangs. In 1999, Chicago Crime Commission researchers put the estimated number of female gang members in the Chicago area at 16,000 – 20,000. Mostly associates in the established male street gang, girls range from hardcore members to "groupies" looking for a good time and someplace to hang out. Law enforcement has documented their participation in all forms of violence. Their involvement, however, has not even come close to that of their male counterparts.

Girls making gang signs.

Why do girls join gangs?

Girls join gangs for the same reasons most boys do, because of multiple factors and circumstances that have existed throughout their life: financial opportunity, identity and status, peer pressure, family dysfunction and protection. However, some girls readily admit they join because they are bored and look to gangs for a social life — looking for fun and excitement — a means to find parties and meet boys. Regrettably for those who naively join expecting harmless social rewards, they may discover too late the actual violent nature of street gang existence.

Still, others join, simply, because gangs are there in the neighborhood and are viewed as an every day way of life. And perhaps the most disturbing impact of female association with street gang members is that eventually the relationship may result in children — children who are then growing up indoctrinated into the gang way of life.

It is not unheard of for girls to slide into gang involvement as early as age eight. Those that enter at this age and up to ten years of age often have family who are gang members or have experienced a strong gang presence in their neighborhood. At this age, the girl may begin to hang around the gang, learn gang culture, experiment with drugs and engage in low level criminal activity.

Ages eleven through twelve represent the more likely age at which a girl may enter a gang, usually to gain recognition from older females. By then, they may begin skipping school, drinking, experimenting with drugs, performing low-level crimes and engaging in sexual activity.

The prime age at which females will undergo their gang initiation appears to be around the ages of thirteen through fourteen. At this time, they may be quite active in property crime, such as larceny/theft, motor vehicle theft, and burglary, as well as weapons offenses and violent assaults. They are very likely engaging in sexual activity and some are getting pregnant.

CASE EXAMPLE:

February 24, 2006. Chicago Police "Operation Stingray" targeted an open air drug market in the Grand Central (25th) Police District controlled by the Insane Spanish Cobras street gang and run by a female member of the gang. Police shut down the market and arrested 14 of 15 targets in the investigation, including Lydia Conley, 23, who allegedly managed and operated the drug spot in the 2000 block of North Lawndale Avenue. Police estimate the market generated between $5,000 to $8,000 in profits a day. The drug spot was within 1,000 feet of two schools, a church, two parks, a senior citizen complex and a YMCA. Police made 15 undercover drug purchases and seized more than $1,100 in crack cocaine and two weapons as part of the investigation.

Ages fifteen through eighteen usually represent the hardcore years of female gang activity. Crimes committed, such as robbery and aggravated assault, peak at age fifteen and remain consistently high through this age period. Murders peak at around age eighteen.

Age nineteen and up, the female gang members face several options. If they have children, they may assume responsibility for paying bills and caring for the children. In order to do so they may continue to sell drugs, go into the sex trade industry or further participate in criminal activity. Indeed, statistics have shown that in this age range, female criminal activities peak in the form of white collar crimes such as fraud, forgery, counterfeiting and drug violations. Another path may lead to becoming a gang leader or advisor to young gang members. Younger girls will consider the leader or advisor to be an "OG" or "old gangster." The leader may be married to an active gang member and still socialize with and perform acts of crime for the gang. However, as she gets older that activity will often dissipate. Quite possibly, an older female gang member will find legitimate employment and advance her education. Those who do usually develop different interests and friends, causing them to drift away from their old gang and eventually leave it altogether.

Initiation

Initiation of a "wannabe" or outsider into the gang, marking full-fledged membership, may take several forms. The method is dependent upon the gang. In some cases, the initiate may select the method; in others, it will be dictated to her. They can generally be classified into four types: 1) "Violated" or "jumped in" refers to a physical beating the candidate must absorb to prove her toughness, loyalty and commitment to the gang; 2) The "Mission Method" simply requires the girl to commit a criminal act, perhaps ride along on a drive-by shooting or even be dropped off deep in enemy territory and forced to get out alive; 3) "Sexed in" is not the most common, but certainly the least respected initiation in which a female may elect to participate in sex with a gang member; however, both girls and boys alike look down on this initiation, and those that elect this course are usually typecast and have

extremely low status; and 4) "Walked in" or "blessed in" is reserved only for those girls who have had generations of family as gang members, who have a family member in good gang standing, or who have grown up in the neighborhood, are well known, respected and have proven their loyalty beyond question.

Roles

Functions of women in gangs vary depending on the individual's personality and the dynamics of the gang she joins. Typically she will fall into one of four membership categories: 1) auxiliary members of male gangs; 2) a female member of a co-ed gang; 3) members of autonomous all-female gangs; or 4) a female leader in a co-ed gang. In Chicago, the vast majority of female gang members may be categorized as being auxiliary members of male gangs. Although a few may rise to be marginally independent of some male authority and set rules for other girls in the gang, they are usually of lower status, subservient to male gang objectives, and depending on the gang culture, are usually treated with little respect by their male peers, who in some gangs view them as weak. Nonetheless, they perform integral gang duties such as serving as drug and weapons couriers, lookouts, luring rivals for ambushes and providing alibis. As members of a co-ed gang, they may achieve much higher status, because the male will trust them with sensitive matters such as stashing drugs, weapons and money. In the latter, they may launder large amounts of cash for the gang. They may also act as liaisons between the streets and members in prison. Some authorities believe that they may be the primary players in drug operations in that direction. Female leaders within co-ed gangs usually retain authority over the female portion of the gang and seldom rise to equal their male counterparts when it comes to decision making. They usually have a bond with a high-ranking male, they may be a family member, or perhaps a long time gang member who grew up in the neighborhood and who has proven their ability and loyalty beyond question. In some cases, they may actually run the business of a male counterpart, if the latter is incarcerated. Authorities believe that autonomous all-female gangs, while more common in Los Angeles, could be a future threat to Chicago youth. Auxilary members of male gangs may tire of subordination and strike out on their own assuming more authoritative roles.

All-female groups do exist. They are not yet classified as true street gangs, but are headed in that direction. The most common group of women, party crews, are groups of females who socialize and party together. They are not loyal to any one gang, but will go to whichever group is throwing the best parties or whomever they are most attracted to at any given moment.

There are no rules, allegiance, rituals, or hierarchy within the party crews. Benign as they might seem, regrettably, they put themselves in positions that may eventually provide the cohesion and tendencies common to street gangs.

Example: When a party crew infringes on the territory claimed by female auxiliary members of another gang, the party crew is forced to defend itself. Retaliations ensue and the cycle of violence begins. In some cases, party crews have branched out into the sale of certain drugs. Unfortunately, the trade exposes them to extreme danger with established street gangs who have long organized and tightly controlled the trade. The party crews may then be forced to commit loyalty to a gang, pay a street tax or risk being killed.

Some girls who appear to be gang members are wannabes. More commonly referred to as "groupies," they tag along with gang members, wear gang colors, sometimes engage in criminal activities, but retain their independence and have not been through any initiation.

Law enforcement and others must monitor female gang activity closely so as to avoid female gangs from following in the footsteps of the powerful male gangs.

The roles that girls in gangs may play are extensive and may include:

- holding and transporting drugs and guns as law enforcement are less likely to search women

- acting as information and contraband couriers to and from prisons

- finding strategic employment: infiltrating law enforcement or county clerk's offices to secure intelligence on gang member targets or witnesses acting against their own members; working for law firms in order to facilitate communications to members who are imprisoned; working for temp services and a host of other companies in order to get personal information on the general public (e.g. credit card numbers, etc.) for white collar fraud schemes; or working in bookstores in order to hide contraband (e.g. drugs) mailed to prison inmates

- acting as lures with rival gang members to secure information or set them up for a murder or a violent hit

- criminal support to include selling drugs, robbery, burglary, car jacking, car theft, drive-by shootings, etc.

- purchasing weapons

- hiding money

- and providing behind the scenes domestic support

CHICAGO NEIGHBORHOODS MAP

Source: Dream Town Realty Inc. • *www.DreamTown.com*

Throughout the report, Chicago neighborhoods are referenced.
This map provides a clearer idea of where these areas are located.

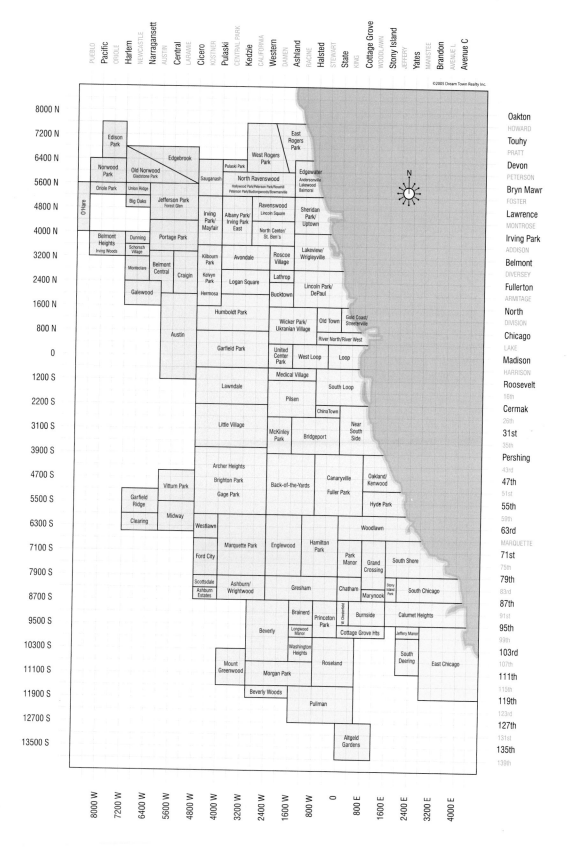

SECTION 2

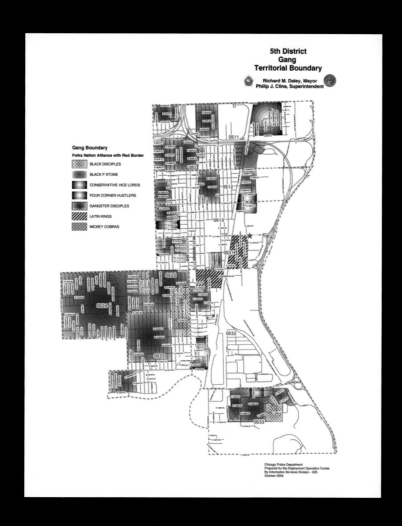

**5th District
Gang
Territorial Boundary**

Richard M. Daley, Mayor
Philip J. Cline, Superintendent

Gang Boundary
Folks Nation Alliance with Red Border

BLACK DISCIPLES

BLACK P STONE

CONSERVATIVE VICE LORDS

FOUR CORNER HUSTLERS

GANGSTER DISCIPLES

LATIN KINGS

MICKEY COBRAS

Chicago Police Department
Prepared for the Deployment Operation Center
By Information Services Division - GIS
October 2004

Chicago Gang Maps, Organizational Structure and Leadership

1ST DISTRICT GANG TERRITORIAL BOUNDARY

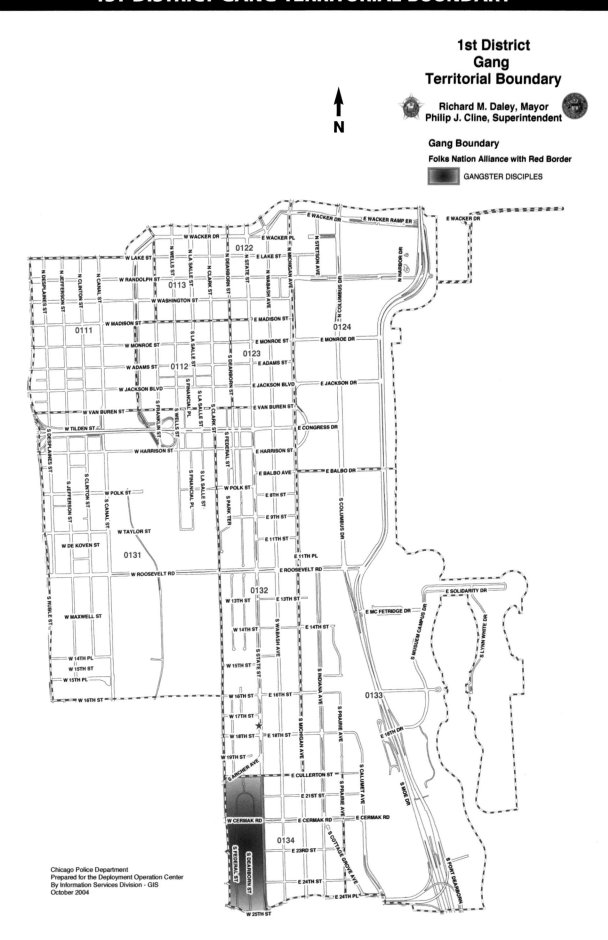

**1st District
Gang
Territorial Boundary**

Richard M. Daley, Mayor
Philip J. Cline, Superintendent

Gang Boundary

Folks Nation Alliance with Red Border

GANGSTER DISCIPLES

Section Two

Chicago Police Department
Prepared for the Deployment Operation Center
By Information Services Division - GIS
October 2004

2ND DISTRICT GANG TERRITORIAL BOUNDARY

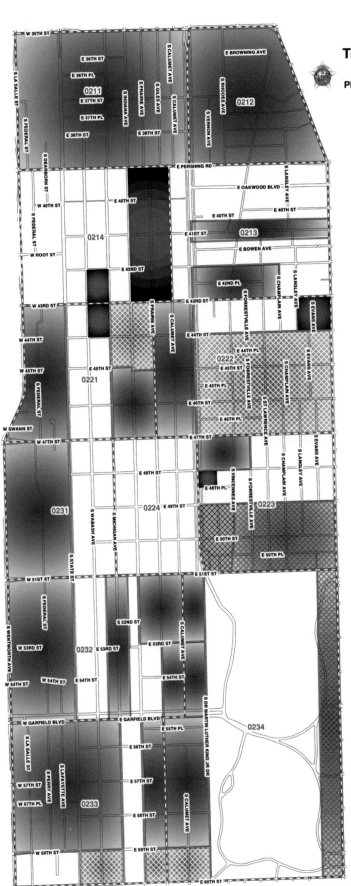

2nd District Gang Territorial Boundary

Richard M. Daley, Mayor
Philip J. Cline, Superintendent

Gang Boundary

Folks Nation Alliance with Red Border

- BLACK DISCIPLES
- BLACK P STONE & MICKEY COBRAS
- GANGSTER DISCIPLES
- MAFIA INSANE VICE LORDS
- MICKEY COBRAS

N

Chicago Police Department
Prepared for the Deployment Operation Center
By Information Services Division - GIS
October 2004

3RD DISTRICT GANG TERRITORIAL BOUNDARY

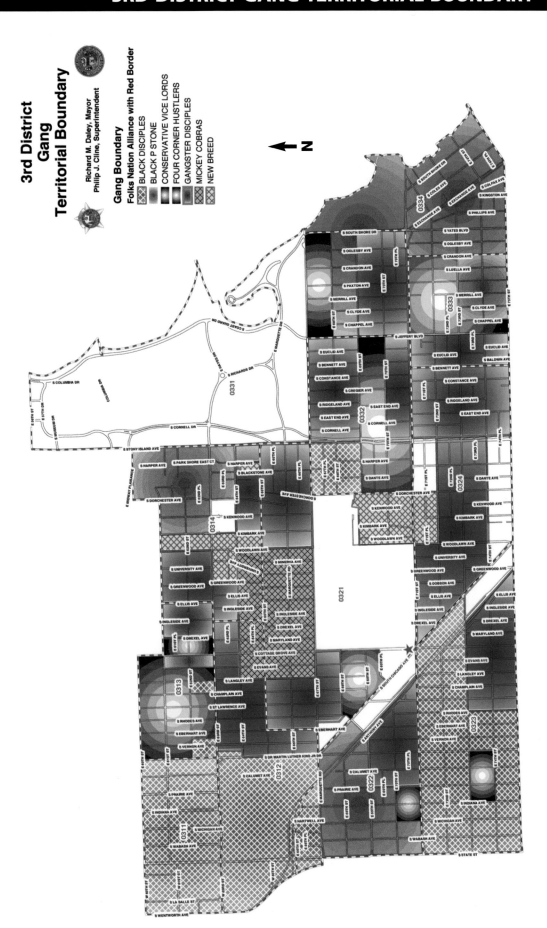

3rd District
Gang
Territorial Boundary

Richard M. Daley, Mayor
Philip J. Cline, Superintendent

Gang Boundary
Folks Nation Alliance with Red Border
- BLACK DISCIPLES
- BLACK P STONE
- CONSERVATIVE VICE LORDS
- FOUR CORNER HUSTLERS
- GANGSTER DISCIPLES
- MICKEY COBRAS
- NEW BREED

N

Chicago Police Department
Prepared for the Deployment Operation Center
By Information Services Division - GIS
October 2004

Section Two

4TH DISTRICT GANG TERRITORIAL BOUNDARY

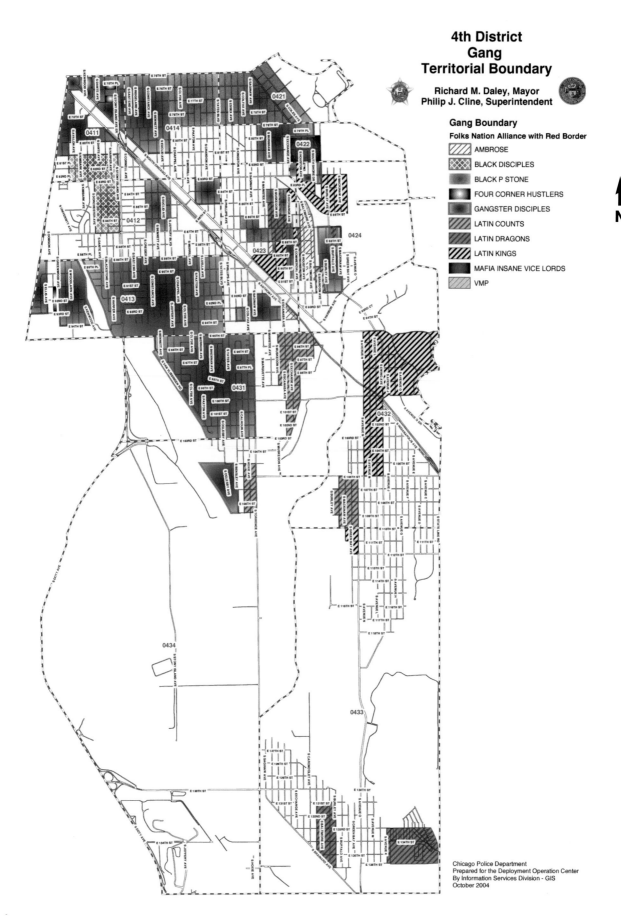

4th District Gang Territorial Boundary

Richard M. Daley, Mayor
Philip J. Cline, Superintendent

Gang Boundary

Folks Nation Alliance with Red Border

- AMBROSE
- BLACK DISCIPLES
- BLACK P STONE
- FOUR CORNER HUSTLERS
- GANGSTER DISCIPLES
- LATIN COUNTS
- LATIN DRAGONS
- LATIN KINGS
- MAFIA INSANE VICE LORDS
- VMP

N

Chicago Police Department
Prepared for the Deployment Operation Center
By Information Services Division - GIS
October 2004

Section Two

5TH DISTRICT GANG TERRITORIAL BOUNDARY

**5th District
Gang
Territorial Boundary**

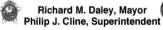

Richard M. Daley, Mayor
Philip J. Cline, Superintendent

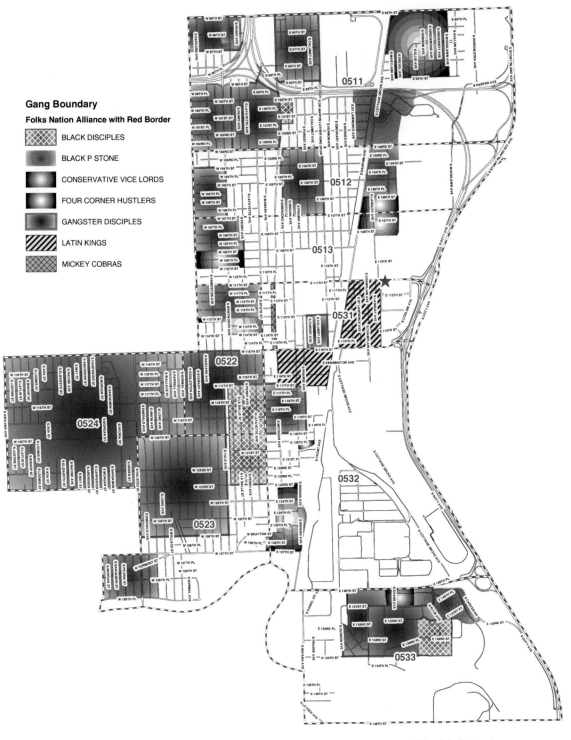

Gang Boundary

Folks Nation Alliance with Red Border

- BLACK DISCIPLES
- BLACK P STONE
- CONSERVATIVE VICE LORDS
- FOUR CORNER HUSTLERS
- GANGSTER DISCIPLES
- LATIN KINGS
- MICKEY COBRAS

Chicago Police Department
Prepared for the Deployment Operation Center
By Information Services Division - GIS
October 2004

6TH DISTRICT GANG TERRITORIAL BOUNDARY

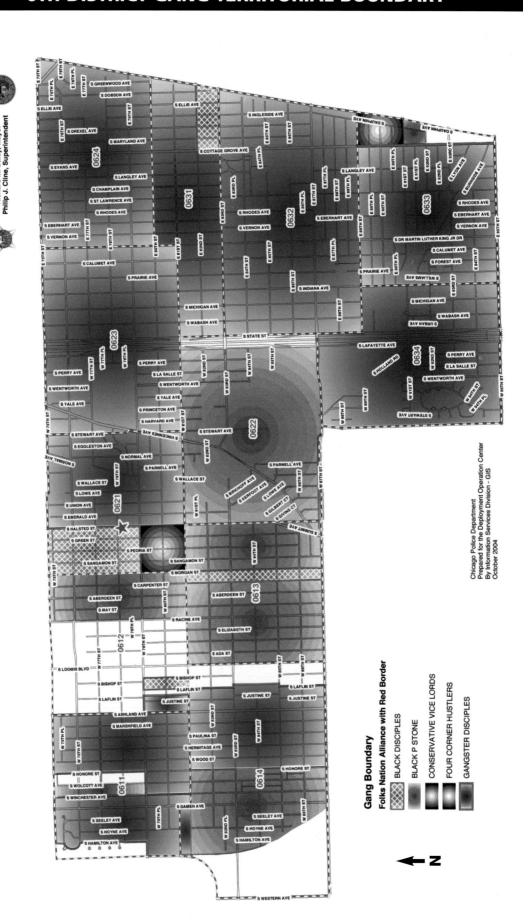

6th District
Gang
Territorial Boundary

Richard M. Daley, Mayor
Philip J. Cline, Superintendent

Section Two

Gang Boundary
Folks Nation Alliance with Red Border

- BLACK DISCIPLES
- BLACK P STONE
- CONSERVATIVE VICE LORDS
- FOUR CORNER HUSTLERS
- GANGSTER DISCIPLES

Chicago Police Department
Prepared for the Deployment Operation Center
By Information Services Division - GIS
October 2004

7TH DISTRICT GANG TERRITORIAL BOUNDARY

7th District
Gang
Territorial Boundary
Richard M. Daley, Mayor
Philip J. Cline, Superintendent
Gang Boundary
Folks Nation Alliance with Red Border
BLACK DISCIPLES
BLACK P STONE
CONSERVATIVE VICE LORDS
GANGSTER DISCIPLES
RUBENITES
Chicago Police Department
Prepared for the Deployment Operation Center
By Information Services Division - GIS
October 2004
N
0711
0712
0713
0714
0715
0722
0723
0724
0725
0726
0731
0732
0733
0734
0735

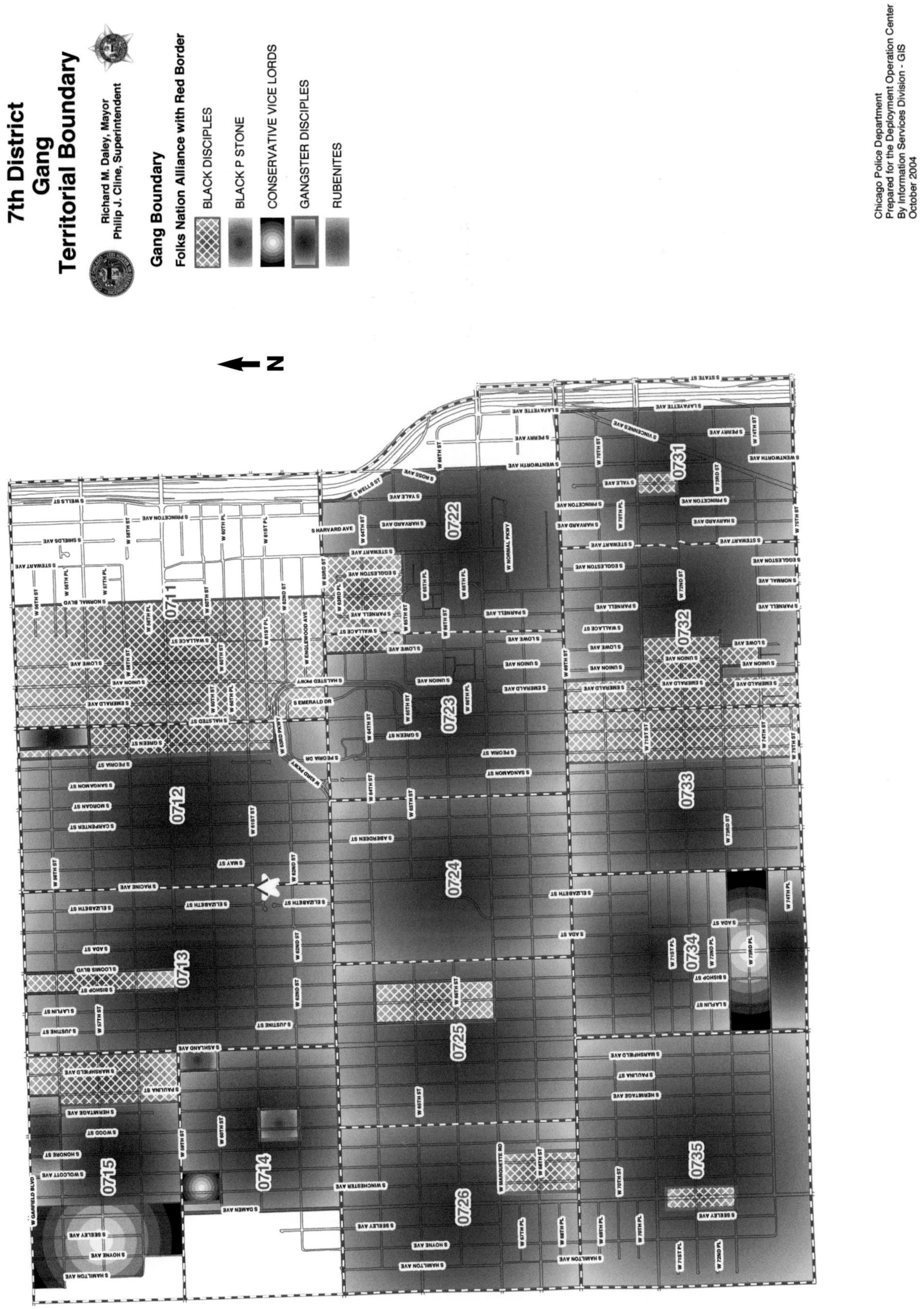

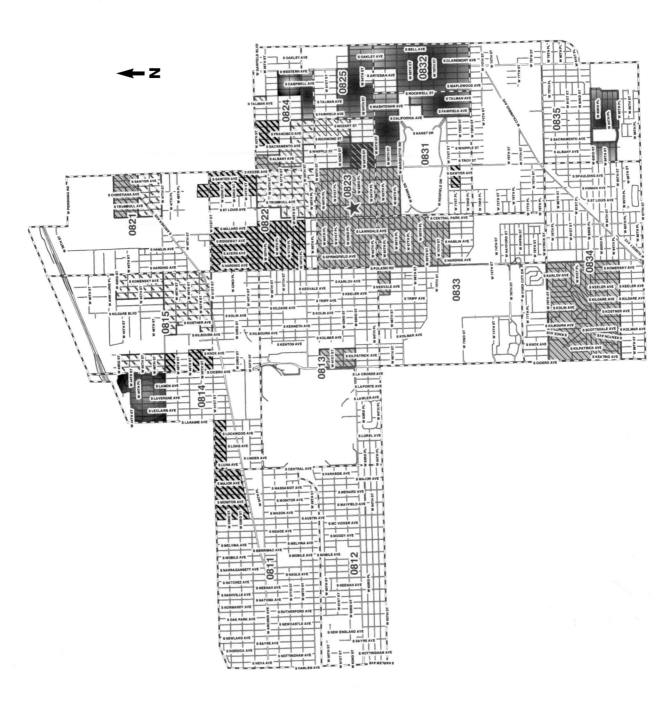

8th District Gang Territorial Boundary

Richard M. Daley, Mayor
Philip J. Cline, Superintendent

Gang Boundary

Folks Nation Alliance with Red Border

- AMBROSE
- CITY KNIGHTS
- CONSERVATIVE VICE LORDS
- GANGSTER DISCIPLES
- LATIN KINGS
- MANIAC LATIN DISCIPLES
- PARTY PEOPLE
- SATAN DISCIPLES
- TRAVELING VICE LORDS
- TWO-SIX

Chicago Police Department
Prepared for the Deployment Operation Center
By Information Services Division - GIS
October 2004

Section Two

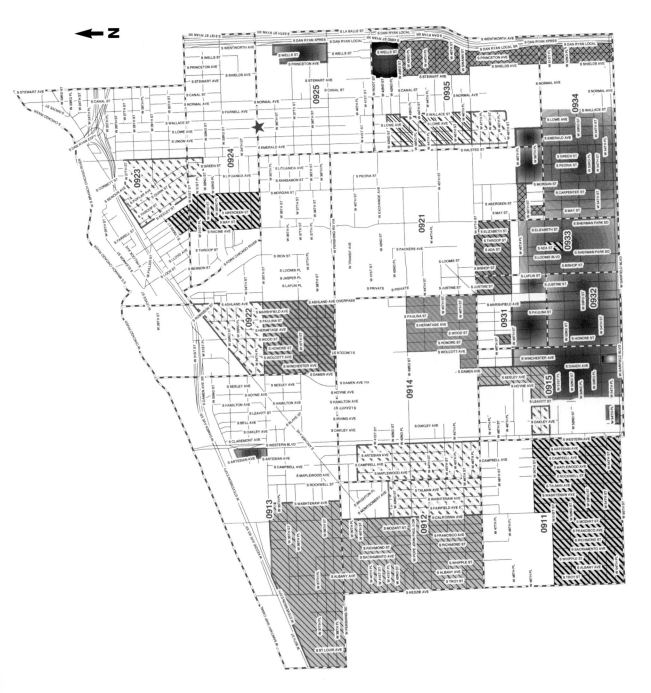

9th District Gang Territorial Boundary

Richard M. Daley, Mayor
Philip J. Cline, Superintendent

Gang Boundary
Folks Nation Alliance with Red Border

- BLACK P STONE
- CONSERVATIVE VICE LORDS
- GANGSTER DISCIPLES
- INSANE CULLERTON DEUCES
- LA RAZA
- LATIN COUNTS
- LATIN KINGS
- LATIN SAINTS
- MAFIA INSANE VICE LORDS
- MICKEY COBRAS
- SATAN DISCIPLES
- SPANISH COBRAS
- TWO-SIX

Chicago Police Department
Prepared for the Deployment Operation Center
By Information Services Division - GIS
October 2004

Section Two

10TH DISTRICT GANG TERRITORIAL BOUNDARY

Section Two

10th District Gang Territorial Boundary

Richard M. Daley, Mayor
Philip J. Cline, Superintendent

Gang Boundary

Folks Nation Alliance with Red Border

- AMBROSE
- BLACK SOULS
- CONSERVATIVE VICE LORDS
- GANGSTER DISCIPLES
- INSANE CULLERTON DEUCES
- LATIN KINGS
- MIX UNKNOWN & TRAVELING VICE LORDS
- NEW BREED
- SATAN DISCIPLES
- TRAVELING VICE LORDS
- TWO-SIX
- TWO-TWO BOYS

← N

Chicago Police Department
Prepared for the Deployment Operation Center
By Information Services Division - GIS
October 2004

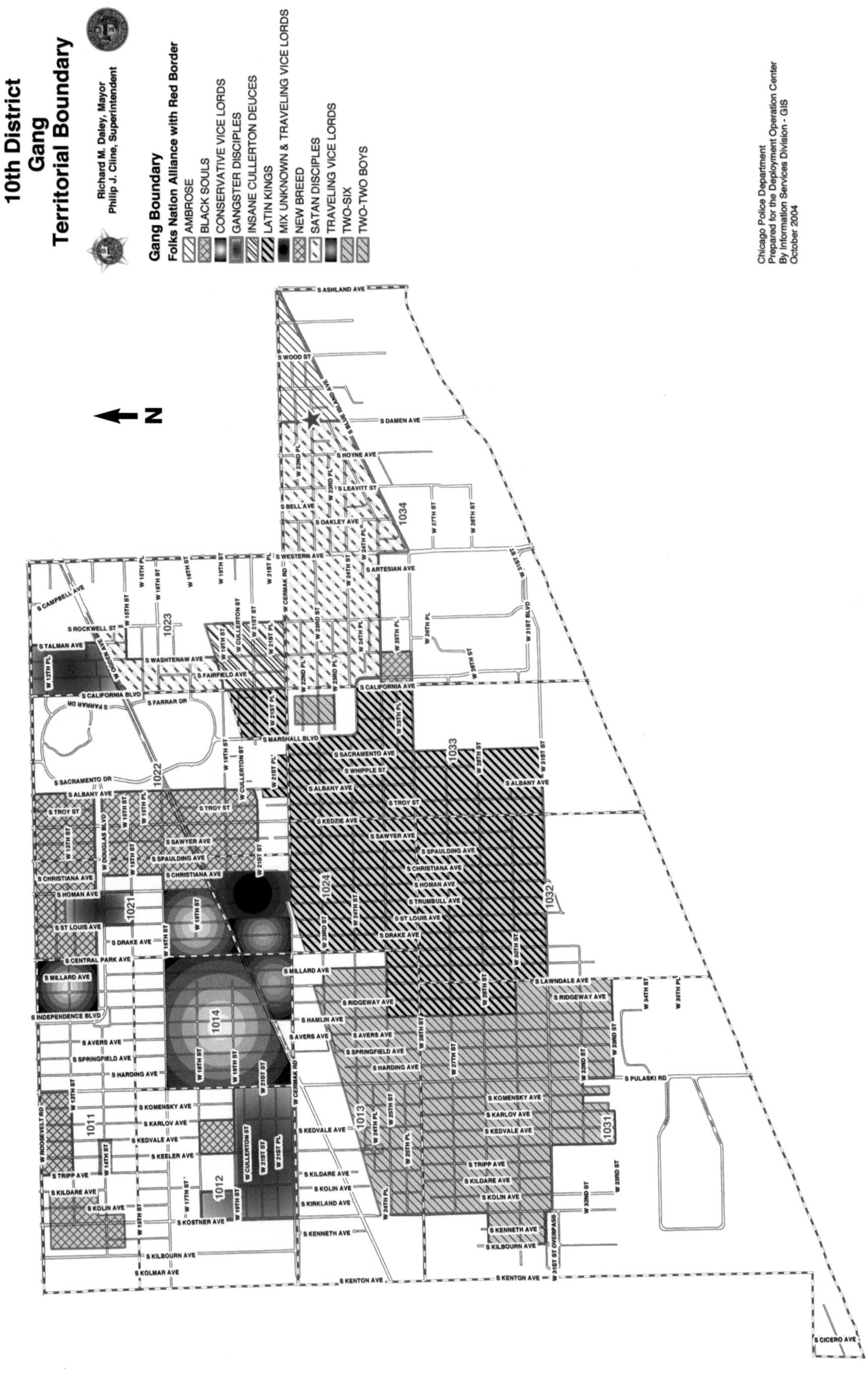

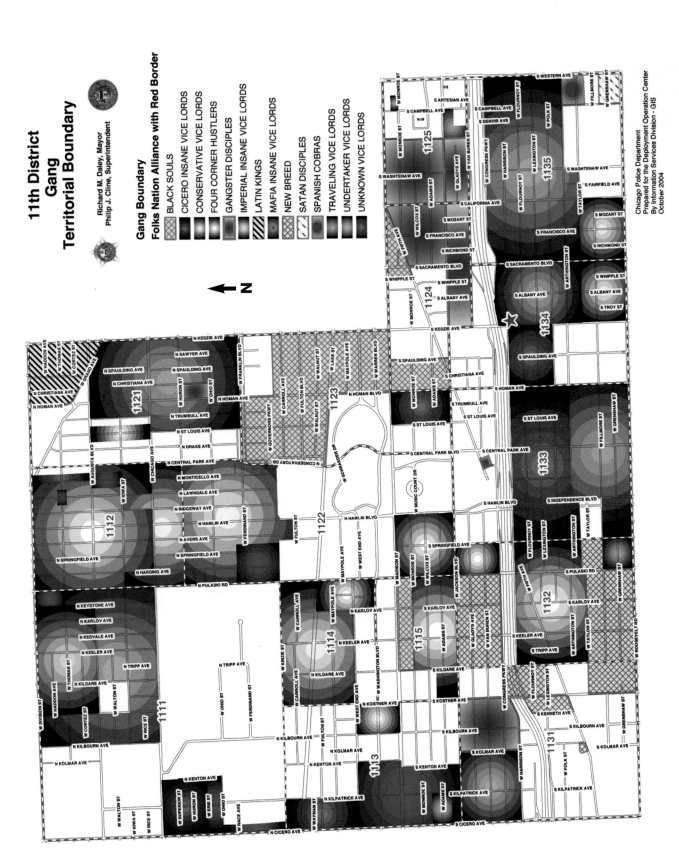

11th District Gang Territorial Boundary

Richard M. Daley, Mayor
Philip J. Cline, Superintendent

Gang Boundary
Folks Nation Alliance with Red Border

- BLACK SOULS
- CICERO INSANE VICE LORDS
- CONSERVATIVE VICE LORDS
- FOUR CORNER HUSTLERS
- GANGSTER DISCIPLES
- IMPERIAL INSANE VICE LORDS
- LATIN KINGS
- MAFIA INSANE VICE LORDS
- NEW BREED
- SATAN DISCIPLES
- SPANISH COBRAS
- TRAVELING VICE LORDS
- UNDERTAKER VICE LORDS
- UNKNOWN VICE LORDS

N

Chicago Police Department
Prepared for the Deployment Operation Center
By Information Services Division - GIS
October 2004

Section Two

12TH DISTRICT GANG TERRITORIAL BOUNDARY

**12th District
Gang
Territorial Boundary**

Richard M. Daley, Mayor
Philip J. Cline, Superintendent

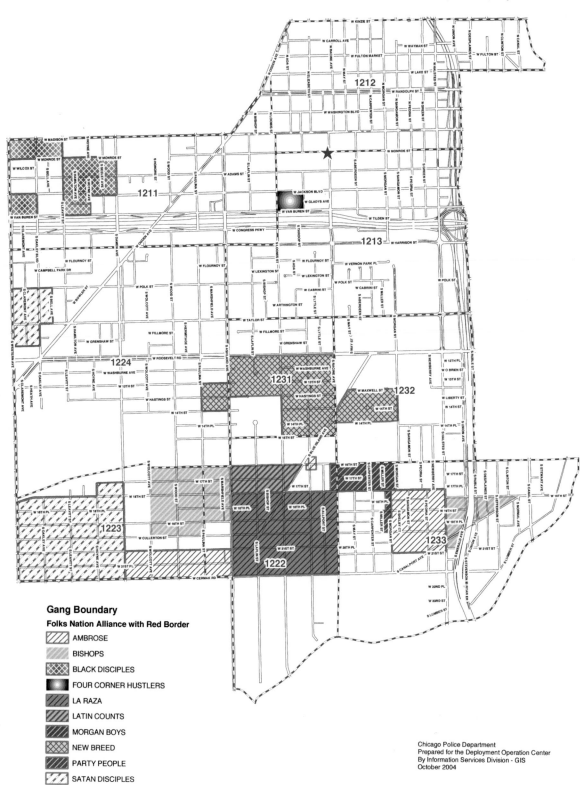

Gang Boundary

Folks Nation Alliance with Red Border

- AMBROSE
- BISHOPS
- BLACK DISCIPLES
- FOUR CORNER HUSTLERS
- LA RAZA
- LATIN COUNTS
- MORGAN BOYS
- NEW BREED
- PARTY PEOPLE
- SATAN DISCIPLES

N

Chicago Police Department
Prepared for the Deployment Operation Center
By Information Services Division - GIS
October 2004

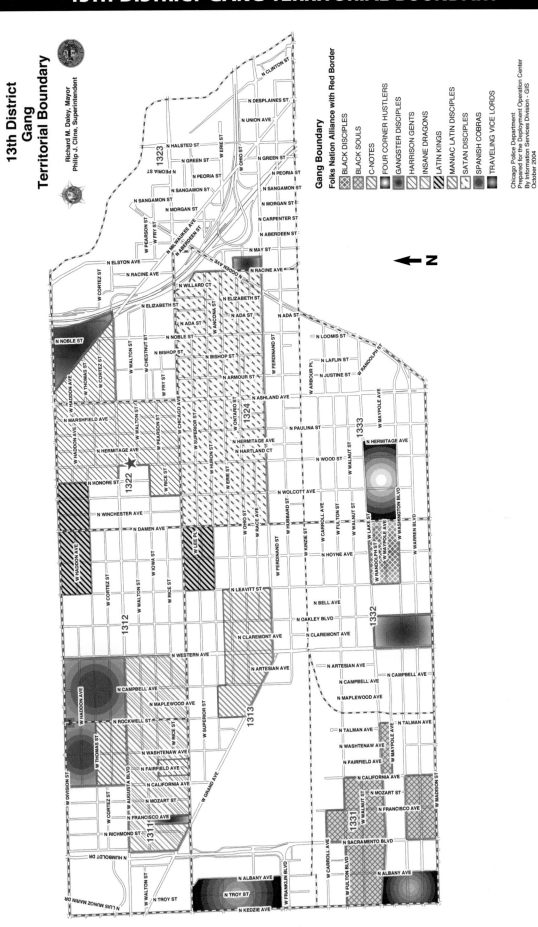

13th District Gang Territorial Boundary

Richard M. Daley, Mayor
Philip J. Cline, Superintendent

Gang Boundary

Folks Nation Alliance with Red Border

- BLACK DISCIPLES
- BLACK SOULS
- C-NOTES
- FOUR CORNER HUSTLERS
- GANGSTER DISCIPLES
- HARRISON GENTS
- INSANE DRAGONS
- LATIN KINGS
- MANIAC LATIN DISCIPLES
- SATAN DISCIPLES
- SPANISH COBRAS
- TRAVELING VICE LORDS

Chicago Police Department
Prepared for the Deployment Operation Center
By Information Services Division - GIS
October 2004

Section Two

14TH DISTRICT GANG TERRITORIAL BOUNDARY

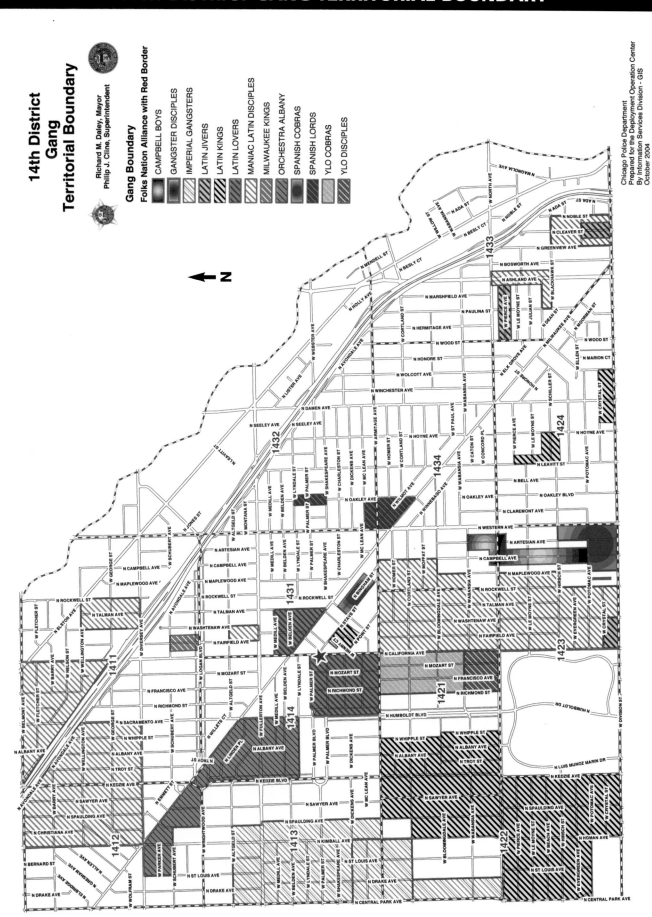

14th District Gang Territorial Boundary

Richard M. Daley, Mayor
Philip J. Cline, Superintendent

Gang Boundary
Folks Nation Alliance with Red Border

- CAMPBELL BOYS
- GANGSTER DISCIPLES
- IMPERIAL GANGSTERS
- LATIN JIVERS
- LATIN KINGS
- LATIN LOVERS
- MANIAC LATIN DISCIPLES
- MILWAUKEE KINGS
- ORCHESTRA ALBANY
- SPANISH COBRAS
- SPANISH LORDS
- YLO COBRAS
- YLO DISCIPLES

Chicago Police Department
Prepared for the Deployment Operation Center
By Information Services Division - GIS
October 2004

Section Two

15TH DISTRICT GANG TERRITORIAL BOUNDARY

N

15th District Gang Territorial Boundary

Richard M. Daley, Mayor
Philip J. Cline, Superintendent

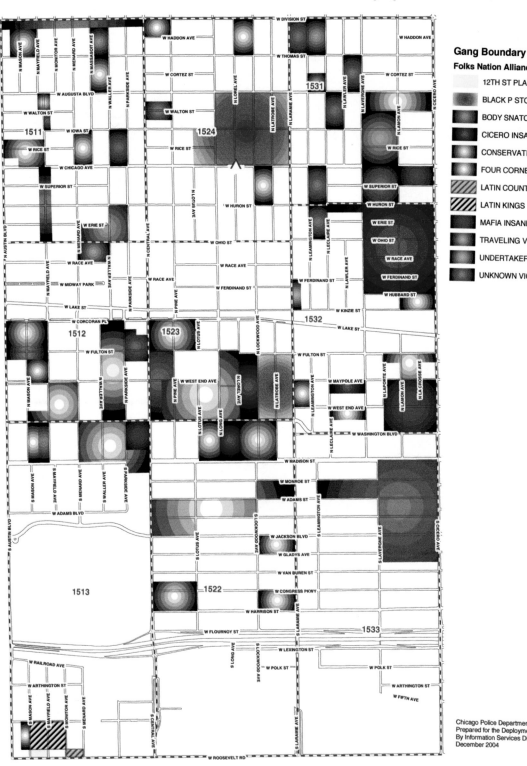

Gang Boundary

Folks Nation Alliance with Red Border

	12TH ST PLAYERS
	BLACK P STONE
	BODY SNATCHERS
	CICERO INSANE VICE LORDS
	CONSERVATIVE VICE LORDS
	FOUR CORNER HUSTLERS
	LATIN COUNTS
	LATIN KINGS
	MAFIA INSANE VICE LORDS
	TRAVELING VICE LORDS
	UNDERTAKER VICE LORDS
	UNKNOWN VICE LORDS

Chicago Police Department
Prepared for the Deployment Operation Center
By Information Services Division - GIS
December 2004

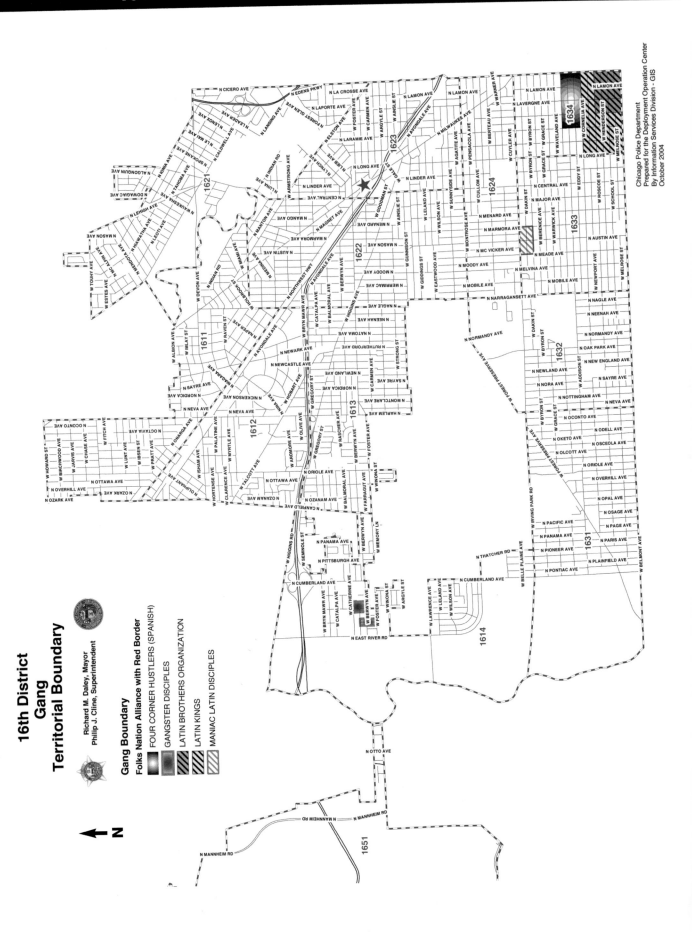

16th District Gang Territorial Boundary

Richard M. Daley, Mayor
Phillip J. Cline, Superintendent

Gang Boundary
Folks Nation Alliance with Red Border
FOUR CORNER HUSTLERS (SPANISH)
GANGSTER DISCIPLES
LATIN BROTHERS ORGANIZATION
LATIN KINGS
MANIAC LATIN DISCIPLES

Chicago Police Department
Prepared for the Deployment Operation Center
By Information Services Division - GIS
October 2004

17TH DISTRICT GANG TERRITORIAL BOUNDARY

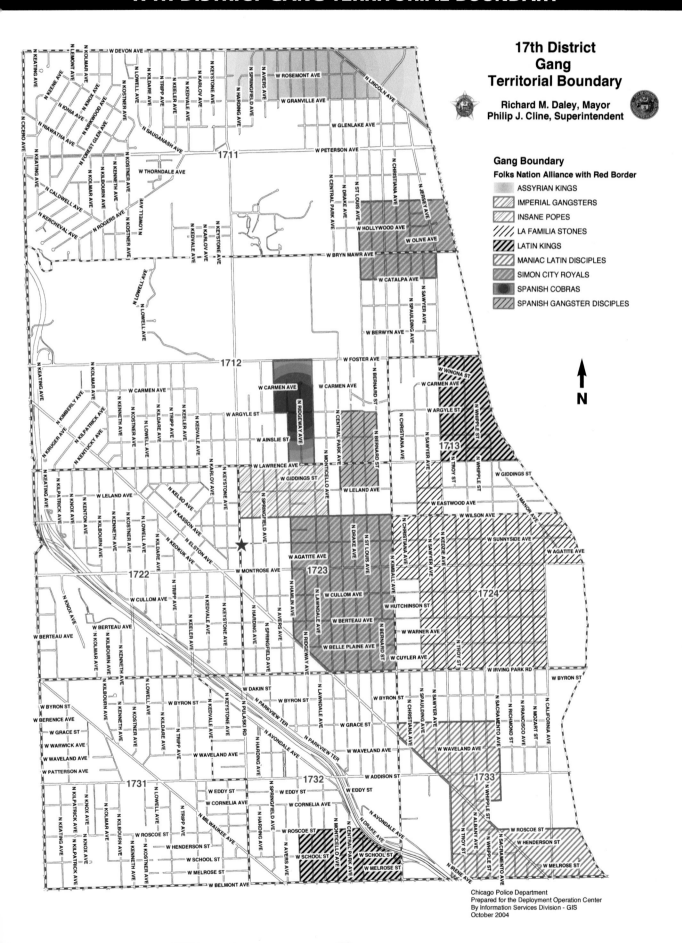

**17th District
Gang
Territorial Boundary**

Richard M. Daley, Mayor
Philip J. Cline, Superintendent

Gang Boundary
Folks Nation Alliance with Red Border

ASSYRIAN KINGS
IMPERIAL GANGSTERS
INSANE POPES
LA FAMILIA STONES
LATIN KINGS
MANIAC LATIN DISCIPLES
SIMON CITY ROYALS
SPANISH COBRAS
SPANISH GANGSTER DISCIPLES

Chicago Police Department
Prepared for the Deployment Operation Center
By Information Services Division - GIS
October 2004

Section Two

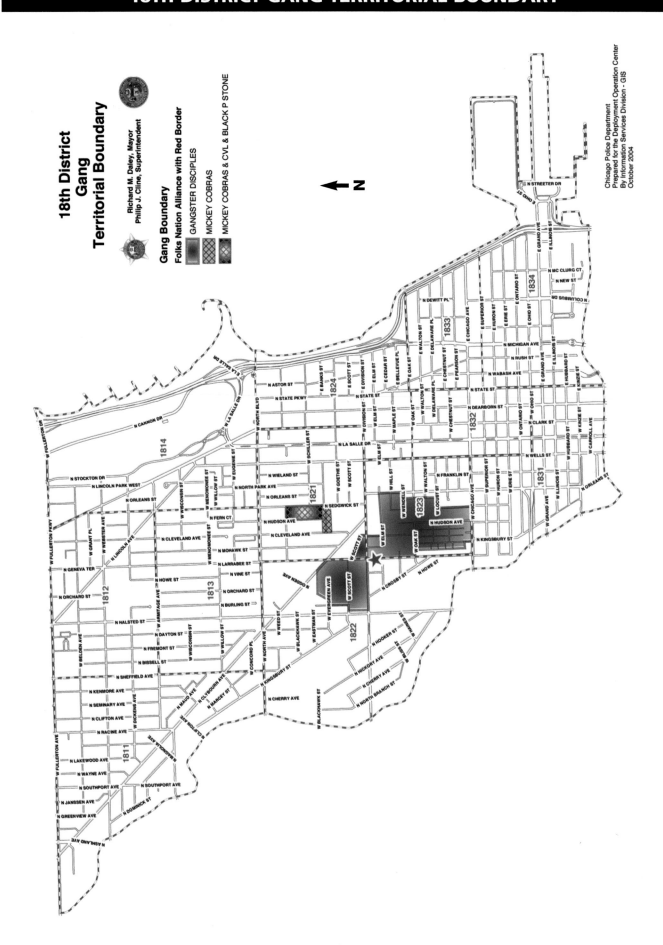

18th District
Gang
Territorial Boundary

Richard M. Daley, Mayor
Philip J. Cline, Superintendent

Gang Boundary

Folks Nation Alliance with Red Border

GANGSTER DISCIPLES

MICKEY COBRAS

MICKEY COBRAS & CVL & BLACK P STONE

Chicago Police Department
Prepared for the Deployment Operation Center
By Information Services Division - GIS
October 2004

19TH DISTRICT GANG TERRITORIAL BOUNDARY

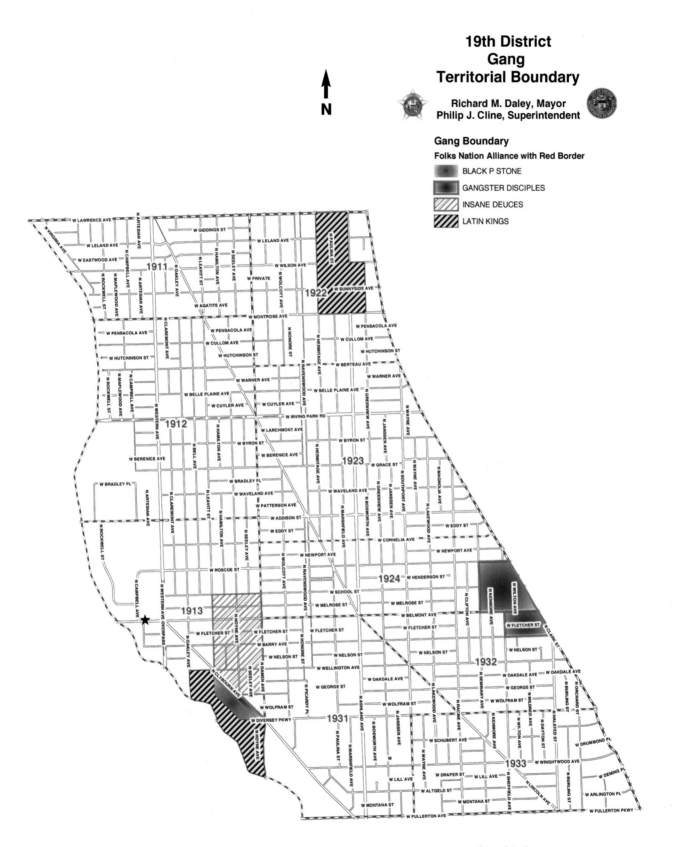

**19th District
Gang
Territorial Boundary**

Richard M. Daley, Mayor
Philip J. Cline, Superintendent

Gang Boundary
Folks Nation Alliance with Red Border

BLACK P STONE
GANGSTER DISCIPLES
INSANE DEUCES
LATIN KINGS

N

Chicago Police Department
Prepared for the Deployment Operation Center
By Information Services Division - GIS
October 2004

20TH DISTRICT GANG TERRITORIAL BOUNDARY

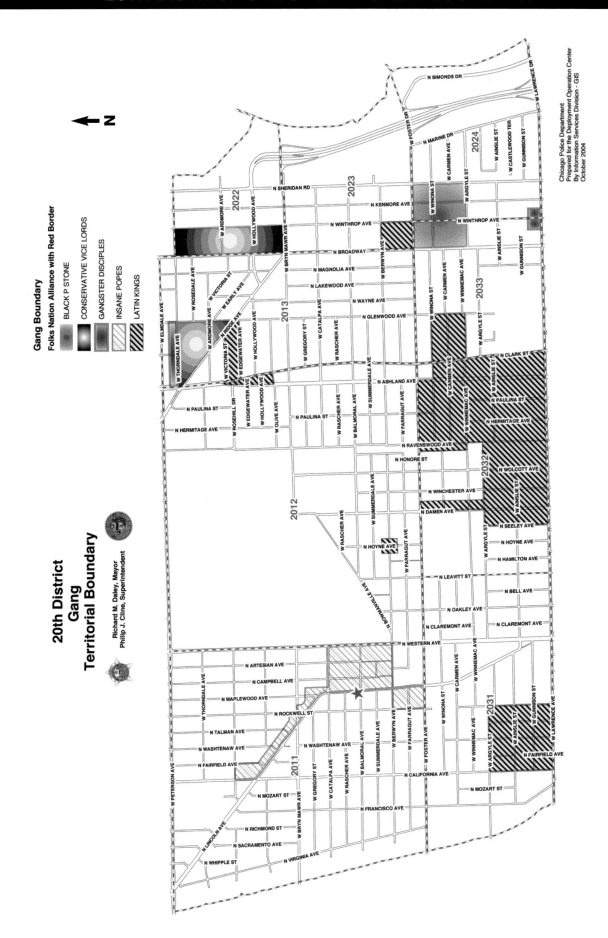

21ST DISTRICT GANG TERRITORIAL BOUNDARY

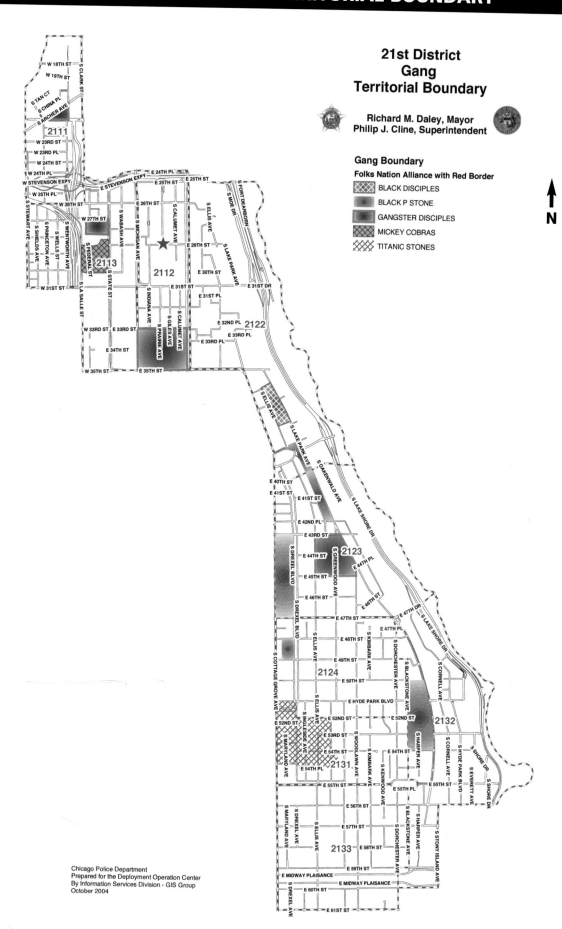

**21st District
Gang
Territorial Boundary**

Richard M. Daley, Mayor
Philip J. Cline, Superintendent

Gang Boundary
Folks Nation Alliance with Red Border

- BLACK DISCIPLES
- BLACK P STONE
- GANGSTER DISCIPLES
- MICKEY COBRAS
- TITANIC STONES

N

Section Two

Chicago Police Department
Prepared for the Deployment Operation Center
By Information Services Division - GIS Group
October 2004

22ND DISTRICT GANG TERRITORIAL BOUNDARY

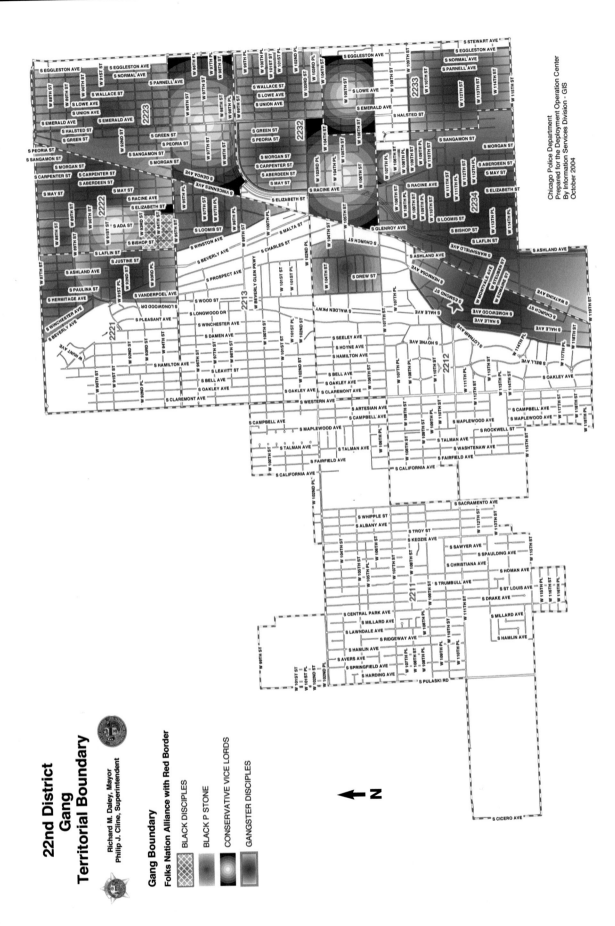

Chicago Police Department
Prepared for the Deployment Operation Center
By Information Services Division - GIS
October 2004

22nd District Gang Territorial Boundary

Richard M. Daley, Mayor
Philip J. Cline, Superintendent

Gang Boundary
Folks Nation Alliance with Red Border

BLACK DISCIPLES
BLACK P STONE
CONSERVATIVE VICE LORDS
GANGSTER DISCIPLES

N

Section Two

23RD DISTRICT GANG TERRITORIAL BOUNDARY

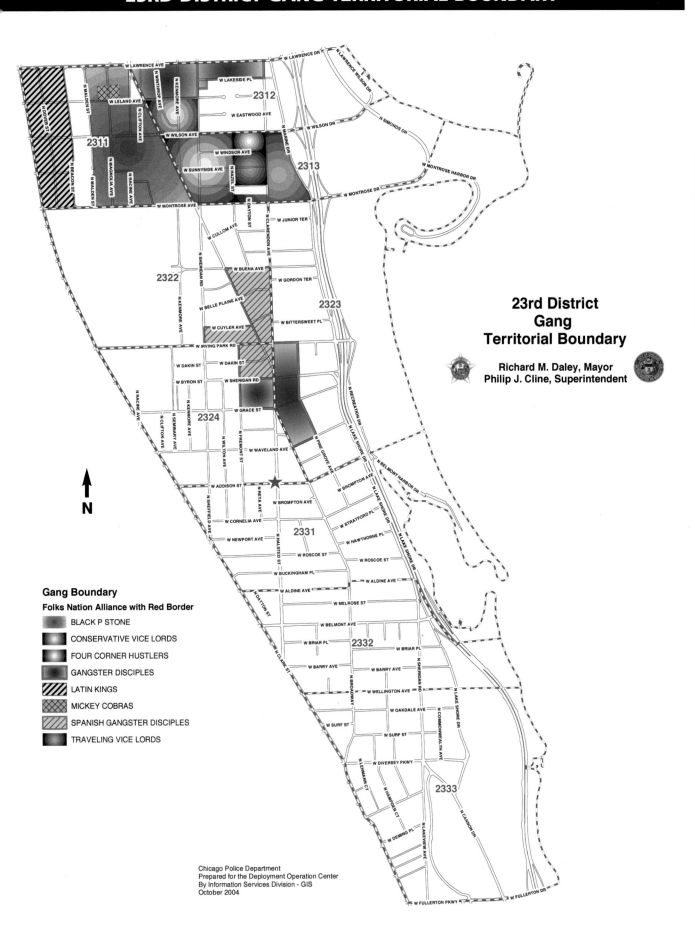

**23rd District
Gang
Territorial Boundary**

Richard M. Daley, Mayor
Philip J. Cline, Superintendent

Gang Boundary

Folks Nation Alliance with Red Border

- BLACK P STONE
- CONSERVATIVE VICE LORDS
- FOUR CORNER HUSTLERS
- GANGSTER DISCIPLES
- LATIN KINGS
- MICKEY COBRAS
- SPANISH GANGSTER DISCIPLES
- TRAVELING VICE LORDS

Chicago Police Department
Prepared for the Deployment Operation Center
By Information Services Division - GIS
October 2004

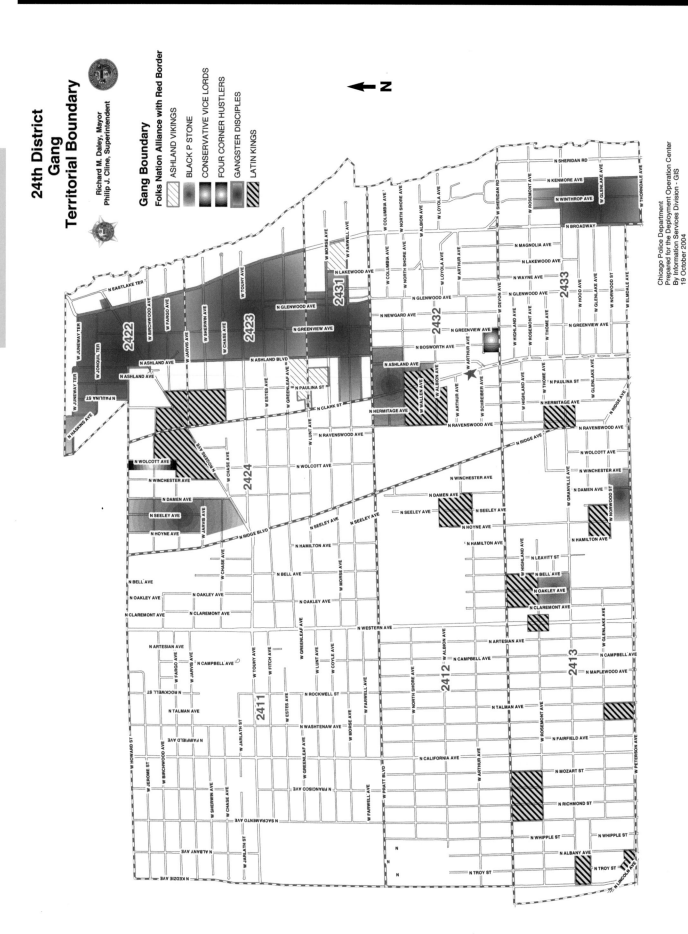

25TH DISTRICT GANG TERRITORIAL BOUNDARY

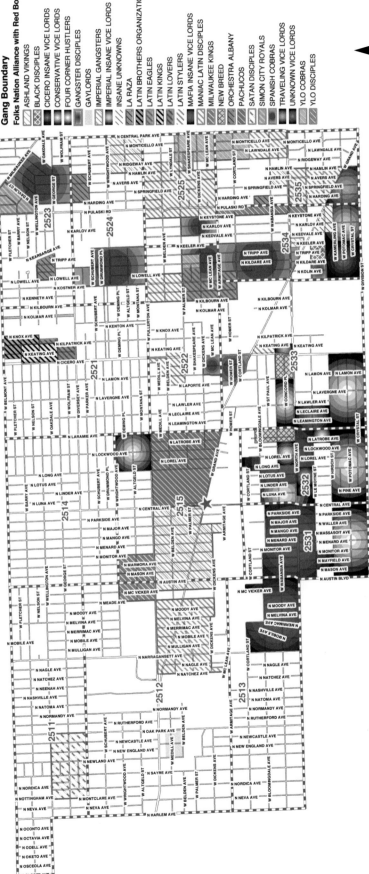

25th District Gang Territorial Boundary

Richard M. Daley, Mayor
Philip J. Cline, Superintendent

Gang Boundary
Folks Nation Alliance with Red Border

- ASHLAND VIKINGS
- BLACK DISCIPLES
- CICERO INSANE VICE LORDS
- CONSERVATIVE VICE LORDS
- FOUR CORNER HUSTLERS
- GANGSTER DISCIPLES
- GAYLORDS
- IMPERIAL GANGSTERS
- IMPERIAL INSANE VICE LORDS
- INSANE UNKNOWNS
- LA RAZA
- LATIN BROTHERS ORGANIZATION
- LATIN EAGLES
- LATIN KINGS
- LATIN LOVERS
- LATIN STYLERS
- MAFIA INSANE VICE LORDS
- MANIAC LATIN DISCIPLES
- MILWAUKEE KINGS
- NEW BREED
- ORCHESTRA ALBANY
- PACHUCOS
- SATAN DISCIPLES
- SIMON CITY ROYALS
- SPANISH COBRAS
- TRAVELING VICE LORDS
- UNKNOWN VICE LORDS
- YLO COBRAS
- YLO DISCIPLES

N

Chicago Police Department
Prepared for the Deployment Operation Center
By Information Services Division - GIS
October 2004

Section Two

71

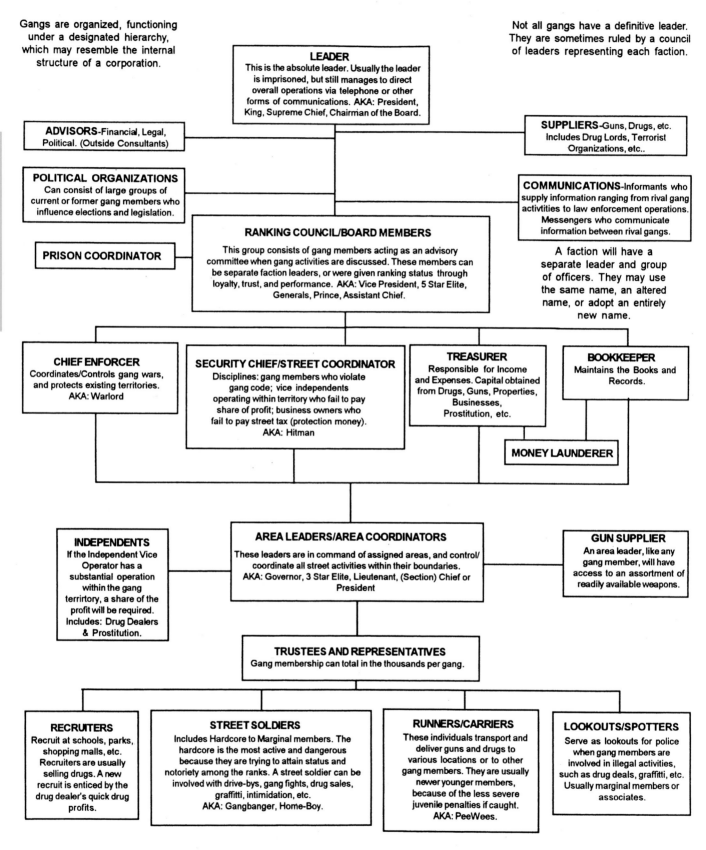

Gangs are organized, functioning under a designated hierarchy, which may resemble the internal structure of a corporation.

Not all gangs have a definitive leader. They are sometimes ruled by a council of leaders representing each faction.

Section Two

LEADER
This is the absolute leader. Usually the leader is imprisoned, but still manages to direct overall operations via telephone or other forms of communications. AKA: President, King, Supreme Chief, Chairman of the Board.

ADVISORS-Financial, Legal, Political. (Outside Consultants)

SUPPLIERS-Guns, Drugs, etc. Includes Drug Lords, Terrorist Organizations, etc..

POLITICAL ORGANIZATIONS
Can consist of large groups of current or former gang members who influence elections and legislation.

COMMUNICATIONS-Informants who supply information ranging from rival gang activtities to law enforcement operations. Messengers who communicate information between rival gangs.

PRISON COORDINATOR

RANKING COUNCIL/BOARD MEMBERS
This group consists of gang members acting as an advisory committee when gang activities are discussed. These members can be separate faction leaders, or were given ranking status through loyalty, trust, and performance. AKA: Vice President, 5 Star Elite, Generals, Prince, Assistant Chief.

A faction will have a separate leader and group of officers. They may use the same name, an altered name, or adopt an entirely new name.

CHIEF ENFORCER
Coordinates/Controls gang wars, and protects existing territories.
AKA: Warlord

SECURITY CHIEF/STREET COORDINATOR
Disciplines: gang members who violate gang code; vice independents operating within territory who fail to pay share of profit; business owners who fail to pay street tax (protection money).
AKA: Hitman

TREASURER
Responsible for Income and Expenses. Capital obtained from Drugs, Guns, Properties, Businesses, Prostitution, etc.

BOOKKEEPER
Maintains the Books and Records.

MONEY LAUNDERER

INDEPENDENTS
If the Independent Vice Operator has a substantial operation within the gang terrirtory, a share of the profit will be required. Includes: Drug Dealers & Prostitution.

AREA LEADERS/AREA COORDINATORS
These leaders are in command of assigned areas, and control/coordinate all street activities within their boundaries.
AKA: Governor, 3 Star Elite, Lieutenant, (Section) Chief or President

GUN SUPPLIER
An area leader, like any gang member, will have access to an assortment of readily available weapons.

TRUSTEES AND REPRESENTATIVES
Gang membership can total in the thousands per gang.

RECRUITERS
Recruit at schools, parks, shopping malls, etc. Recruiters are usually selling drugs. A new recruit is enticed by the drug dealer's quick drug profits.

STREET SOLDIERS
Includes Hardcore to Marginal members. The hardcore is the most active and dangerous because they are trying to attain status and notoriety among the ranks. A street soldier can be involved with drive-bys, gang fights, drug sales, graffitti, intimidation, etc.
AKA: Gangbanger, Home-Boy.

RUNNERS/CARRIERS
These individuals transport and deliver guns and drugs to various locations or to other gang members. They are usually newer younger members, because of the less severe juvenile penalties if caught.
AKA: PeeWees.

LOOKOUTS/SPOTTERS
Serve as lookouts for police when gang members are involved in illegal activities, such as drug deals, graffitti, etc. Usually marginal members or associates.

Gang structures vary from gang to gang. Structure depends on size of membership and the extent of illegal activity with which the gang is involved. The above structure depicts a well organized street gang.

ORGANIZATIONAL STRUCTURE AND LEADERSHIP OF CHICAGO'S LARGEST GANGS

Today, gangs are significantly more structured within the corrections facilities than in the streets. Most law enforcement sources agree that, in Chicago, gang structures have been significantly weakened due to successful police operations and the greed of younger members. The desire to make more money has become more important than following gang rules. Sources also believe that in Chicago's suburbs these gang structures may be more solid.

BLACK DISCIPLES

According to the Chicago Police, there are approximately 1,300 recorded Black Disciples in Chicago.

Black Disciples Rank Structures in the institution and on the streets are as follows:

Institution	Street
Director	King
Cell House Director	Don
Security	Board of Directors
Treasurer	Minister
Co-Minister	
Director	
Soldier	

Black Disciples Reputed Leadership:

Eddie McKenzie was once third in command of the BDs. Intelligence from Chicago Police Area One Gang Unit, along with the IDOC Intelligence Unit, notes that McKenzie may be in control of the BDs for the City of Chicago.

BLACK GANGSTER (or NEW BREED or BREED)

According to the Chicago Police, there are approximately 463 recorded Black Gangsters in Chicago.

Black Gangsters Rank Structure:

Don
King
Commander
Prince
Chief
Field Marshall
General

BLACK P STONES/EL RUKN

According to the Chicago Police, there are approximately 1,900 recorded Black P Stones in Chicago.

Black P Stones Rank Structure:

Black P Stones	El Rukn
Chief Prince (Jeff Fort)	Chief Imam (Jeff Fort)
Crown Prince	Crown Prince & Abdullah
Prince or Grand Sheikh	Emir
Akbar or Asst. Grand Sheikh	Wazir
General or Chairman	Sharieff
Ranger Military Force or Lawman	Mufti
Membership	Membership

FOUR CORNER HUSTLERS

According to the Chicago Police, there are approximately 1,550 recorded Four Corner Hustlers in Chicago.

Four Corner Hustlers Council:

Supreme Minister
Minister of Justice
Minister of the Exterior
Minister of the Interior
Minister of Finance
Minister of Vanguard
Minister of Command and Communications
Minister of Literature
Minister of Secretarial

According to law enforcement sources, it is reputed that the Four Corner Hustlers recognize the following individuals as Five Star Universal Supreme Chief Elites. The Supreme status gives them supreme authority within their structure.

Rufus "Weasel" Simms
John "Peanut" Walton
Larry Ford
Curtis "Noon" Henderson
Raymond "Ray Ray" Longstreet
Morris Ledell "Hodari Joe" Carr
Jerome "Head" Murray
Shawn "Shakey Shawn" Betts
Darnell "Cinque" Bryant

GANGSTER DISCIPLES

According to the Chicago Police, there are approximately 7,400 recorded Gangster Disciples in Chicago.

Gangster Disciples Rank Structure

Chairman
Assistant Chairman
Board Members
    Finance and Communications Committee
Governors or Regents
Coordinators or Street Enforcers
Foot Soldiers

LATIN KINGS

According to the Chicago Police, there are approximately 2,700 recorded Latin Kings in Chicago.

Latin Kings Nation Rank Structure

National Leadership
Coronas
Nation Advisor
Regional Officers

Chapter or Set Leadership
Inca
Cacique
Chapter Crown Council (7 members)
    Chapter Crown Council Chairman
    Council Members
Enforzador (Enforcer)
Tesorero (Treasurer)
Secretario (Secretary)
Investigador (Investigator)
Member or Foot Soldier

VICE LORDS

According to the Chicago Police, there are approximately 3,600 recorded Vice Lords in Chicago.

Vice Lords Chain of Command

Chief Elite
Minister of Justice
Elites
Minister of Command
Lieutenant (assistant to the MOC)
Minister

Vice Lords Reputed Leadership:

Conservative Vice Lords — Reputed Leadership

Kenneth Shannon/Shoulders, aka "Shine", A 5 Star Universal Supreme Elite, was elected into the leadership position (Chief) after the murder in 2000 of Leader Elbert "Pierre" Mahone. Shannon was elected by a Conservative Vice Lords council to oversee Conservative Vice Lords street operations.

Cicero Insane Vice Lords — Reputed Leadership

Martin "King Bean" Rocket was once identified as the Chief of street operations.

Lance "Godfather" Harris is a Prince.

Corey "Richie Rich" Gilmore was identified as a 5 Star Universal Chief Elite. On Saturday June 12, 2004, Gilmore was shot 7 times and severely wounded. At the time of the shooting, Gilmore had numerous Universal Elites working under his direction. Gilmore is believed to have connections to a large-scale supply line of quality heroin.

Ebony Vice Lords — Reputed Leadership

The Ebony Vice Lords charter was approved by Supreme Chief Samuel "Madhi" Smith. They were formed under the direction of the Clay Brothers. The Clay Family is considered the Royal Family of the Ebony Vice Lords.

Arter "Pharaoh" Clay – a founder and a national leader

David "King David" Clay – a king/founder

Roosevelt "Valdez" Clay – a national leader

Jerry Clay, aka "Ghost"

Harold Clay – brother

Eddie Clay – brother

Melvin Clay

Executioner Vice Lords — Reputed Leadership

This old but elite group of Vice Lords was founded by Fred Gage, Sr. and since only Gage, Sr. could appoint membership into the Executioner Vice Lords, the shrinking ranks of this group now consist only of a few older members who have now aligned themselves with other Vice Lord factions.

Edward "Big Spicy" Spicer – a 5 Star Universal Elite (now a Conservative Vice Lord)

Earl "Mongoose" Good (now a Conservative Vice Lord)

Imperial Insane Vice Lords — Reputed Leadership

Sidney "Don Sid" Hughes was the National leader from 1975-1981. During this time, Sidney was also referred to as "Prince Symphony Sid" and "Prince Shy Ku Auton." He was the Chief Overseer of the set on 13th and Ashland. Hughes is believed to currently be in an advisor's role and he's been discharged from the Illinois Department of Corrections (IDOC).

Mathew "DJ" Williams was recognized as the National Leader of the Imperial Insane Vice Lords from 1981 through 2002. It is believed that he has currently turned the leadership of the Nation over to Joseph Faulkner, Anthony Pettigrew and Sammy Hodges and that he will assume an advisor's role.

John "China Joe" Lofton was recognized as a Don, a Prince and an Enforcer. It is believed that his age and a heroin addiction have kept him from any further growth as a national level leader.

Joe "Lil Joe" Faulkner is a 5 Star Universal Chief Elite and is currently one of three National Overseers for the Imperial Insane Vice Lords' street operations.

Anthony Pettigrew is a 5 Star Universal Elite, paroled out of IDOC in July 2003 and is believed to be one of the three Imperial Insane Vice Lord Chiefs overseeing street operations.

Sammy Hodges is a 5 Star Universal Elite from the vicinity of Cicero and Erie and is believed to be one of the three Imperial Insane Vice Lord Chiefs overseeing street operations.

Mafia Insane Vice Lords — Reputed Leadership

King Troy "KT" Martin is the National Level Leader of the Mafia Insane Vice Lords. In May of 2004, he was arrested and taken off the streets in a criminal drug conspiracy operation titled "Day Trader 2." Martin is awaiting prosecution.

Derrick "Skullbone" Griffin is the Nation's Prince and their number two man for the MIVL Nation. Griffin at one time was the Personal Security

Man/Chief Enforcer for a Four Corner Hustler narcotics giant identified as Rufus "Weasel" Sims.

Calvin "Chief Goob" Hunt was a Chief Overseer on the west side in the late 80s and mid-to-late 1990s. Hunt was incarcerated from 1991 through April of 1994. Hunt was the overseer of a large narcotics distribution network that worked in the North Avenue vicinity.

Kenneth "Ken" Myrick was one of two 5 Star Universal Chief Elites under Calvin Hunt.

Lenorris "B" Bolden was one of two 5 Star Universal Chief Elites under Calvin Hunt.

Lee "Twan" Day is the nation's best kept secret. He is a Prince and was largely responsible for their street level growth in the mid 1980s and early 1990s. He was identified as Troy "KT" Martin's right hand man at one time. Day's murder conviction was overturned and he was released from the Illinois Department of Corrections on January 23, 2003. He is currently incarcerated in federal prison.

Gregory "Mafia Boo" Hudgins is a 5 Star Universal Elite and Chief of MIVL operations. Hudgins was the Chief Overseer of four narcotics locations and was arrested in May of 2004.

Wesley "Ke Ke" Hawkins was originally a Conservative Vice Lord but flipped Mafia Insane Vice Lord in the mid-1990s. He is a 5 Star Universal Elite and was the overseer of the Mafia operations on Chicago's west side from the late 1990s through the early 2000s. Hawkins is considered a dangerous man and those in the Nation are very respectful in his presence.

Renegade Vice Lords — Reputed Leadership

Dewayne "Popalo" Thornton was a Chief Enforcer at the time of his brother's death (the former Nation Chief). He became the next Chief for the Renegades. Thornton was released from the IDOC in August 1996.

Ivory "Ali"/"Allah" Dillard is a 5 Star Universal Elite from the Rockwell Garden Housing Development.

Traveler Vice Lords — Reputed Leadership

Andrew "Bay Bay" Patterson, a former National Level Leader and 5 Star Universal Supreme Chief Elite, is sentenced to life in prison for running a multimillion-dollar crack cocaine and heroin operation on Chicago's west side.

Robert Patterson, TVL leader, was also sentenced to life in prison for running a multimillion-dollar crack cocaine and heroin operation on Chicago's west side. Prosecutors estimate the narcotics sales totaled at least $36 million over that nearly four-year period.

Samuel "Spanky" Barnes/Ricky Baker is one of the original founders and ranking members of this gang. Baker still has the respect of many of the high ranking Vice Lord elders and is considered the Chief of Chiefs.

James "King Dickie" Milton was recognized as a National Level Leader in the 1990s.

Jettie "Bo Didley" Williams has been recognized as a National Level Leader. Williams has been in and out of the IDOC for three decades and was last released from the IDOC in February 2004.

Eddie "Cisco" Wells was one of the original founding members and was a former TVL Prince.

Terry "T-Fly" Young was a former Berwyn Police Officer. Young was an influential 5 Star Universal Elite Chief and is currently serving a federal sentence.

Darren "Fat Man" Jones is a 5 Star Universal Chief Elite and the heir apparent to the TVL thrown. Jones was discharged from the IDOC on August 18, 2005.

Edward Lee "Pac-Man" Jackson Jr. was a former Chicago Police Officer in the 15th District and was allegedly working for the TVL nation. He was arrested and indicted as the leader of a group of corrupt police known as the "Austin 7." Jackson received a 115-year sentence and is currently serving federal time. Other CPD Officers that worked under Jackson were identified as:

M.L. Moore (received a 109-year sentence);

Alexander Ramos (received a 49-year sentence);

Cornelius Tripp (received a 15-year sentence); and

James P. Young (received a 9-year sentence).

Undertaker Vice Lord — Reputed Leadership

Eddie "Hi Neef" Richardson is the King and National Founder. Richardson is currently serving a federal sentence for a criminal drug conspiracy case.

Curt Kirkland was also instrumental in laying the foundation for the Undertaker Vice Lord Nation. His ranking status was that of a King/Prince or Chief.

Carman "Redman" Tate was the original Prince and Chief. Tate was a narcotics specialist and he's currently serving a lengthy federal sentence.

Unknown Vice Lords — Reputed Leadership

Willie "Al Uqdah" Lloyd at one time called himself "The King of Kings" and claimed dominion over the entire Vice Lord Nation. On February 22, 2001, Lloyd was released from the Federal Correctional Institution in Bastrop, Texas. On August 20, 2003, Willie Lloyd was shot six times near Garfield Park, the third assassination attempt against the King of Kings. According to the Illinois Department of Corrections, a published article in the Austin Voice in May of 2001 claimed that "Lloyd is the founder of the Unknown Vice Lords and supreme ruler of the entire Vice Lord Nation. He is known as the most ruthless and violent street gang leader the west side has ever seen, despite spending 29 of his 50 years in various prisons." In 1996, former Austin District Commander Leroy O'Shield declared that every murder committed in the 15th district could be linked directly to orders from Willie Lloyd. By 1970, Lloyd already had an extensive arrest record for various offenses including criminal trespass, auto theft, aggravated battery, murder, armed robbery, sexual assault and unlawful use of a weapon. During Lloyd's many incarcerations, the Unknown Vice Lords had grown in large part due to the successful recruiting and oversight of their Prince, "Baby Tye" Tyrone Williams. On March 26, 1993 Willie Lloyd had Baby Tye's brother, Cordell Williams, kidnapped and held for ransom as he extorted money and a vehicle from Tyrone Williams. On March 27, 1993, the Williams' brothers were taken into custody for the shooting of Victor Nichols on the eastbound Eisenhower Expressway. The incident on the Eisenhower was an attempt to kill Lloyd.

Tyrone "Baby Tye" Williams is a Prince/National Level Leader who was the Chief Overseer of the Unknown Vice Lord Nation during most of Willie Lloyd's incarceration. Williams has generations of Unknown Vice Lords who are still very loyal to him. Williams is currently incarcerated in Tamms.

Source: Chicago Police Department

BLACK P STONES/ EL RUKN

Daryl Abney
Nation Leader/Gangster Stones

MANIAC LATIN DISCIPLES

Johnny Almovodar
Nation Prince

FAMILIA STONES

Robert Anderson
Nation Leader

TWO SIX

David Ayala
Nation Leader

FOUR CORNER HUSTLER

Shawn Betts
Nation Prince

CONSERVATIVE VICE LORDS

Ramiro Brown
City-Wide Chief

BLACK P STONES/ EL RUKN

John Burnom
Institutional Leader

IMPERIAL GANGSTERS

Ronald Carrasquillo
Nation King

LATIN COUNTS

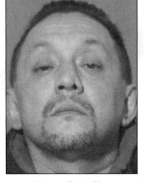

Juan Castillo
Nation Prince

EBONY VICE LORDS

Arter Clay
Nation King

EBONY VICE LORDS

Roosevelt Clay
Nation Leader

IMPERIAL GANGSTERS

David Colon
Institutional Leader

LATIN KINGS

Gustavo Colon
Nation Leader

SPANISH GANGSTER DISCIPLES

David Cruz
Nation Leader

NEW BREEDS/ BLACK GANGSTERS

George Davis
Leader

INSANE DRAGONS

Eduardo Delgado
Institutional Leader

NEW BREEDS/ BLACK GANGSTERS

Jeffery Denson
Nation Prince

YLO-C

Jimmy Diaz
Institutional Leader

BLACK P STONES/ EL RUKN

Randy Dillard
Nation Leader/Rubenites

UNDERTAKER VICE LORDS

Kerry Dockery
3rd Generation King

BLACK P STONES/ EL RUKN

Robert East
Nation Leader/Titanic Stones

LATIN DRAGONS

Roberto Fernandez
Chief

FOUR CORNER HUSTLER

Larry Ford
Senior Advisor

BLACK P STONES/ EL RUKN

Jeff Fort
Nation King

LEADERSHIP OF CHICAGO AREA GANGS

Source: Chicago Police Department

BLACK DISCIPLES

Jerome Freeman
Nation King

MANIAC LATIN DISCIPLES

Francisco Garcia
Institutional Leader/Prince

RENEGADE VICE LORDS

Henry Gaston
Nation King

GAYLORDS

William Giles
Institutional Leader

LATIN KINGS

Raul Gonzalez
Nation Leader

LA RAZAS

Jose Gutierrez
Nation King

AMBROSE

Peter Guzman
Nation Leader

POPES

Michael Hamilton
Nation Leader

CICERO INSANE VICE LORDS

Anthony Harris
Nation King

MAFIA INSANE VICE LORDS

Wesley Hawkins
Chief

GANGSTER DISCIPLES

Melvin Haywood
Nation Leader

INSANE UNKNOWNS

Ruben Hernandez
Institutional Leader

LEADERSHIP OF CHICAGO AREA GANGS

Source: Chicago Police Department

INSANE UNKNOWNS

Keith Hoddenback
Nation Leader

GANGSTER DISCIPLES

Larry Hoover
Nation Leader "Chairman"

MAFIA INSANE VICE LORDS

Calvin Hunt
Nation Prince

IMPERIAL GANGSTERS

Geraldo Iglesias
Institutional Leader

LATIN EAGLES
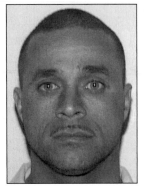
Thomas Jimenez
Nation Leader

CONSERVATIVE VICE LORDS

Willie Johnson
Nation Leader

TRAVELING VICE LORDS

Darren Jones
Nation Leader

BLACK SOULS

Willie Jones
Nation King/ Egyptian Cobra Souls

IMPERIAL INSANE VICE LORDS

Willie Jones
Nation Leader

BLACK P STONES/ EL RUKN

Jackie Kelly
Nation Leader/Jet Black Stones

LATIN SAINTS

Joe Krentkowski
Nation King

NEW BREEDS/ BLACK GANGSTERS

Fontaine Lewis
Prince of Princes

Section Two

Source: Chicago Police Department

Section Two

UNKNOWN VICE LORDS

Willie Lloyd
Nation King

IMPERIAL INSANE VICE LORDS

Leonard Lofton
Nation Leader

FOUR CORNER HUSTLER

Ray Longstreet
Nation Leader

MAFIA INSANE VICE LORDS

Troy Martin
Nation King

MILWAUKEE KINGS

Joseph Matos
Institutional Leader

BLACK SOULS

Sam McKay
Nation Leader/
Gangster Black Souls

INSANE DRAGONS

Luis Mejias
Nation Leader

LA RAZAS

Benjamin Monteca
Institutional Leader

SATAN DISCIPLES

Elliot Montes
Institutional Leader

MILWAUKEE KINGS

Efrain Morales
Nation Leader

IMPERIAL GANGSTERS
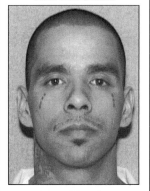
Mario Navarro
Institutional Leader

SIMON CITY ROYALS
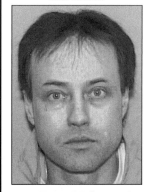
Brian Nelson
Nation Leader

LEADERSHIP OF CHICAGO AREA GANGS

Source: Chicago Police Department

Section Two

LA RAZAS

Alberto Pacheco
Nation King

LATIN LOVERS

Nelson Padilla
Nation Leader

TRAVELING VICE LORDS

Andrew Patterson
Nation Leader

ASHLAND VIKINGS

Edwin Perez
Nation Prince

AMBROSE

Willie Perez
Institutional Leader

INSANE DRAGONS

Billy Phillips
Institutional Leader

ORCHESTRA ALBANY

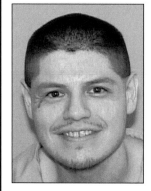

Vincent Reyna
Institutional Leader

UNDERTAKER VICE LORDS

Eddie Richardson
Nation King

LATIN COUNTS

Manuel Rios
Nation Leader

PUERTO RICAN STONES

Jose Rivera
Nation Leader

HARRISON GENTS

Luis Rivera
Nation Leader

YLO-D

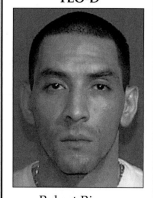

Robert Rivera
Nation Leader

LEADERSHIP OF CHICAGO AREA GANGS

Source: Chicago Police Department

CICERO INSANE VICE LORDS

Martin Rocket
Nation Prince

SPANISH COBRAS

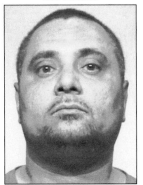

Adam Rodriguez
Institutional Leader

LATIN STYLERS

Johnny Rodriguez
Institutional Leader

LATIN JIVERS

Ramiro Rodriguez
Institutional Leader

SPANISH GANGSTER DESCIPLES

Enrique Romero
Nation Leader

LATIN LOVERS

Mark Rosado
Institutional Leader

SPANISH COBRAS

Eduardo Rosario
Institutional Leader

GAYLORDS

Darryl Rowe
Institutional Leader

BISHOPS

Jaime Salinas
Institutional Leader

TWO SIX

Francisco Sanchez
Nation Leader/
IDOC Latin Folks Leader

SPANISH COBRAS

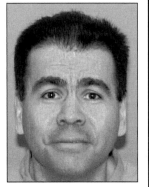

Annibal Santiago
Nation Leader

SPANISH COBRAS

Melvin Santiago
Institutional Leader

Source: Chicago Police Department

Section Two

SIMON CITY ROYALS

David Shinley
Institutional Leader

BISHOPS

Martin Silva
Nation Leader

MAFIA INSANE VICE LORDS

Donell Simons
Nation Leader

INSANE UNKNOWNS

Edwin Suarez
Institutional Leader

UNDERTAKER VICE LORDS

Carmen Tate
Nation Leader

RENEGADE VICE LORDS

John Taylor
Institutional Leader

YLO-C

Efrain Torres
Nation Leader

LA RAZAS

Osvaldo Torres
Institutional Leader

SATAN DISCIPLES

Jose Trejo
Nation Leader

BLACK P STONES/ EL RUKN

Watkeeta Valenzuela
Nation Prince

SATAN DISCIPLES

Larry Vargas
Leader

SATAN DISCIPLES

Loren Vargas
Leader

Section Two

SPANISH COBRAS

Manuel Vasquez
Institutional Leader

AMBROSE

Paulino Villagomez
Nation Prince

SATAN DISCIPLES

Agapito Villalobos
King

BLACK SOULS

William Earl Weaver
Leader

HARRISON GENTS

Antoine Wells
Nation Leader

UNDERTAKER VICE LORDS

Joseph Westmoreland
4th Generation King

TRAVELING VICE LORDS

Jettie Williams
Nation Supreme Elite

IMPERIAL INSANE VICE LORDS

Matthew Williams
Nation Prince

UNKNOWN VICE LORDS

Tyrone Williams
Nation Leader

TRAVELING VICE LORDS

Terry Young
Nation Leader

LATIN KINGS

Augustine Zambrano
Leader

MANIAC LATIN DISCIPLES

Fernando Zayas
Nation Prince

CONVICTION INFORMATION ON CHICAGO GANG LEADERS

Source: Chicago Police Department

PCS = Possession of a Controlled Substance
DCS = Delivery of a Controlled Substance
PDCS = Possession to Deliver a Controlled Substance
UUW = Unlawful Use of a Weapon
PSMV = Possession of a Stolen Motor Vehicle
MDCS = Manufacturing/Delivery of a Controlled Substance

NAME	IR#	GANG	DOB	REPUTED TITLE	CONVICTIONS	PRISON
ABNEY, Daryl	319256	Black P Stones/Gangster Stone	06 Apr 54	Nation Leader	Murder	
ALMOVODAR, Johnny	867107	Maniac Latin Disciples	10 May 70	Nation Prince	Murder/Armed Violence	TAMMS
ANDERSON, Robert	1186359	La Familia Stones	10 Jul 78	Nation Leader	Aggravated Battery/PSMV	
AYALA, David	586465	Two Six	08 Jul 63	Nation Leader	Murder	TAMMS
BETTS, Shawn	703655	Four Corner Hustlers	10 Mar 67	Nation Prince	Involuntary Manslaughter	
BROWN, Ramiro	1096042	Vice Lord/Conservative	27 Mar 73	City Wide Chief	MDCS	
BURNOM, John	507127	Black P Stone/ElRukn	19 Jul 60	Institution Leader	Murder	MENARD
CARRASQUILLO, Ronald	476577	Imperial Gangsters	04 May 58	Nation King	Murder	DANVILLE
CASTILLO, Juan	441549	Latin Counts	17 Dec 56	Nation Prince	Voluntary Manslaughter/UUW	
CLAY, Arter	318561	Vice Lord/Ebony	16 Mar 54	Nation King	MDCS	Parole
CLAY, Roosevelt	362150	Vice Lord/Ebony	12 Oct 55	Nation Leader	Murder/Armed Robbery	MENARD
COLON, David	849182	Imperial Gangsters	03 Jan 71	Institution Leader	Murder	MENARD
COLON, Gustavo	286645	Latin Kings	09 Aug 53	Nation Leader	Murder	
CRUZ, David	833876	Spanish Gangster Disciples	16 Jul 70	Nation Leader	Attempted 1st Degree Murder	
DAVIS, George	5130	Black Gangsters/NewBreed	24 May 38	Leader	Voluntary Manslaughter/Armed Robbery	
DELGADO, Eduardo	1064076	Insane Dragons	24 Jan 75	Institution Leader	Murder	STATEVILLE
DENSON, Jeffrey	583694	Black Gangsters/NewBreed	20 Feb 61	Nation Prince	Attempted Murder	MENARD
DIAZ, Jimmy	619730	YLO - C	26 Sep 64	Institution Leader	UUW Felon/PCS/Aggravated Battery	
DILLARD, Randy	179280	Black P Stones/Rubenites	24 May 49	Nation Leader	Robbery/Rape/Burglary	
DOCKERY, Kerry	634161	Vice Lord/Undertaker	22 Jan 64	3rd Generation.King	Kidnapping/Armed Robbery	
EAST, Robert	308816	Black P Stones/Titan.Stones	29 Jun 54	Nation Leader	Murder	
FERNANDEZ, Roberto.	1008269	Latin Dragons	17 Mar 74	Chief	Aggravated Assault/Possession of a Firearm	
FORD, Larry	313846	Four Corner Hustlers	24 Nov 52	Senior Advisor	Robbery/Burglary	
FORT, Jeff	80328	Black P Stones/El Rukn	20 Feb 47	Nation King	Conspiracy Criminal Acts	MARION USP
FREEMAN, Jerome	257924	Black Disciples	05 Nov 51	Nation King	PCS/Armed Robbery	
GARCIA, Francisco	655625	Maniac Latin Disciples	08 Nov 66	Institution Leader/Prince	Aggravated Battery/PCS	TAMMS
GASTON, Henry	666147	Vice Lord/Renegade	09 Dec 65	Nation King	Robbery/Burglary	
GILES, William	460061	Gaylords	27 Mar 58	Institution Leader	Murder/PCS/Theft	
GONZALEZ, Raul	244087	Latin Kings	20 Dec 50	Nation Leader	Murder	
GUTTIERREZ, Jose	924725	La Razas	18 Aug 72	Nation King	Attempted Murder/Aggravated Battery	
GUZMAN, Peter	636239	Ambrose	17 Mar 65	Nation Leader	Murder	TAMMS
HAMILTON, Michael	661854	Popes	13 May 65	Nation Leader	Aggravated Battery	
HARRIS, Anthony	289463	Vice Lords/Cicero Insane	20 Aug 53	Nation King	PCS/UUW	
HAWKINS, Wesley	634230	Vice Lord/Mafia Insane	17 Jun 64	Chief	UUW by Felon/Aggravated Battery	

Source: Chicago Police Department

PCS = Possession of a Controlled Substance
DCS = Delivery of a Controlled Substance
PDCS = Possession to Deliver a Controlled Substance
UUW = Unlawful Use of a Weapon
PSMV = Possession of a Stolen Motor Vehicle
MDCS = Manufacturing/Delivery of a Controlled Substance

NAME	IR#	GANG	REPUTED TITLE	DOB	CONVICTIONS	PRISON
HAYWOOD, Melvin	***	Gangster Disciples	Nation Leader	11 Dec 49	Murder	Parole
HERNANDEZ, Ruben	880079	Insane Unknowns	Institution Leader	30 Jan 72	Murder	PONTIAC
HODDENBACK, Keith	727885	Insane Unknowns	Nation Leader	17 Jul 63	Murder	DANVILE
HOOVER, Larry	190647	Gangster Disciples	Chairman	30 Nov 50	Murder	FLORENCE USP
HUNT, Calvin	845177	Vice Lord/Mafia Insane	Nation Prince	24 Aug 69	Conspiracy PDCS	
IGLESIAS, Geraldo	764637	Imperial Gangsters	Institution Leader	21 Jul 68	Murder	DIXON
JIMENEZ, Thomas	576630	Latin Eagles	Nation Leader	13 Jan 63	Attempted Murder/Armed Robbery	DIXON
JOHNSON, Willie	133769	Vice Lord/Conservative	Nation Leader	23 Feb 49	Murder/Armed Robbery	
JONES, Darren	783978	Vice Lord/Traveling	Nation Leader	21 Feb 68	Armed Violence/DCS	
JONES, Willie	230577	Black Souls/Egyptian Cobras	Nation King	02 Feb 52	Murder/Armed Robbery	STATEVILLE
JONES, Willie	358350	Vice Lord/Imperial Insane	Nation Leader	24 Nov 55	UUW/Burglary	
KELLY, Jackie	336285	Black P' Stones/Jet Black Stones	Nation Leader	15 Aug 54	Murder	
KRENTKOWSKI, Joe	150405	Latin Saints	Nation King	10 Apr 49	Attempted Murder/Aggravated Battery/Rape	
LEWIS, Fontaine	969411	Black Gangsters/New Breed	Prince of Princes	04 Dec 73	Murder-2nd Degree	
LLOYD, Willie	197015	Vice Lord/Unknown	Nation King	13 Dec 50	Murder-2nd Degree/UUW by a Felon	
LOFTON, Leonard	564318	Vice Lord/Imperial Insane	Nation Leader	04 Jul 61	UUW/PCS/Attempted Armed Robbery	
LONGSTREET, Ray	593946	Four Corner Hustlers	Nation Leader	03 Aug 64	Aggravated Battery	
MARTIN, Troy	324833	Vice Lord/Mafia Insane	Nation King	07 Nov 54	Murder	
MATOS, Joseph	1305792	Milwaukee Kings	Institution Leader	09 Sep 82	Aggravated UUW/PCS/Attempted Armed Robbery	
McKay, Sam	360473	Gangster Black Souls	Nation Leader	02 Apr 57	Murder/Aggravated Kidnapping	MENARD
MEJIAS, Luis	766795	Insane Dragons	Nation Leader	11 Apr 68	MDCS	TAMMS
MONTECA, Benjamin	820369	La Razas	Institution Leader	04 Nov 68	Murder	LAWRENCE
MONTES, Elliot	1163376	Satan Disciples	Institution Leader	09 Oct 79	Murder	PONTIAC
MORALES, Efrain	902158	Milwaukee Kings	Nation Leader	24 Aug 72	Murder	TAMMS
NAVARRO, Mario	866488	Imperial Gangsters	Institution Leader	11 Sep 71	Murder/Armed Robbery	DANVILLE
NELSON, Brian	643250	Simon City Royals	Nation Leader	24 Sep 64	Murder/Armed Robbery	TAMMS
PADILLA, Nelson	697822	Latin Lovers	Nation Leader	05 Sep 64	Aggravated Battery/MDCS	
PATTERSON, Andrew	377477	Vice Lord/Traveling	Nation Leader	31 Mar 56	Armed Robbery	
PEREZ, Edwin	570746	Ashland Vikings	Nation Prince	20 Sep 62	Burglary/MDCS	Parole
PEREZ, Willie	807442	Ambrose	Institution Leader	01 Jul 69	MDCS	
PHILLIPS, Billy	556216	Insane Dragons	Institution Leader	28 Jan 62	Aggravated Robbery	LOGAN
REYNA, Vincent	***	Orchestra Albany	Institution Leader	07 Nov 71	Murder/Aggravated Battery	TAMMS
RICHARDSON, Eddie	380352	Vice Lord/Undertaker	Nation King	27 Feb 56	Aggravated Battery	
RIVERA, Jose	580953	Puerto Rican Stones	Nation Leader	16 Apr 63	Murder	WESTERN IL

CONVICTION INFORMATION ON CHICAGO GANG LEADERS

Source: Chicago Police Department

PCS = Possession of a Controlled Substance
DCS = Delivery of a Controlled Substance
PDCS = Possession to Deliver a Controlled Substance
UUW = Unlawful Use of a Weapon
PSMV = Possession of a Stolen Motor Vehicle
MDCS = Manufacturing/Delivery of a Controlled Substance

NAME	IR#	GANG	REPUTED TITLE	DOB	CONVICTIONS	PRISON
RIVERA, Robert	745517	YLO - D	Nation Leader	22 Nov 67	Aggravated Intimidation by Gang/UUW	Parole
ROCKETT, Martin	337659	Vice Lord/Cicero Insane	Nation Prince	26 Feb 59	PCS/UUW Felon	Parole
RODRIGUEZ, Adam	530903	Spanish Cobras	Institution Leader	04 Mar 60	Attempted Murder/UUW By Felon	
RODRIGUEZ, Johnny	1037990	Latin Stylers	Institution Leader	07 Jan 76	Murder/UUW	
RODRIGUEZ, Ramiro	1075569	Latin Jivers	Institution Leader	14 Sep 76	Aggravated Battery w/ Firearm	
ROMERO, Enrique	1176912	Spanish Gangster Disciple	Nation Leader	29 Mar 76	Armed Robbery	LAWRENCE
ROSADO, Mark	841327	Latin Lovers	Institution Leader	01 Feb 71	Attempted Murder	Parole
ROSARIO, Eduardo	619691	Spanish Cobras	Institution Leader	27 Oct 63	Murder	Parole
ROWE, Darryl	503428	Gaylords	Institution Leader	15 Sep 61	Robbery/MDCS	
SALINAS, Jaime	781501	Bishops	Institution Leader	05 Oct 59	Attempted Murder	
SANCHEZ, Francisco	733380	Two Six	Nation Leader	20 Aug 66	Murder	TAMMS
SANTIAGO, Annibal	466158	Spanish Cobras	Nation Leader	13 Apr 58	Murder	TAMMS
SANTIAGO, Melvin	707607	Spanish Cobras	Institution Leader	20 Mar 67	Murder	***
SILVA, Martin	692668	Bishops	Nation Leader	09 Oct 63	Murder	
SIMONS, Donell	632912	Vice Lord/Mafia Insane	Nation Leader	31 May 64	Attempted Murder/Armed Violence & Robbery	
SUAREZ, Edwin	642961	Insane Unknowns	Institution Leader	20 Feb 65	Murder	PINCKNEYVILLE
TATE, Carmen	431502	Vice Lord/Undertaker	Nation Leader	16 Feb 54	Federal Firearm Violation	
TAYLOR, John	700731	Vice Lord/Renegade	Institution Leader	30 Jul 66	Murder/Armed Robbery	DANVILLE
TORRES, Efrain	704741	YLO - C	Nation Leader	10 Feb 66	UUW/Home Invasion/PCS	
TORRES, Osvaldo	948193	La Razas	Institution Leader	01 Aug 73	Aggravated Battery/Aggravated Criminal Sexual Assault	MENARD
TREJO, Jose	834555	Satan Disciples	Nation Leader	05 Feb 71	Murder	HILL
VARGAS, Larry	756873	Satan Disciples	Leader	17 Jul 68	Aggravated UUW/PCS	
VARGAS, Loren	785208	Satan Disciples	Leader	17 Jul 68	Aggravated Battery	
VASQUEZ, Manuel	638114	Spanish Cobras	Institution Leader	05 Oct 63	Murder	Parole
VILLAGOMEZ, Paulino	480319	Ambrose	Nation Prince	16 Jan 59	Murder	
VILLALOBOS, Agapito	307195	Satan Disciples	King	03 May 55	Armed Robbery/Aggravated Battery	
WEAVER, William Earl	246944	Black Souls	Leader	23 Jul 52	Murder/Criminal Drug Conspiracy	
WELLS, Antoine	764576	Harrison Gents	Nation Leader	05 Jan 69	Armed Violence	Parole
WESTMORELAND, Joseph	704093	Vice Lord/Undertaker	4th Generation King	29 May 66	UUW by Felon/Armed Violence	
WILLIAMS, Jettie	451384	Vice Lord/Traveling	Nation Supreme Elite	09 Mar 58	Attempted Murder/Armed Violence/UUW	
WILLIAMS, Matthew	319080	Vice Lord/Imperial Insane	Nation Prince	07 Feb 53	UUW/PCS/Bribery	
WILLIAMS, Tyrone	586007	Vice Lord/Unknown	Nation Leader	12 Mar 63	Murder	TAMMS
ZAMBRANO, Augustine	483589	Latin Kings	Leader	15 Mar 59	Attempted Murder/Aggravated Battery	
ZAYAS, Fernando	561410	Maniac Latin Disciples	Nation Prince	24 Nov 61	Murder	TAMMS

SECTION 3

Gangs In The Suburbs and Suburban Gang Maps

Deadly Migration

by Anne Keegan

Sureno 13 photo provided by West Chicago Police Department.

Chicago Police are cracking down on drugs and murder. So gangs are following the dollar signs to suburbs and small towns.

"We are seeing a gang migration out of Chicago. The vast majority of it is heading south, some west. Black gangs, Hispanic gangs, some whites. It started three years ago when a number of big gang leaders wanted to get out from the watchful eye of the Chicago police. So they moved out to places where nobody knew who they were and the police departments were small and ill-equipped. They figured they could get away with more out there without being caught."

Michael Smith, deputy chief of special prosecutions, Cook County state's attorney's office

"Everyone I talk to is looking for a small town. The small towns don't know the tricks yet. In Chicago these days you got one good year, maybe, when you can buy yourself a Corvette and a motorcycle. One good summer selling drugs, then the police close the spot down, close the whole neighborhood down, and for one good summer you catch 30 years on a drug conspiracy. Chicago ain't playing games no more. In a small town you can play games forever."

"DRE," Chicago gang member, now living in Indiana

Well, things are starting to change in Chicago. And as they change there, an awful lot of other places are going to be affected. Cities miles down the interstate, suburbs just across the city line, towns, little and big, near and sometimes far, are going to have to face this fact.

There is a migration, subtle but real. And it's becoming noticeable. The notorious Chicago street gangs are heading out to newer and, in may cases, more naive pastures. "Like the old-time gypsies," says one Chicago street cop, "when it gets too hot, they move away from the heat and out of town." The migration is discernible, not just to Chicago police, but to destination towns that are starting to become concerned about this influx of outsiders with big city ways.

The reasons for the movement are complex, for it isn't limited to Illinois; it's happening nationwide. Chicago, however, has lost patience with the organized crime that has evolved as gangs become more sophisticated and network out to suburbs and rural areas, which enables them to profit from America's insatiable appetite for illegal drugs. Chicago simply wants them gone.

Chicago's straight-talking new chief of patrol, James Maurer, has 10,000 troops under his command who are enforcing his warning: We'll make it so unprofitable for you to operate a dope spot on the street in this city that you will have no choice but to move to Iowa.

"We have the worst gang problem in the country," Maurer says. "But the message is out. Their heyday is over. We are going to close down their street operations and give them no choice but to stay out of business or move somewhere else. We're going to make it so hard for them to sell drugs here that it will be like trying to open a candy shop on a diabetic ward."

Section Three

This time, Chicagoans are starting to believe it. The newly appointed Chicago police superintendent, Philip Cline, has begun implementing many new aggressive procedures, which are making it more than uncomfortable for Chicago's deeply embedded street gangs to continue to wreak havoc in that city's neighborhoods.

Between 60 percent and 70 percent of the murders in Chicago are attributed to gangs. Their presence has caused the city to become, among other things, America's murder capital. That status had not made Mayor Richard Daley at all happy. He wants that changed and the problem fixed now. But it's not so easy. Gangs, drugs and guns are inextricably intertwined, and have been for years. More guns were confiscated in Chicago last year — over 10,000 — than any other city in America.

"You can't talk about a gang problem without talking about the narcotic problem. You can't talk about the narcotic problem without talking about the gun problem," says Michael Smith, deputy chief of special prosecutions in the Cook County state's attorney's office. "You can't peel one off from the other. And the result of all three is violence and death."

"Gangs aren't just a bunch of teenagers hanging out on the corner anymore," says Commander Mike Cronin of Chicago's gang intelligence unit. "They are not street gangs anymore. They are a business. In the 30 years that I have been on the street, they've gone from gang banging and shooting at each other to selling dope and turning it into big business.

"Gangs aren't about gang colors anymore like they used to be. They are all about one color — green — the color of money. Street gangs have become dope crews. Gangs are beyond graffiti."

Gang leaders no longer boast they are gang leaders to admit to gang affiliations, says Cronin. They don't wear hats cocked to one side or jewelry hanging off their necks. "They want to be anonymous. That's why they started moving out, where nobody knows them or what they are doing.

"They don't drive flamboyant cars. Instead, they often rent them. They buy nice houses whose lawns are mowed. They look like a working guy and don't want to attract attention. When they move out to the suburbs, or a smaller town, they aren't touching the drugs themselves that much, so it's hard to catch them.

"There's a guy named 'Psycho' who runs a street [drug] operation in Chicago, but he's out in one of the Iowa towns. The police there know all about him. He has a $250,000 home, but they can't catch him doing anything illegal out there. He still comes here to Chicago, don't get me wrong, and he's still a leader with the New Breeds selling narcotics. The narcotics unit just shut down one of his spots for the second time but didn't get him. He's one of many like that."

Gangs have evolved over decades from social to corporate, says John Firman, director of research for the International Association of Chiefs of Police in Washington, D.C. "In the major cities, where there have traditionally been gangs, the police have gang units and [have] learned more and developed some savvy, so the logical questions for the gang leaders is, 'Where can I go and get out of the spotlight?' Especially when you have a big brawny police force after you. They move to the smaller town. The problem is there are 14,000 police departments in America with less then 24 officers. They are scraping for resources. How are they going to deal with the gang problem?"

"What is going to hurt gangs eventually is the Homeland Security technology developed because of the need for intelligence sharing among agencies. Well, that intelligence sharing doesn't have to be limited to terrorists, it can include gangs. Big police agencies will be able to web in [link to] the little ones with information. But, if I am a small town officer and I'm not watching out on my beat, then the gang problem is going to sneak up on me, web or not."

DuPage County Assistant State's Attorney Paul Marchese says, "As long as I have been here — and that is seven years — the majority of the gang members came from Chicago."

"This gang migration is across the collar counties around Chicago, and it has grown," says Marchese, who heads that county's gang prosecution unit. "For them, there is less emphasis on territory and more on making money."

Looking at a map of Illinois, with stars to mark the existence of a gang of some kind, there is nary a county that is not part of the galaxy — a vast Milky Way, whose great center is Chicago, with rogue offshoots trailing all the way down to the Ohio River.

A 2003 study conducted by the Gang Crime Prevention Center out of the office of the Illinois attorney general queried more than 1,000 police officers statewide in 290 jurisdictions, and the majority of the individual officers and their agencies reported gang migration in their districts. In one phase of the study, 86 percent of the agencies reported migration into their gang population.

The study found that gangs are a major presence in communities throughout Illinois. Respondents from 22 law enforcement agencies reported an average of five gangs and 67 gang members in their jurisdictions. The number of gangs in individual jurisdictions ranged from none to 80, and the number of members per gang ranged from none to 3,445.

Respondents to the study agreed on three reasons for migration into local gangs: 83 percent of the agencies cited family moving into the area; 69 percent stated the reason was to be near family or friends; 37 percent credited an expanding drug market.

"Therefore," the report stated, "the primary reasons for individuals to migrate to gangs are for non-gang related reasons. For the most part, gang members move for the same reasons that non-gang members move."

Gang experts in Chicago might agree in part with that conclusion, but they have a different perspective. "Of course, when they go, they have to have somewhere to go," says Commander Cronin. "They don't just throw a dart at the map and head out. They know somebody there. A girlfriend, a cousin, a friend they met in the penitentiary. When they are from Chicago, they commute back and forth — Minneapolis, Des Moines, Indianapolis and back to Chicago."

Commander Wayne Wiberg, who headed Chicago's narcotics unit, says, "We can see some of them going, but they are not going away, like disappearing, just moving."

"I've talked to some officers from the towns outside Chicago and they hate us because they say we're sending them these guys, and I respond, 'Believe me. I'd like to send you more,'" says Wiberg, who now works in the police academy. "They get these gang members out of Chicago and all of sudden they have a drug problem. Not just people living there who are using drugs, but people living there that are selling."

Officer Bruce Malkin is with a five-man unit that works gangs in West Chicago, a DuPage County suburb. He is seeing a large migration of Hispanic gangs into the Midwest from California. West Chicago, population 25,000, has had five murders in the last three years and four out of the five where gang-related. His unit, which is large for a small force, was approved by citizen referendum to deal with escalating gang violence.

"The key to comprehending what is happening with the gangs is street intelligence," he says. "You have to know what to look for in order to find it. A lot of these gangs now are not overt in the way they act."

There are several reasons why some gang leaders and lower-echelon gang members are migrating out of the inner city of Chicago. One reason is the systematic tearing down of the high-rise public housing projects whose dank hallways and empty apartments became rat warrens and hideaways for the gangs. They served not only as incubators of gang crime but as recruitment centers for the very young, and often were as impenetrable to law enforcement as a moated medieval castle with its drawbridge raised.

The second reason is the massive gentrification of the city that has spilled out to Chicago's notorious West Side. Though small in geographic size, the West Side and surrounding neighborhoods are responsible annually for one percent of all murders in the free world, says Maurer. On its eastern rim, where broken skeletons of houses and sagging two flats once lined the streets, new condominiums have sprouted by the hundreds. Yuppies have replaced the poor. Briefcase-carrying whites now stand on corners where thugs used to hang. The gangs have moved somewhere, perhaps only blocks away, for the West Side's Fillmore Police District is still considered one of the most dangerous sections of real estate in America. Where all these thousands and thousands of displaced or migrating people have gone, nobody is sure. There is no census for gang members.

Then there are the moves that the new police superintendent is making. Cline reactivated a gang intelligence unit and promoted to its head a veteran of the street and an old hand with gangs, Mike Cronin, who, when he stops a young gang member on the street, often had locked up his father, arrested his grandfather and may have known his grandmother when she was selling marijuana out of a candy store. What Cronin is looking for is intelligence on drugs, guns and, most important, murder.

Cline has taken the 25 district tactical units — which he says "are the young hard chargers" who often had been used for frivolous details such as parades — and now sends them as a concentrated battalion to problem areas. He has ordered the top brass — all commanders — to be out on the street Friday and/or Saturday nights when gang violence has its highest potential so that they can see for themselves what is going on rather than just reading a report about it while sitting at a desk on Monday morning.

Every three weeks, he starts a street corner conspiracy case on a drug spot using undercover body wires and videotaping equipment. Once the corner operation is raided and shut down, it stays down. Cline puts blinking "blue light" cameras on a pole on the corner and a squad that sits there watching. And to cover these closed-down drug spots and others still in operation, Cline has ordered 1,000 desk-bound officers to spend some time on the street. Once every five weeks for one week, they rotate out on the street and sit on drug spots, in uniform, in a marked car. It puts a serious damper on business.

Flashing blue lights with revolving cameras have been installed on the main West Side thoroughfares where gangs have traditionally gathered, and occasionally rioted. On a Saturday night, and a warm one for February, there was no one hanging around or loitering, even near the eerily blinking blue lights. Big brother, the police, or somebody was watching.

Things are indeed starting to change in Chicago. And what happens there, in the city with the greatest gang violence problem in America, could have repercussions throughout the state and beyond.

As "Dre," a former Chicago gang member says, "They are moving out to make more money cause you don't get caught. Besides, you might be a punk in Chicago, but you're a chief in a small town.'

"There is a need for a national gang strategy," says prosecutor Smith. "This could become an epidemic because there are no borders for gangs, and it's not just a problem of big cities like Chicago anymore. Big city police departments are experienced, the smaller ones aren't. The answer to how to deal with this problem is as complex as the problem itself."

Anne Keegan is a Chicago writer who was a Chicago Tribune reporter for more than 25 years. She is currently writing On the Street Doing Life, a book about police and gangs on Chicago's West Side.

The Chicago Crime Commission developed, distributed and collected a Suburban Street Gang Survey. The survey analysis follows.

SUBURBAN POLICE DEPARTMENT RESPONSE

Gang Picnic in Suburban Cook County.
Source: Cook County Sheriff's Police.

In total, 81 Chicago area suburban police departments responded to the Chicago Crime Commission survey (some twice, in that two different people filled out surveys). As is common with surveys, not all surveys are completely filled out. To analyze the results in greater detail, the suburbs were divided into geographic areas: North (30 responses), West (31 responses) and South (20 responses).

■ Street gang activity is widespread. With the exception of some more affluent suburbs and some that are far outlying from the City and other gang affected areas, most suburban police departments have contact with street gangs and there is street gang activity. In most cases, when there is gang activity, police note that they have contact with multiple gangs. In some cases, the police department notes over a dozen gangs in their area.

■ Street gang activity appears to be on the rise in the suburbs, with 31 of the responding departments reporting an increase.

■ In some cases the problem is quite large, in terms of estimated street gang members in the suburb. There are an estimated 3000 in Waukegan, 2000 in Cicero and 1800 in Aurora, for example.

■ Data on individual gang presence by suburb, given the above, is hard to summarize across the 81 suburbs. Table 1 (see page 96) tabulates the number of times each gang was mentioned as one of the three worst in the suburb or as an emerging gang in the suburb (by area). In the northern suburbs, the Latin Kings have the largest presence, which is not surprising given their northside roots, with the Gangster Disciples and the Sureno 13s coming in a somewhat distant second. The Latin Kings also have the largest west suburban presence, followed by the Gangster Disciples, the Latin Counts, the Sureno 13s and the Vice Lords. This is again not surprising, given the large Latino communities in the area and which gangs are the strongest in the City. The Gangster Disciples and, interestingly, the Latin Kings are both widespread in the south suburbs, followed by the Vice Lords, Four Corner Hustlers and the Two Six gangs.

■ The Sureno 13s are far and away the most prominent of the newly emerging gangs, both in the northern and western suburbs. In the south suburbs, a variety of biker gangs and miscellaneous street gangs are noted by police departments as newly emerging.

Section Three

TABLE 1
CCC Suburban Gang Survey 2005 — Gangs (Top Three and Emerging) by Area

North (Top Three Gangs)	# Of Suburbs Reporting Gang as a "Top Three" Gang
Acros	1
Black P Stone	3
Dragons	1
Gangster Disciples	11
Insane Deuces	1
Insane Unknowns	1
Latin Counts	1
Latin Disciples	1
Latin Kings	26
La Razas	2
Pachucos	1
Renegade Disciples	1
Russian (Ad Hoc)	1
Satan Disciples	3
Spanish G. D.'s	5
Sureno 13s	11
Surenos Locos Tres.	1
Vampires	1
Vice Lords	3
Fourteens	3
Four Corner Hustlers	1
Thirteens	2
Two-Six	2

South (Top Three Gangs)	
Ambrose	2
Arabian Posse	1
Aryan Brotherhood	1
Black P Stone	1
Gangster Disciples	12
Goon Squad	1
Insane Vice Lords	1
Latin Counts	3
Latin Kings	11
Outlaws	1
Satan G. D.'s	3
Vice Lords	5
Four Corner Hustlers	4
Two-Six	4

West (Top Three Gangs)	
Ambrose	1
Gangster Disciples	9
B. G. D.	1
Imperial Gangsters	4
Insane Deuces	1
Insane Dragons	1
Insane Popes	2
Latin Counts	7
Latin Disciples	1
Latin Kings	24
Latin Saints	1
La Razas	1
Maniac Latin Disc.	2
Maniac Sureno 13s	1

Pachucos	1
Satan Disciples	1
Simon City Royals	2
Sin City Boys	1
Sureno 13s	6
Vice Lords	6
18th St.	1
Fourteens	1
Four Corner Hustlers	2
Thirteens	1
Twelfth St. Players	1
2-2 Boys	1
Two-Six	3

North (Emerging Gangs)	# Of Suburbs Reporting Gang as an Emerging Gang
Acros	1
Black P Stones	1
Bloods	1
Boxwood Boys	1
Brazers	1
Latin Counts	1
La Raza	1
Norteno 14s	2
Renegade Disciples	1
Russian (Ad Hoc)	1
Skin Heads	1
Sureno 13s	6
Sureno Locos Tres.	1
Vampires	1

South (Emerging Gangs)	
Goon Squad	1
Hells Angels (bikers)	1
Insane Vice Lords	1
Lithuanians	1
Lockport Thugs	1
Outlaws (bikers)	2
Mickey Cobras	1
Satan Disciples	2
True Players	1
Vice Lords	1
14th St. Posse	1
Four Corner Hustlers	1

West (Emerging Gangs)	
G Unit Girls	1
Insane Dragons	2
Imperial Gangsters	1
Insane Popes	1
Latin Counts	1
Latin Saints	1
Maniac Sureno 13	3
Original Crew	1
Sin City Boys	1
Sureno 13s	5
18th St.	1
4th Gen. Messiahs	3

TABLE 2

CCC Suburban Gang Survey 2005 — Suburban Street Gang Criminal Activities

Gang Activity	# Of North Depts. Reporting Activity (n=30)	# Of West Depts. Reporting Activity (n=31)	# Of South Depts. Reporting Activity (n=20)	Total (n=81)
Drug Distribution	18	20	16	54
Homicide	6	6	3	15
Criminal Sexual Assault	3	3	3	9
Aggravated Assault	16	12	4	32
Robbery	13	13	7	33
Theft	16	13	9	38
Burglary	15	13	8	36
Motor Vehicle Theft	10	13	7	30
Arson	4	5	3	12
Gun Trafficking	6	5	3	14
Real Estate/Mortgage Fraud	0	0	0	0
Kidnapping	3	2	0	5
Identity Theft	1	1	3	5
Illegal Immigration	8	2	0	10
Counterfeiting	0	2	1	3
Dog Fighting	2	3	2	7
Prostitution	1	2	1	4
Human Trafficking	0	0	0	0
Money Laundering	1	2	0	3
Terrorism	0	0	0	0
High Tech Crime	0	1	1	2
Other	1	2	3	6

■ Regarding criminal activities, distribution of drugs is by far the most common focus of the street gangs. Fifty-four of the suburbs (see Table 2 above) reported it, with this being the most common (in terms of the percentage of suburbs reporting it) in the southern area.

■ Violence (aggravated assault) goes hand in hand with narcotics as a gang activity, especially in the northern suburbs, but much less so in the southern suburbs. Fifteen departments reported gang related homicides, resulting in 17 juvenile deaths in total (four of which were near a school).

■ As the number of gang members increases in a suburb, murder and other violent activities also seem to increase.

■ No suburban police officers were killed by gang members, but nine suburbs (six in the northern area) reported that officers or school officials were injured by gang members.

■ Gangs are involved in a wide range of criminal activities, not just illegal narcotics. In suburbs where street gangs are involved in narcotics trafficking, they also are very frequently engaged in robbery, theft, burglary and motor vehicle theft. These activities seem to go hand in hand in what could perhaps be described as a set of basic street gang activities. Motor vehicle theft is most active in the southern and western suburbs, perhaps given their proximity to south suburban chop shops and the fact that auto theft has traditionally been centered in the south suburbs.

- Less common gang crimes are sexual assault, arson, gun trafficking and illegal immigration. The latter is most common in the northern suburbs (and appears more prevalent in the Latino community).

- At the other end of the spectrum, no suburban departments report real estate fraud, human trafficking or terrorist activities by street gangs.

- Activities in the category marked "Other" on the survey and reported in Table 2 include home invasion, insurance fraud, destruction of property, mob action and graffiti.

- The surveys indicate that as gang presence becomes stronger (measured by the number of members) in a suburb, their activities become broader and more sophisticated. The latter types of activities include money laundering, I. D. theft, illegal immigration and high tech crime. This should be useful information to suburbs with increased gang presence. Not only will they see more of the common types of gang related crimes, but they should also expect to see greater violence and more sophisticated types of street gang activities.

- Regarding narcotics seizure, the responding departments seized all of the usual types of illegal narcotics: cannabis, cocaine, heroin, prescription drugs, ecstasy and methamphetamines.

- All types of weapons, including handguns, were also seized.

- In terms of increased or decreased presence of drugs in the suburbs, most suburbs report increases of one type or another. Table 3 summarizes the net increase for each type of drug. That is, for each drug the figure equals the number of suburbs reporting an increase minus the number reporting a decrease. Several police departments reported an increase in drug trafficking overall. Drug trafficking is increasing at a greater rate in the southern and western suburbs than elsewhere.

- Various departments report successful prosecutions of gang members during the last two years. These vary from convictions for murder and drug dealing to battery. West suburban

TABLE 3

DRUG TYPE	# OF DEPARTMENTS REPORTING INCREASE
Cannabis	11
Heroin	7
Cocaine	5
Crack	9
Methamphetamines	5
Ecstasy	1
Prescription Drugs	2
Drugs Overall	6

departments have been especially successful in this respect recently. By region, the reporting departments break down as noted in Table 4 on page 99.

- Regarding methods of communication used by street gangs (beyond face to face conversation and other basic methods of communication not covered by the survey), it appears that virtually all gangs use cell phones and heavily use the related function of text messaging. E-mails, chat rooms and websites are common, but less so. The responses are summarized in Table 5 on page 99.

- Only one suburban department reports any interest by street gang members in politics and there is only one case where gang members

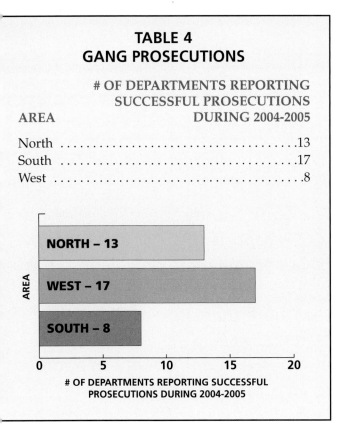

TABLE 4
GANG PROSECUTIONS

AREA	# OF DEPARTMENTS REPORTING SUCCESSFUL PROSECUTIONS DURING 2004-2005
North	13
South	17
West	8

NORTH – 13
WEST – 17
SOUTH – 8

OF DEPARTMENTS REPORTING SUCCESSFUL
PROSECUTIONS DURING 2004-2005

appear to be interested in criminal justice. Five departments note links between street gangs and other organized crime groups, four of these being drug trafficking organizations.

The most frequently reported obstacle to combating street gangs is a lack of police resources. Not far behind is lack of cooperation by victims and witnesses, sometimes due to fear and intimidation. Also cited, but less frequently, is the lack of solid information on gang activities and ineffective sentencing by the courts.

The most successful law enforcement responses to street gangs can be divided into three categories: 1) community education and presentation of information, 2) creation of special gang focused police units, and 3) the implementation of response strategies, such as sweeps and saturation of trouble areas. Cooperation with other agencies, including the federal government, was mentioned somewhat less often.

■ Regarding gangs in the schools, the major reported problems are graffiti and fights between gang members and with others. Less common is the problem of gang members being apprehended in schools with weapons. Responses to problems in school include primarily informational programs for teachers, placing officers in the schools, zero tolerance programs in the schools and school imposed restrictions on dress and the use/carrying of other items, such as cell phones.

■ Suburban departments find that young people join gangs for a variety of reasons: self-protection/power/self-interest (money and drugs), prestige (including a media-created sense of gangbanger status)/low self-esteem/sense of belonging, lack of good alternatives, family issues/problems and peer/neighborhood pressure.

■ On the subject of parole and parole-related recommendations, only a few departments responded. The most frequent response was that paroled gang members should not be allowed to have contact with other gang members and that this rule should be strictly enforced. Suburban police also suggested that: 1) paroled gang members should be forced to register with authorities; 2) there should otherwise be better information available about gang members; and 3) the parole laws should be more strictly enforced and there should be stiffer penalties for parole violations by gang members.

TABLE 5
GANG COMMUNICATION

COMMUNICATION METHOD USED BY GANGS	# OF DEPARTMENTS REPORTING COMMUNICATION METHOD AS ONE USED BY GANGS
Cell Phones	70
Text Messaging	49
Faxes	5
E-mail	23
Chat Rooms	20
Websites	21
Radio Stations	3
Party Lines	13
OTHER	
Graffiti	2
Walkie-Talkies	8
Instant Messages	1

- Regarding the general recommendations these police departments would like to see the CCC put in its report, again only a few departments responded to this specific question. The most frequent recommendations concerned providing much stiffer punishment for gang-related offenses, including a suggestion that illegal immigrants who are repeat gang offenders be deported, and also enforcing more strenuously the parole laws for gang members who are out on parole.

Other than the suburban police departments, several other agencies responded to the survey: FBI, ATF, the Illinois State Police, five county police forces, the Cook County State's Attorney's office and the College of DuPage. These agencies, with the exception of the latter, cover a much broader domain than the individual town/village departments and have different perspectives on some issues.

For example, they are able in some cases to apply different statutes or have a different focus — think in terms of broad cooperative efforts across suburbs/areas — than the individual suburban police. On quite a few of the questions, however, their responses are quite similar to those of the suburban departments, such as which gangs are prevalent, what crimes they commit and what technologies they use.

These agencies note gang involvement in politics/criminal justice fields much more frequently than do the individual suburban departments. Information secured from these other agencies, from this survey, and through other means is provided here and throughout this report.

Cook County Sheriff's Office and Cook County State's Attorney's Office

Historically, street gangs in suburban Cook County have always been affiliated with Chicago's gangs.

The Cook County Sheriff's Office (CCSP) reports that Chicago's gangs have become more prevalent in the suburbs, with intelligence showing that more than 50% of Chicago's street gang leadership now resides in suburban Cook County. In addition to an escalation in gang activity, Cook County Sheriff's Police note a substantial escalation in suburban murders and other violent crime.

The Cook County State's Attorney's Office (CCSA) estimates approximately 100,000 gang members in their area. Combined CCSP and CCSA survey data rated the following gangs as the worst: Gangster Disciples, Vice Lords, Latin Kings, Black P Stones, Black Disciples, Four Corner Hustlers, Maniac Latin Disciples, Two Sixers, Satan Disciples, Ambrose, Insane Popes, Sureno 13s and Imperial Gangsters. The Milwaukee Kings and Latin Dragons were noted as newly emerging gangs. Sixty-one guns in 2005 and 80 guns in 2004 were confiscated by the CCSP Gang Crimes Narcotic Unit alone. In 2005, the CCSP confiscated 693,000 grams of cocaine, 5,000 grams of heroin, 1,345,000 grams of cannibis, 1,500 units of ecstacy and 45,000 grams of methamphetamine. Over two million dollars in U.S. currency was confiscated in 2005.

The most successful CCSA gang-related prosecutions in the years 2004 – 2005 were People vs. Jacky Burks, et al., a case involving the firebombing and killing of a four-year old by a gang and the People vs. Jose Martinez case which involved a Satan Disciple who shot and killed an innocent man who was giving money to a homeless man. The Satan Disciples believed him to be a rival gang member. In both cases, the sentence was natural life. The CCSP noted that they have undertaken numerous street corner conspiracy cases involving multiple defendants. These prosecutions have resulted in a conviction rate of over 90%.

Gang crimes noted by the CCSP and the CCSA are: drug distribution, homicide (including one murdered juvenile), robbery, theft, burglary, motor vehicle theft, arson, gun trafficking, mortgage and real estate fraud, kidnapping, identity theft, illegal immigration, counterfeiting, dog fighting, money laundering and high-tech crime.

The CCSP reported major differences between the gangs in the City and the gangs in the suburbs as: 1) suburban gangs tend to be more racially diverse than in the city and 2) they tend to use open air drug markets for drug sales in the City more often, while in the suburbs they prefer selling illegal drugs primarily from inside homes or apartments. The CCSP, like law enforcement in the City, agrees that gangs are more often crossing over the boundaries once set by long existing rivalries in order to work together towards higher profits through their illegal activities. For example, it is not uncommon today to see Gangster Disciples dealing with Vice Lords regarding the acquisition and selling of narcotics and cannabis.

Suburban gangs frequently employ young gang members to conduct street sales. In one CCSP investigation, an undercover police officer purchased crack cocaine from a 12-year old boy selling drugs for the Vice Lords at an open air market in Maywood, Illinois.

According to the Cook County Sheriff's Police, suburban gang members frequently put property and vehicles in another person's name or use leased or rental vehicles when engaged in criminal activity in order to avoid the forfeiture laws in the event they are arrested. Furthermore, the use of sophisticated "traps" or hidden compartments in vehicles is very common as a means for gang members to hide narcotics, money and weapons.

Another obstacle facing Cook County Sheriff's Police is the expansion and migration of gang members as law enforcement has jurisdictional boundaries to which suburban street gangs are not bound by when conducting their criminal activities. In addition, it is difficult for police to determine the level of involvement of a specific gang member, since there is an abundance of fringe members and "wanna be" gang members amongst the hard core members. Hard core gang members, in particular, are more likely to try and avoid detection by wearing white tee-shirts. The purpose of the white tee-shirt is twofold: 1) it makes the identification of the gang member difficult when police are conducting surveillance as all members are dressed alike; and 2) it is a signal to customers that they are selling drugs.

DuPage County Sheriff's Office

The DuPage County Sheriff's Office does not see an increase in gang activity or in drug distribution in their County compared to three years ago. The office estimates 5,000 gang members in their area with the following gangs rated as the worst (in order given): Latin Kings, Gangster Disciples, Sureno 13s, Vice lords, Satan Disciples, Latin Counts, Four Corner Hustlers and the Nortenos 14. The 18th Street Gang and the Latin Dragons were noted as newly emerging gangs. Fourteen guns were confiscated in 2004 and 6 guns in 2005. Marijuana, cocaine, heroin and meth have also been confiscated in 2004 and 2005. The DuPage County Sheriff's Office's most successful gang-related prosecution was a drug conspiracy case with eight Class X felony arrests. Gang crimes noted include: drug distribution, aggravated assault, robbery, theft, burglary, motor vehicle theft, arson, gun trafficking, identity theft and prostitution. The DuPage County Sheriff's Office started the Anti-Gang Tactical Team (ATAC) which enrolled all town TAC officers into a working relationship for the enhanced sharing of intelligence.

Kane County Sheriff's Department

The Kane County Sheriff's Department reports an increase in street gang activity and an increase in drug distribution today compared to three years ago. The Department estimates about 150 gang members are active in Kane County and another 300 reside in the local prison. The Department rates the following gangs (in order given) as the worst gangs in their area: Latin Kings, Ambrose, Deuces, Maniac Latin Disciples, Vice Lords, Gangster Disciples and Sureno 13s. Sureno 13s are a new, emerging gang. Within the county jail, numerous home made weapons, such as shanks, have been confiscated. Illegal drugs, including powder and crack cocaine, cannibis, heroin, meth, vicodin and MDMA (ecstasy), were confiscated in 2005 by the Department. The Kane County Sheriff's Department works with the FBI in a gang task force and, in the Spring of 2005, they conducted a sweep that resulted in the arrest of over 20 Latin Kings and Latin Homeboys, who have been charged federally. One Illinois Department of Corrections guard was killed by gangs since January of 2004. Drug distribution and homicide have been identified as gang activities in Kane County, and the Department notes that there are other gang related crimes, but that these crimes are not separated out by whether there is gang involvement or not. In addition to some of the communication methods noted elsewhere in this report, the Kane County Sheriff's Office reports that Latin Kings have been known to meet during local soccer games.

Lake County Sheriff's Department

The Lake County Sheriff's Department reports an increase in street gang activity and in illegal drug distribution today compared to three years ago. The Department estimates that between 2,000-3,000 gang members are active in Lake County and rates the following gangs (in order given) as the worst gangs in their area: Sureno 13s, Latin Kings, Gangster Disciples, Vice Lords, Aryan Nation ("Skin Heads"), Insane Deuces, Renegades, Four Corner Hustlers and the Latin Maniac Disciples. MS13s, Sureno 13s, Insane Deuces and the Renegades are newly emerging gangs. A total of 144 guns were confiscated in 2004. From January to September 2005, 135 guns were confiscated. Illegal drugs, including cannibis, cocaine, heroin and crack cocaine, have been confiscated by the Sheriff's Department in 2004 and 2005. Gang activities in Lake County have included: drug distribution, homicide, criminal sexual assault, aggravated assault, identity theft, counterfeiting, prostitution and money laundering. The Sheriff's Department has a two-prong approach to confront gang activity, which includes gathering information on active gang members (sharing with local, state and federal agencies) and taking a zero tolerance approach. The most successful prosecutions noted in the survey for the years 2004-2005 involved aggravated battery cases, shooting investigations, homicide and narcotics investigations, and vandalism and graffiti cases.

McHenry County Sheriff's Office

The McHenry County Sheriff's Office does not see an increase in gang activity or an increase in illegal drug distribution in McHenry County compared to three years ago. The Office has recorded 1500 gang members in their County's gang database. The following gangs are rated as the worst gangs in their County (in order given): Latin Kings, Nortenos 14, Sureno 13s, Skinheads, Outlaws Motor Cycle Gang, Latin Dragons, Gangster Disciples, Cross Roads Motor Cycle Gang and Sojourner Motor Cycle Gang. The McHenry Sheriff's Office has seen an emergence of area groups that wear gang colors, but they believe these are not true gang members. The Office confiscated two guns in 2004 and no guns in 2005. Heroin, cocaine and cannibis were confiscated by the Sheriff's Office in 2004 and 2005. The most successful gang-related prosecution in 2004-2005 was a mob action case. Gang-related criminal activities noted on the survey include drug distribution, aggravated assault, burglary and aggravated battery.

Will County Sheriff's Office

Will County did not return the survey.

CCC Suburban Gang Survey 2005 — North (Gang Crimes)

* = two responses   Y = Yes   N = No

Community	Reported Increase In Gang Crime In Last 3 Years	Reported Gang Members	Guns Confiscated 2004	Guns Confiscated 2005	Illegal Drugs	Homicide	Sexual Assault	Aggrav. Assault	Robbery	Theft	Burglary
Algonquin	N	30	0	0							
Antioch	N	0	1	0							
Arlington Hts.	N	100-150	25-50	25-50	y						
Buffalo Grove	Y	10-20	0	0							
Deerfield	Y	1-5	0	0							
Elgin	N	950	28	25	y	y		y	y	y	y
Elk Grove	N	n/a	0	0							
Evanston	Y	600+	47	22	y	y		y	y	y	
Grayslake	N	30-35	0	0	y					y	
Hanover Park	N	200	6	5	y		y	y	y	y	y
Harvard	Y	50	3	2	y			y	y	y	y
Harwood Heights	N	15-20	0	0							
Highland Park	Y	20-25	1	0	y			y	y	y	y
Hoffman Estates	Y	75	15	n/a	y			y	y	y	y
Lake Forest	N	0	0	0							
Lincolnshire	N	20	3	3							y
McCook	N	0	1	1							
Marengo	N	8-10	0	0							
Morton Grove *	Y	40-80	5	3	y			y	y	y	y
Mount Prospect *	Y	100-200	6	3	y		y	y	y	y	y
Mundelein	Y	25	1	3	y	y		y		y	y
Northbrook *	Y	3	5	5	y			y		y	
Palatine	Y	100	2	2	y	y		y	y	y	y
Park Ridge	N	50	7	10	y	y		y	y	y	y
Streamwood	N	100-125	6	8	y			y	y	y	y
Waukegan	N	3000	62	80	y	y			y	y	y
Wheeling	N	100	13	42	y			y	y	y	y
Wilmette	N	5	6	20							
Woodstock	Y	250	28	14	y	y	y	y	y	y	y
Zion	N	300+	10	10	y			y	y	y	
Subtotal					-18-	-6-	-3-	-16-	-13-	-16-	-15-

103

CCC Suburban Gang Survey 2005 — West (Gang Crimes)

* = two responses   Y = Yes   N = No

Community	Reported Increase In Gang Crime In Last 3 Years	Reported Gang Members	Guns Confiscated 2004	Guns Confiscated 2005	Illegal Drugs	Homicide	Sexual Assault	Aggrav. Assault	Robbery	Theft	Burglary
Aurora	n/a	1800	34	12	y	y	y	y	y	y	y
Bensenville	Y	n/a	28	19	y	y	y	y	y	y	y
Berkeley	Y	100	0	2							
Berwyn	Y	150	14	17	y						
Bloomingdale	N	10	2	1							
Broadview	N	20	10	5							
Burr Ridge	N	0	0	0							
Cicero	Y	2000	n/a	n/a	y	y	y	y	y	y	y
Countryside	N	n/a	0	1	y						
DeKalb	N	100	5	6				y			
Downers Grove	N	50-75	n/a	25							
Elburn	N	1	0	0							
Hinsdale	Y	20	10	10	y						
Hodgkins	N	2	2	0	y						
LaGrange	Y	n/a	n/a	1	y			y	y	y	y
LaGrange Park	N	50-75	4	0							
Lyons	N	50	1	1	y						
Melrose Park	N	150	26	16	y			y	y	y	y
Montgomery	Y	15-20	3	3	y				y	y	y
Naperville	Y	75-100	25	30	y			y	y	y	y
Northlake *	N	12-20	5	4	y	y		y	y	y	y
Riverside	Y	30	4	2				y	y	y	y
Stickney	Y	25	16	1							
Stone Park	N	50	12	10	y	y		y	y	y	y
Warrenville	N	40	5	6	y	y			y	y	y
West Chicago	N	500+	5	15	y						
Westchester	Y	40-50	<5	<5	y			y	y	y	y
Western Springs	n/a	<50	1	0	y						
Westmont	N	30	n/a	n/a							
Wheaton	Y	40-50	2	3	y			y	y	y	y
Woodridge	N	50-100	5	5	y						
Subtotal					-20-	-6-	-3-	-12-	-13-	-13-	-13-

CCC Suburban Gang Survey 2005 — South (Gang Crimes)

* = two responses   Y = Yes   N = No

Community	Reported Increase In Gang Crime In Last 3 Years	Reported Gang Members	Guns Confiscated 2004	Guns Confiscated 2005	Illegal Drugs	Homicide	Sexual Assault	Aggrav. Assault	Robbery	Theft	Burglary
Alsip	Y	100	4	5	y					y	
Burbank	Y	n/a	n/a	n/a	y						
Calumet Park	N	n/a	n/a	n/a	y			y	y	y	y
Coal City	N	20	1	3	y					y	y
Crete	n/a	n/a	<12	<12	y	y	y		y	y	y
Dixmoor	Y	n/a	15	12	y	y	y	y	y	y	y
Evergreen Park	N	n/a	0	0							
Flossmoor	N	n/a	1	2							
Lansing	N	100+	10	8	y				y	y	
Lemont	n/a	<5	3	3						y	y
Lockport	n/a	15-20	2	3	y						
Lynwood	Y	100+	4	3	y	y		y	y	y	y
Oak Lawn	Y	80	60	16	y				y		y
Orland Park	N	<5	41	47	y						
Palos Park	N	n/a	1	0							
Park Forest	Y	300-400	20	25	y		y	y	y	y	y
Richton Park	N	100-150	1	0	y						
Sauk Village	Y	n/a	50	75	y						
Shorewood	N	15-20	0	0	y						
Wilmington	N	3-5	n/a	n/a	y						
Subtotal					-16-	-3-	-3-	-4-	-7-	-9-	-8-

105

CCC Suburban Gang Survey 2005 — North

* = two responses   Y = Yes   N = No

Community	Motor Vehicle Theft	Arson	Gun Trafficking	Real Estate Fraud	Kidnapping	I.D. Fraud	Illegal Immigration	Counterfeiting	Dog Fighting	Vice	Human Trafficking
Algonquin											
Antioch											
Arlington Hts.											
Buffalo Grove											
Deerfield											
Elgin	y	y	y				y				
Elk Grove											
Evanston	y								y		
Grayslake											
Hanover Park	y		y				y				
Harvard											
Harwood Heights											
Highland Park	y		y				y				
Hoffman Estates											
Lake Forest											
Lincolnshire											
McCook											
Marengo											
Morton Grove *	y										
Mount Prospect *	y				y		y				
Mundelein										y	
Northbrook *											
Palatine	y						y				
Park Ridge									y		
Streamwood		y			y						
Waukegan	y	y	y				y				
Wheeling	y	y	y		y		y				
Wilmette											
Woodstock	y					y	y				
Zion			y								
Subtotal	-10-	-4-	-6-	-0-	-3-	-1-	-8-	-0-	-2-	-1-	-0-

CCC Suburban Gang Survey 2005 — West

* = two responses   Y = Yes   N = No

Community	Motor Vehicle Theft	Arson	Gun Trafficking	Real Estate Fraud	Kidnapping	I.D. Fraud	Illegal Immigration	Counterfeiting	Dog Fighting	Vice	Human Trafficking
Aurora	y	y	y								
Bensenville	y										
Berkeley									y		
Berwyn											
Bloomingdale											
Broadview											
Burr Ridge											
Cicero	y	y	y				y				
Countryside											
DeKalb											
Downers Grove											
Elburn											
Hinsdale											
Hodgkins											
LaGrange	y	y	y								
LaGrange Park								y	y		
Lyons	y	y									
Melrose Park	y		y								
Montgomery							y	y		y	
Naperville	y										
Northlake *	y										
Riverside	y				y						
Stickney											
Stone Park	y	y									
Warrenville			y						y	y	
West Chicago											
Westchester	y				y						
Western Springs											
Westmont	y										
Wheaton	y					y					
Woodridge											
Subtotal	-13-	-5-	-5-	-0-	-2-	-1-	-2-	-2-	-3-	-2-	-0-

CCC Suburban Gang Survey 2005 — South

* = two responses   Y = Yes   N = No

Community	Motor Vehicle Theft	Arson	Gun Trafficking	Real Estate Fraud	Kidnapping	I.D. Fraud	Illegal Immigration	Counterfeiting	Dog Fighting	Vice	Human Trafficking
Alsip	y										
Burbank											
Calumet Park									y		
Coal City											
Crete	y	y				y					
Dixmoor	y	y				y		y		y	
Evergreen Park											
Flossmoor											
Lansing											
Lemont	y										
Lockport			y								
Lynwood	y										
Oak Lawn	y										
Orland Park											
Palos Park											
Park Forest	y	y	y			y			y		
Richton Park			y								
Sauk Village											
Shorewood											
Wilmington											
Subtotal	-7-	-3-	-3-	-0-	-0-	-3-	-0-	-1-	-2-	-1-	-0-

CCC Suburban Gang Survey 2005 — North

* = two responses   Y = Yes   N = No

Community	Money Laundering	Terrorism	High Tech Crime	Other	Homicide Details Officers	Juveniles	School Personnel	Personal Injury to Police or School Employees
Algonquin								
Antioch								
Arlington Hts.								y
Buffalo Grove								
Deerfield								
Elgin						1		
Elk Grove								
Evanston						1	3	
Grayslake								
Hanover Park								
Harvard								
Harwood Heights								
Highland Park								
Hoffman Estates								
Lake Forest								
Lincolnshire								
McCook								
Marengo								
Morton Grove *								
Mount Prospect *								y
Mundelein								
Northbrook *								
Palatine								
Park Ridge								
Streamwood	y							y
Waukegan						1		y
Wheeling								y
Wilmette				home invasion				
Woodstock						1		y
Zion								
Subtotal	-1-	-0-	-0-	-1-	-0-	-4-	-3-	-6-

109

CCC Suburban Gang Survey 2005 — West

* = two responses   Y = Yes   N = No

Community	Money Laundering	Terrorism	High Tech Crime	Other	Homicide Details			Personal Injury to Police or School Employees
					Officers	Juveniles	School Personnel	
Aurora	y					4		y
Bensenville								
Berkeley								
Berwyn								
Bloomingdale								
Broadview								
Burr Ridge								
Cicero						7	1	
Countryside								
DeKalb								
Downers Grove								
Elburn								
Hinsdale								
Hodgkins								
LaGrange	y							
LaGrange Park								
Lyons								
Melrose Park								y
Montgomery				home invasion				
Naperville								y
Northlake *						2		
Riverside								
Stickney				graffiti				
Stone Park								
Warrenville								
West Chicago								
Westchester			y					
Western Springs								
Westmont								
Wheaton								
Woodridge								
Subtotal	-2-	-0-	-1-	-2-	-0-	-13-	-1-	-3-

CCC Suburban Gang Survey 2005 — South

* = two responses   Y = Yes   N = No

Community	Money Laundering	Terrorism	High Tech Crime	Other	Homicide Details			Personal Injury to Police or School Employees
					Officers	Juveniles	School Personnel	
Alsip								
Burbank								
Calumet Park								
Coal City								
Crete								
Dixmoor				insurance fraud				
Evergreen Park								
Flossmoor								
Lansing								
Lemont								
Lockport								
Lynwood								
Oak Lawn				mob action, graffiti				
Orland Park								
Palos Park								
Park Forest								
Richton Park				destruction of property				
Sauk Village								
Shorewood								
Wilmington								
Subtotal	-0-	-0-	-1-	-3-	-0-	-0-	-0-	-0-

Section Three

MAYWOOD

Tristan Agee
Mafia
DOB 05-23-85

CHICAGO HEIGHTS

Andre Agnew
Gangster Disciples
DOB 01-11-82

ROBBINS

Leonard L.B. Anderson
Gangster Disciples
DOB 10-03-79

CENTRAL STICKNEY

Pierre A. Anderson
Latin Kings
DOB 11-12-79

ROBBINS

Raymond Anderson
Gangster Disciples
DOB 04-07-78

FORD HEIGHTS

Tracy Bankhead
Gangster Disciples
DOB 11-25-73

MAYWOOD

Carlos Barefield
Four Corner Hustlers
DOB 03-17-72

FORD HEIGHTS

Marvin Bentley
Four Corner Hustlers
DOB 02-16-75

MAYWOOD

Phillip D. Blake
Four Corner Hustlers
DOB 12-22-79

MAYWOOD

Claudius Blackledge
Four Corner Hustlers
DOB 10-19-83

EVANSTON

Gregory Boyd
P-Stones
DOB 07-31-80

CHICAGO HEIGHTS

Marshawri Boyd
Gangster Disciples
DOB 03-03-75

Source: Cook County Sheriff's Police

CHICAGO HEIGHTS

Anthony Brown
Gangster Disciples
DOB 11-15-81

ROBBINS

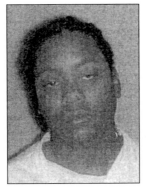

Antwaan Bryant
Renegade Gangster Disciples
DOB 03-21-80

MAYWOOD

Ronald L. Buefort
Mafia
DOB 02-13-81

ROBBINS

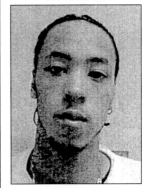

Christopher Clark
Vice Lords
DOB 03-30-82

ROBBINS

Danainie Codenhed
Gangster Disciples
DOB 08-28-74

ROBBINS

Garrett Cogan
Gangster Disciples
DOB 10-03-66

CHICAGO HEIGHTS

Mark Cole
Four Corner Hustler
DOB 09-05-65

MAYWOOD

Nicholas D. Coleman
Mafia
DOB 02-15-85

FORD HEIGHTS

Kevin Drummond
Gangster Disciples
DOB 10-15-80

MAYWOOD

Casanova R. Echols
Four Corner Hustlers
DOB 01-24-83

ROBBINS

Antonio Ellis
Gangster Disciples
DOB 12-01-83

MAINE TOWNSHIP

David Garibay
Latin Kings
DOB 11-18-87

Section Three

Source: Cook County Sheriff's Police

Section Three

ROBBINS

Robert C. Garrett
Gangster Disciples
DOB 01-29-78

MAYWOOD

Mack A. Goodman
Black Gangster Disciples
DOB 10-13-83

ROBBINS

Anthony Gosa
Vice Lords
DOB 10-08-75

ROBBINS

Demetrius Gosa
Vice Lords
DOB 10-07-79

ROBBINS

Ricky Gosa
Vice Lords
DOB 11-24-81

EVANSTON

Richard Hardy
Four Corner Hustlers
DOB 10-26-80

EVANSTON

Michael Henley
P-Stones
DOB 04-02-80

CHICAGO HEIGHTS

Clarence Irons
Vice Lords
DOB 01-28-72

CHICAGO HEIGHTS

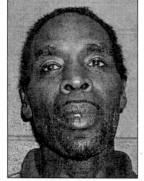

Kyle Irons
Four Corner Hustler
DOB 08-30-55

BROADVIEW

Derry Johnson
Gangster Disciples
DOB 03-06-85

MAYWOOD

Terrence H. Kennebrew
Black Gangster Disciples
DOB 04-18-80

FORD HEIGHTS

Frederick Keys
Four Corner Hustlers
DOB 06-24-75

Source: Cook County Sheriff's Police

CHICAGO HEIGHTS

Tarrante Lackey
Vice Lords
DOB 08-10-80

BROADVIEW

Bryon M. Lanes
Gangster Disciples
DOB 03-18-85

ROBBINS

Francisco Lavine
Renegade Gangster Disciples
DOB 04-31-79

CHICAGO HEIGHTS

Nathan Lee
Gangster Disciples
DOB 02-13-80

EVANSTON

Jonathan Lejman
Vice Lords
DOB 03-01-79

ROBBINS

Phillip Lloyd
Renegade Gangster Disciples
DOB 03-04-73

MAYWOOD

John W. Marshall
Black Gangster Disciples
DOB 03-25-82

FORD HEIGHTS

Ernest McCarter
Four Corner Hustlers
DOB 05-13-79

MAINE TOWNSHIP

Emiledio Montesinos
Sureno 13
01-14-79

MAINE TOWNSHIP

Nelson J. Montesinos
Sureno 13
01-07-80

CENTRAL STICKNEY

Daniel Montoya
Latin Kings
DOB 06-06-82

CENTRAL STICKNEY

David Montoya
Latin Kings
DOB 05-18-84

Section Three

Source: Cook County Sheriff's Police

MAYWOOD

Jermalle S. Morris

Four Corner Hustlers

DOB 03-12-82

CENTRAL STICKNEY

Jason K. Novak

Latin Kings

DOB 10-08-85

CENTRAL STICKNEY

Michael Novak

Latin Kings

DOB 04-25-80

CHICAGO HEIGHTS

Alfred Parker

Gangster Disciples

DOB 08-25-70

CHICAGO HEIGHTS

Calvin Peterson

Vice Lords

DOB 07-14-74

ROBBINS

Terry Pickett

Gangster Disciples

DOB 06-07-77

ROBBINS

Troy Pickett

Gangster Disciples

DOB 01-30-81

MAYWOOD

Donte L. Ray

Four Corner Hustlers

DOB 04-28-82

MAINE TOWNSHIP

Lionel Reyes

Latin Kings

DOB 06-01-84

CHICAGO HEIGHTS

Andre Riggins

Four Corner Hustler

DOB 07-11-84

CHICAGO HEIGHTS

Julius Ringo

Vice Lords

DOB 11-28-80

EVANSTON

Cojuan Ruffin

Four Corner Hustlers

DOB 06-07-75

Section Three

Source: Cook County Sheriff's Police

STREAMWOOD (AREA)	STREAMWOOD (AREA)	STREAMWOOD (AREA)	STREAMWOOD (AREA)

Ricardo Ruiz
Sureno 13
DOB 06-07-88

Edgar Salgado
Sureno 13
DOB 02-15-83

Oscar Salgado
Sureno 13
DOB 08-04-77

Vicente Salgado
Sureno 13
DOB 09-16-81

STREAMWOOD (AREA)	CHICAGO HEIGHTS	EVANSTON	FORD HEIGHTS

Ricardo Salinas
Sureno 13
DOB 06-30-81

Johnny Savage
Gangster Disciples
DOB 03-03-74

Demetrius Shavers
P-Stones
DOB 11-12-81

Tyrone Simpson
Gangster Disciples
DOB 10-26-73

MAINE TOWNSHIP	MAYWOOD	MAINE TOWNSHIP	BROADVIEW

Wayne E. Skippings
Latin Kings
DOB 11-09-86

Michael L. Smith
Mafia
DOB 03-12-78

Omar C. Soriano
Sureno 13
01-29-87

Lawrence Stallings
Four Corner Hustlers
DOB 07-03-78

Section Three

REPUTED SUBURBAN GANG LEADERSHIP

Source: Cook County Sheriff's Police

MAYWOOD

Shawn Stubblefield

Black Gangster Disciples

DOB 05-17-84

MAINE TOWNSHIP

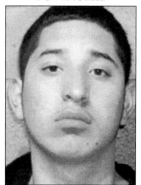

Juan Terrazas

Latin Kings

DOB 11-11-88

MAYWOOD

Michael Q. Turner

Maniac P Stones

DOB 04-25-80

CHICAGO HEIGHTS

Shedrick Turner

Gangster Disciples

DOB 10-16-79

CHICAGO HEIGHTS

Terrance Vaughn

Four Corner Hustler

DOB 12-20-67

CHICAGO HEIGHTS

Hershel Walker

Gangster Disciples

DOB 09-02-80

CHICAGO HEIGHTS

Ricardo Watson

Gangster Disciples

DOB 05-30-76

MAYWOOD

Terrell D. Weasley

Maniac P Stones

DOB 07-28-84

MAYWOOD

Torrance Weatherly

Maniac P Stones

DOB 02-01-79

ROBBINS

Henry L. White

Renegade Gangster Disciples

DOB 10-04-74

FORD HEIGHTS

Cornelius Williams

Four Corner Hustlers

DOB 07-10-79

MAYWOOD

Delvin K. Williams

Maniac P Stones

DOB 02-03-79

Please Note: The following maps highlight only predominant gangs in the area noted. For a listing of gangs by suburb, see the Law Enforcement Directory on pages 246-262.

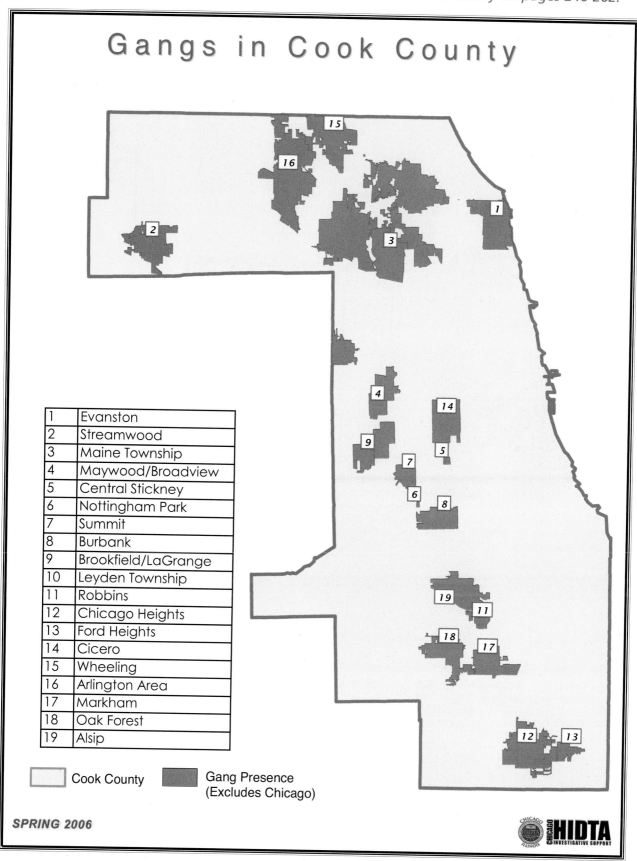

Gangs in Cook County

1	Evanston
2	Streamwood
3	Maine Township
4	Maywood/Broadview
5	Central Stickney
6	Nottingham Park
7	Summit
8	Burbank
9	Brookfield/LaGrange
10	Leyden Township
11	Robbins
12	Chicago Heights
13	Ford Heights
14	Cicero
15	Wheeling
16	Arlington Area
17	Markham
18	Oak Forest
19	Alsip

Cook County

Gang Presence
(Excludes Chicago)

SPRING 2006

Section Three

HIDTA
INVESTIGATIVE SUPPORT
CHICAGO

Please Note: The following map highlights only predominant gangs in the area noted. For a listing of gangs by suburb, see the Law Enforcement Directory on pages 246-262.

Alsip

Predominant Gangs:

Ganster Disciples

Latin Kings

Satan Disciples

SPRING 2006

Please Note: The following map highlights only predominant gangs in the area noted. For a listing of gangs by suburb, see the Law Enforcement Directory on pages 246-262.

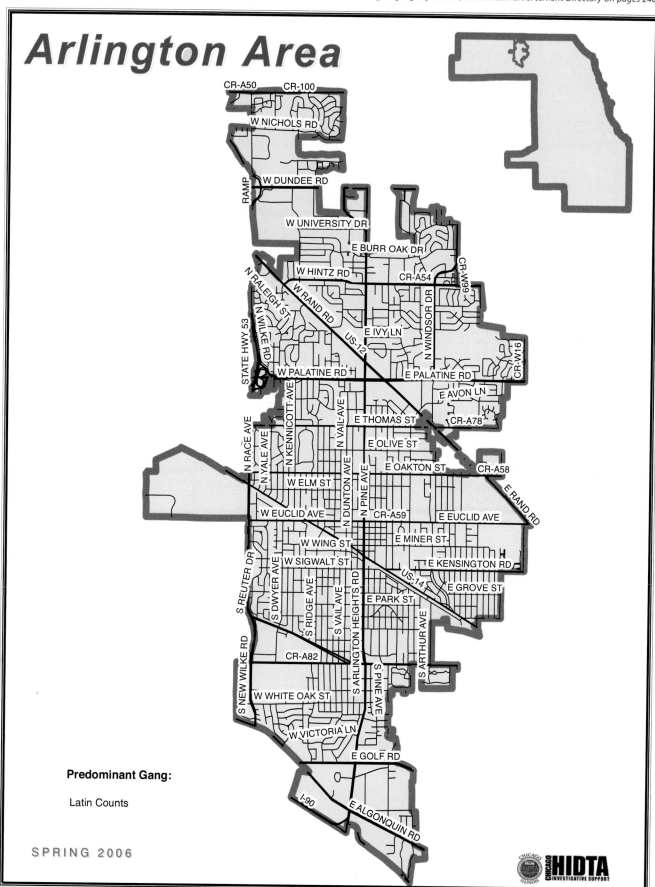

Arlington Area

Section Three

Predominant Gang:

Latin Counts

SPRING 2006

Please Note: The following map highlights only predominant gangs in the area noted. For a listing of gangs by suburb, see the Law Enforcement Directory on pages 246-262.

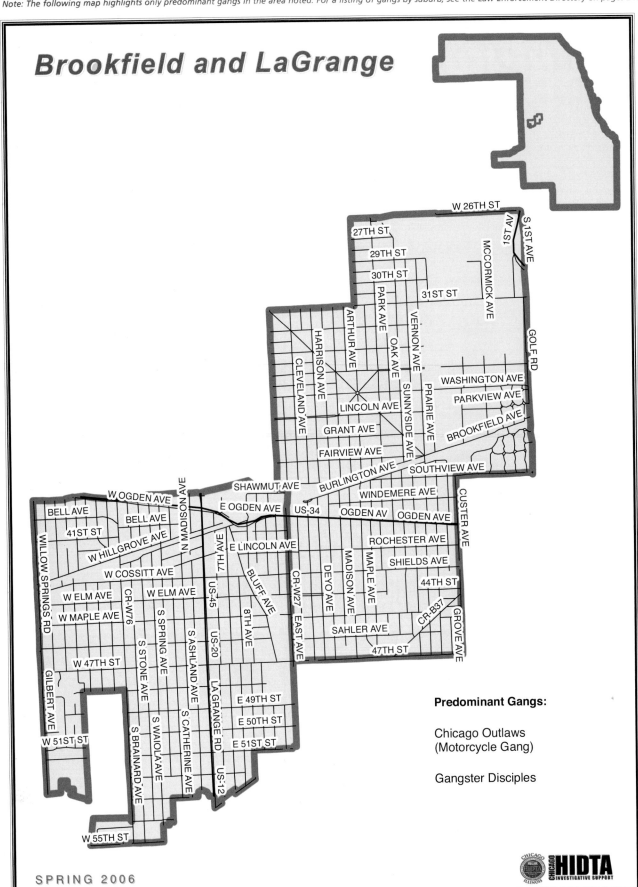

Brookfield and LaGrange

Section Three

Predominant Gangs:

Chicago Outlaws
(Motorcycle Gang)

Gangster Disciples

SPRING 2006

Please Note: The following map highlights only predominant gangs in the area noted. For a listing of gangs by suburb, see the Law Enforcement Directory on pages 246-262.

Burbank

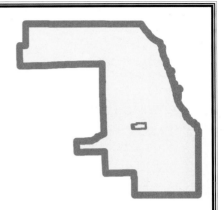

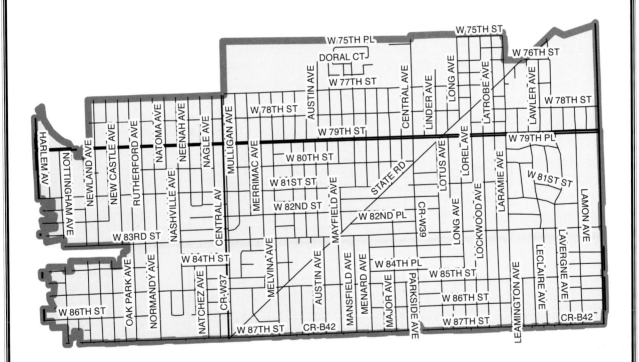

Section Three

Predominant Gangs:

Insane Popes

Ambrose

Latin Kings

Please Note: The following map highlights only predominant gangs in the area noted. For a listing of gangs by suburb, see the Law Enforcement Directory on pages 246-262.

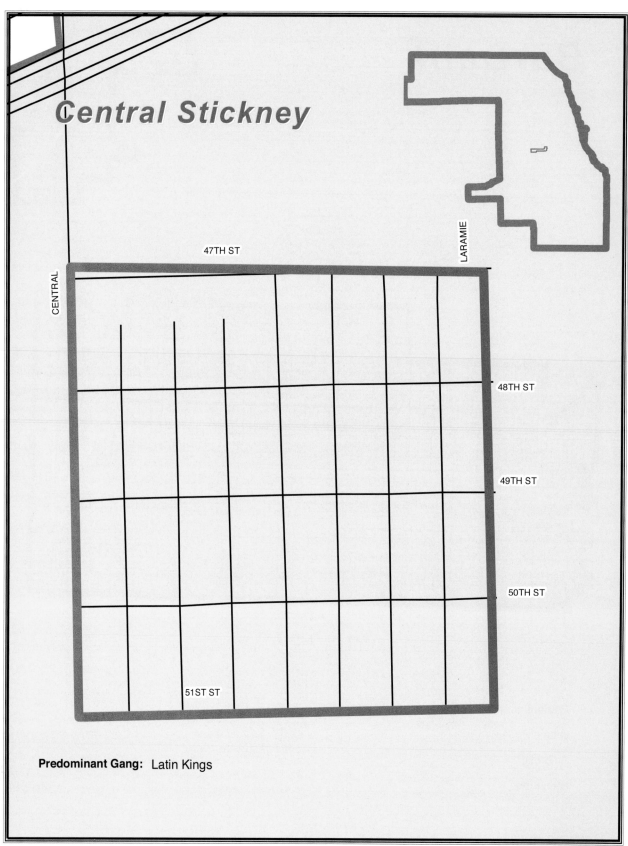

Central Stickney

47TH ST

CENTRAL

LARAMIE

48TH ST

49TH ST

50TH ST

51ST ST

Predominant Gang: Latin Kings

Section Three

Please Note: The following map highlights only predominant gangs in the area noted. For a listing of gangs by suburb, see the Law Enforcement Directory on pages 246-262.

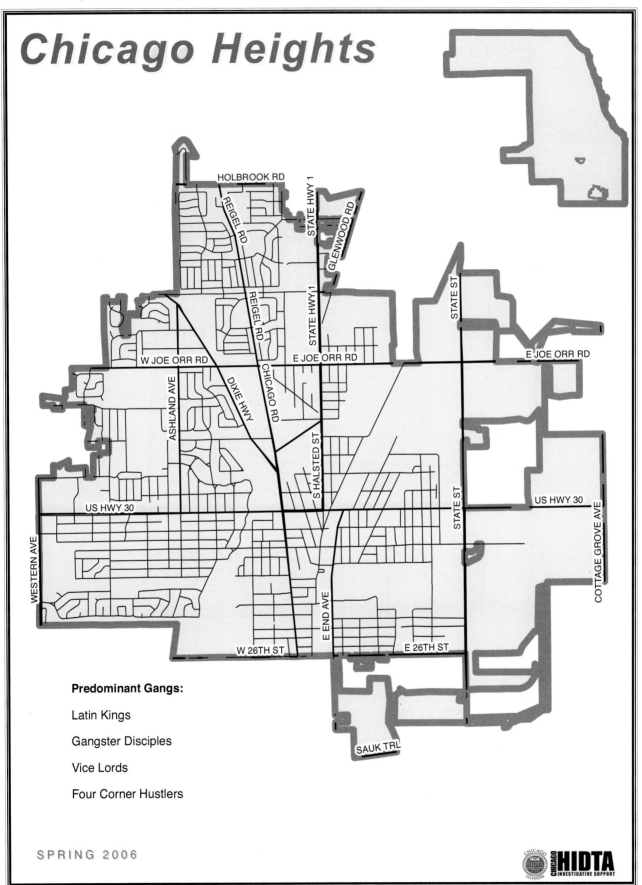

Chicago Heights

Predominant Gangs:

Latin Kings

Gangster Disciples

Vice Lords

Four Corner Hustlers

Section Three

SPRING 2006

Please Note: The following map highlights only predominant gangs in the area noted. For a listing of gangs by suburb, see the Law Enforcement Directory on pages 246-262.

Section Three

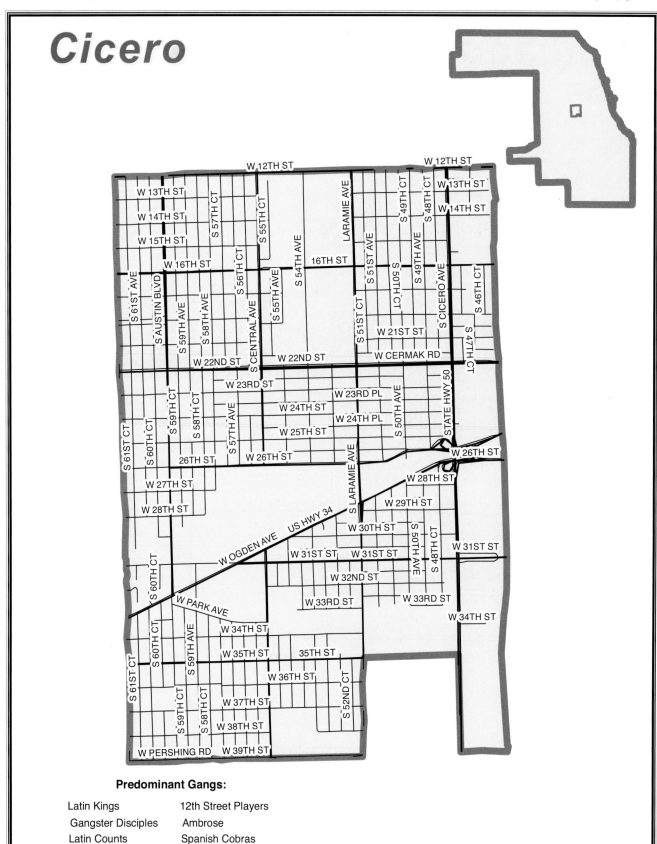

Cicero

Predominant Gangs:

Latin Kings

Gangster Disciples

Latin Counts

12th Street Players

Ambrose

Spanish Cobras

SPRING 2006

CHICAGO HIDTA
INVESTIGATIVE SUPPORT

Please Note: The following map highlights only predominant gangs in the area noted. For a listing of gangs by suburb, see the Law Enforcement Directory on pages 246-262.

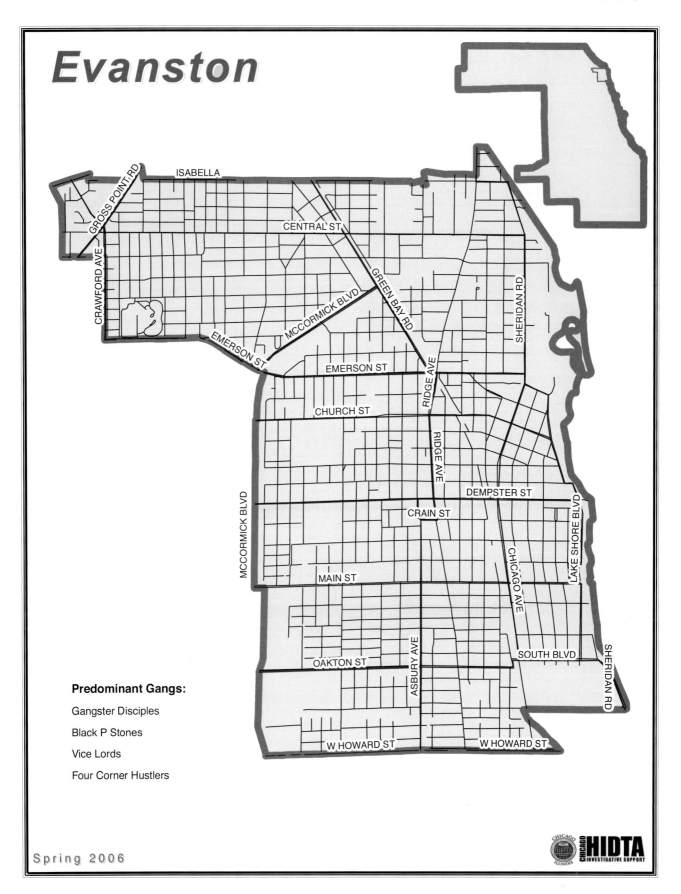

Evanston

ISABELLA

GROSS POINT RD

CENTRAL ST

CRAWFORD AVE

MCCORMICK BLVD

GREEN BAY RD

SHERIDAN RD

EMERSON ST

EMERSON ST

RIDGE AVE

CHURCH ST

RIDGE AVE

MCCORMICK BLVD

DEMPSTER ST

LAKE SHORE BLVD

CRAIN ST

CHICAGO AVE

MAIN ST

OAKTON ST

ASBURY AVE

SOUTH BLVD

SHERIDAN RD

W HOWARD ST

W HOWARD ST

Predominant Gangs:

Gangster Disciples

Black P Stones

Vice Lords

Four Corner Hustlers

Section Three

Spring 2006

CHICAGO HIDTA
INVESTIGATIVE SUPPORT

Please Note: The following map highlights only predominant gangs in the area noted. For a listing of gangs by suburb, see the Law Enforcement Directory on pages 246-262.

Section Three

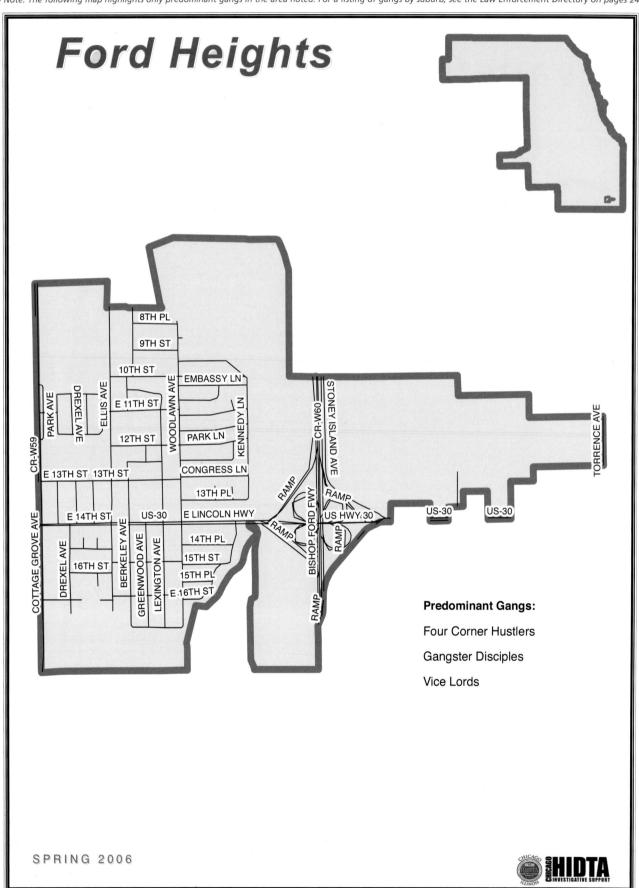

Ford Heights

Predominant Gangs:

Four Corner Hustlers

Gangster Disciples

Vice Lords

SPRING 2006

CHICAGO HIDTA
INVESTIGATIVE SUPPORT

Please Note: The following map highlights only predominant gangs in the area noted. For a listing of gangs by suburb, see the Law Enforcement Directory on pages 246-262.

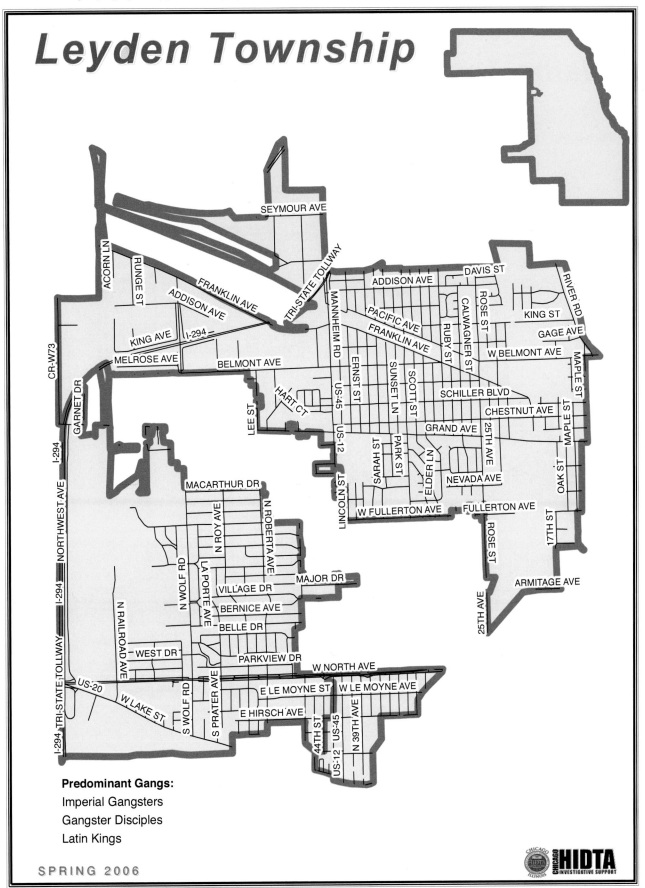

Leyden Township

Section Three

Predominant Gangs:

Imperial Gangsters

Gangster Disciples

Latin Kings

Please Note: The following map highlights only predominant gangs in the area noted. For a listing of gangs by suburb, see the Law Enforcement Directory on pages 246-262.

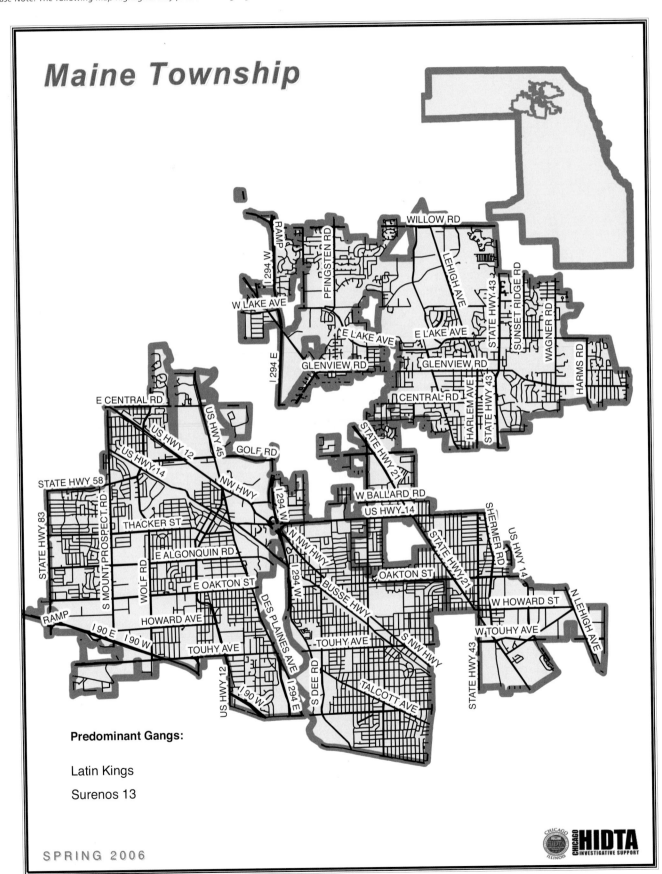

Maine Township

Section Three

Predominant Gangs:

Latin Kings

Surenos 13

CHICAGO HIDTA INVESTIGATIVE SUPPORT

Please Note: The following map highlights only predominant gangs in the area noted. For a listing of gangs by suburb, see the Law Enforcement Directory on pages 246-262.

Markham

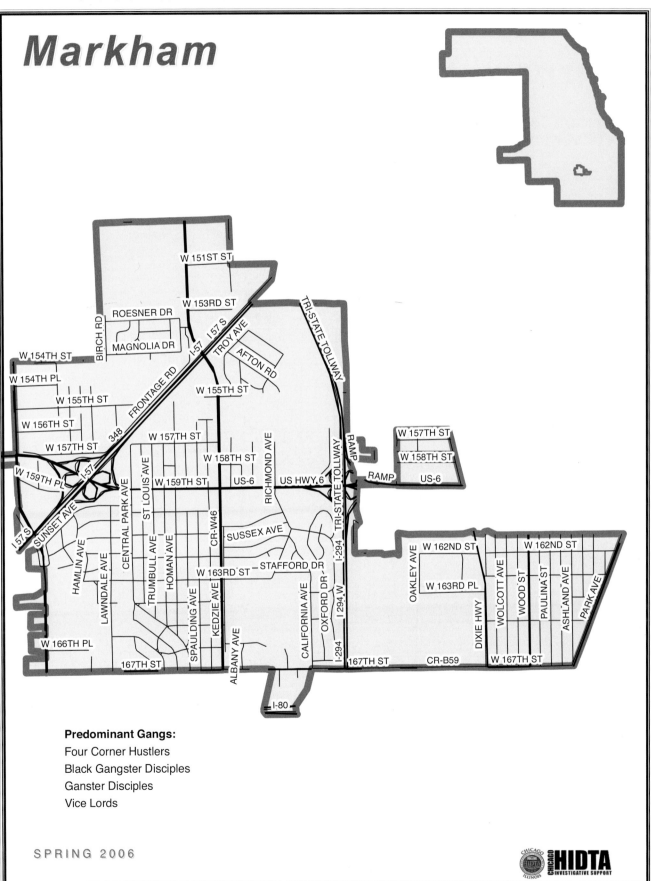

Predominant Gangs:

Four Corner Hustlers

Black Gangster Disciples

Ganster Disciples

Vice Lords

SPRING 2006

Section Three

CHICAGO **HIDTA** INVESTIGATIVE SUPPORT

Please Note: The following map highlights only predominant gangs in the area noted. For a listing of gangs by suburb, see the Law Enforcement Directory on pages 246-26.

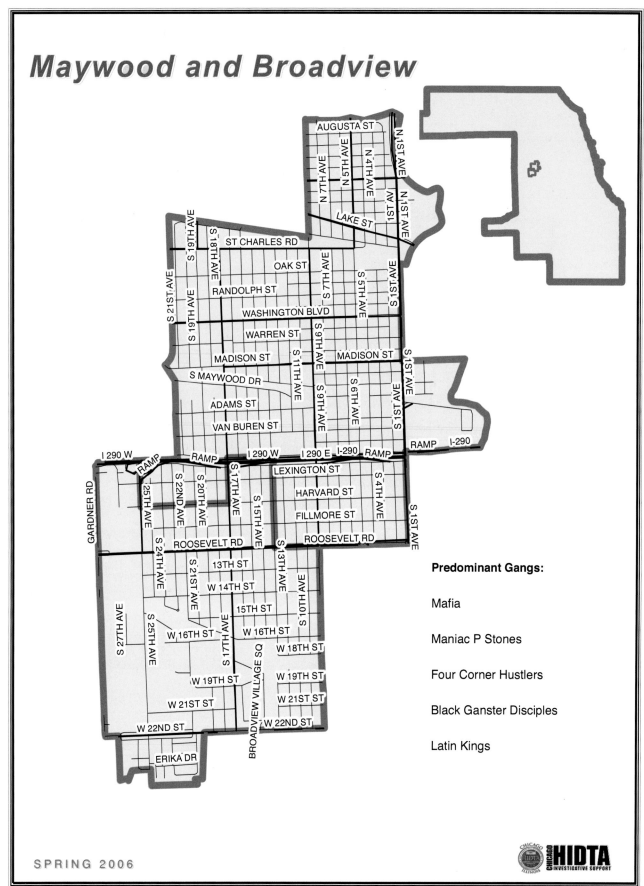

Maywood and Broadview

Predominant Gangs:

Mafia

Maniac P Stones

Four Corner Hustlers

Black Ganster Disciples

Latin Kings

SPRING 2006

CHICAGO **HIDTA**
INVESTIGATIVE SUPPORT

ease Note: The following map highlights only predominant gangs in the area noted. For a listing of gangs by suburb, see the Law Enforcement Directory on pages 246-262.

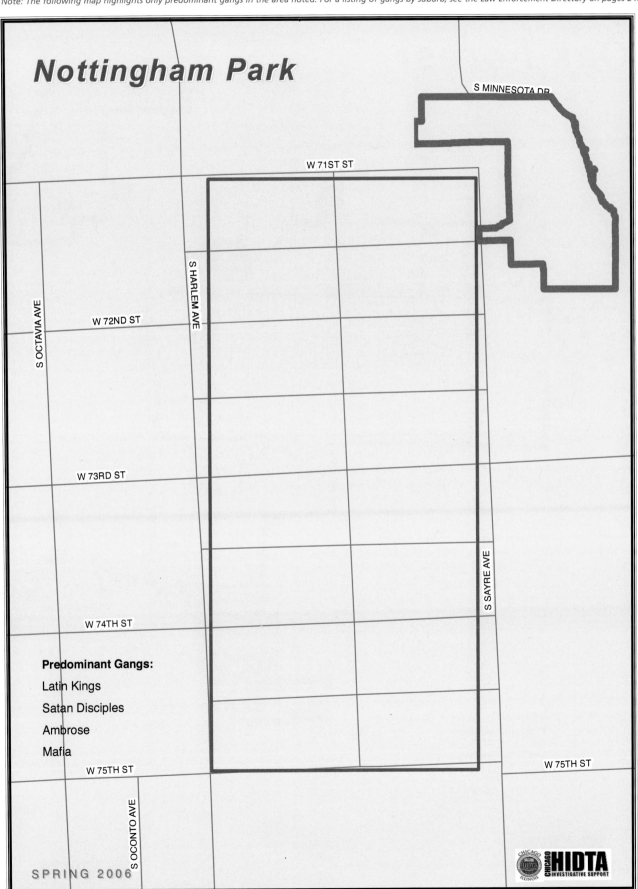

Nottingham Park

S MINNESOTA DR

W 71ST ST

S OCTAVIA AVE

W 72ND ST

S HARLEM AVE

W 73RD ST

S SAYRE AVE

W 74TH ST

Predominant Gangs:

Latin Kings

Satan Disciples

Ambrose

Mafia

W 75TH ST

W 75TH ST

S OCONTO AVE

SPRING 2006

Section Three

Please Note: The following map highlights only predominant gangs in the area noted. For a listing of gangs by suburb, see the Law Enforcement Directory on pages 246-26.

Oak Forest

Predominant Gangs:

Ganster Disciples

Latin Kings

SPRING 2006

Please Note: The following map highlights only predominant gangs in the area noted. For a listing of gangs by suburb, see the Law Enforcement Directory on pages 246-262.

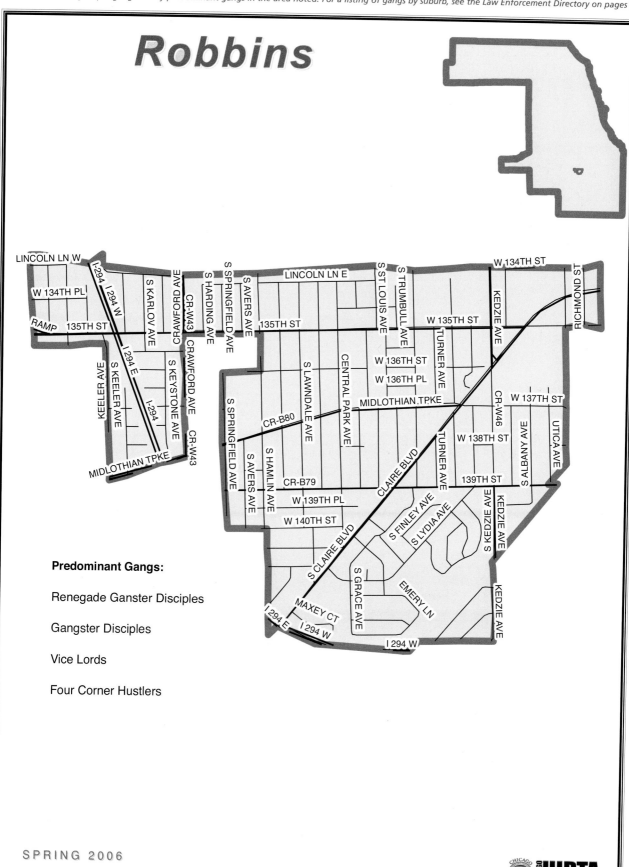

Robbins

Section Three

Predominant Gangs:

Renegade Ganster Disciples

Gangster Disciples

Vice Lords

Four Corner Hustlers

HIDTA
INVESTIGATIVE SUPPORT
CHICAGO ILLINOIS

Please Note: The following map highlights only predominant gangs in the area noted. For a listing of gangs by suburb, see the Law Enforcement Directory on pages 246-262

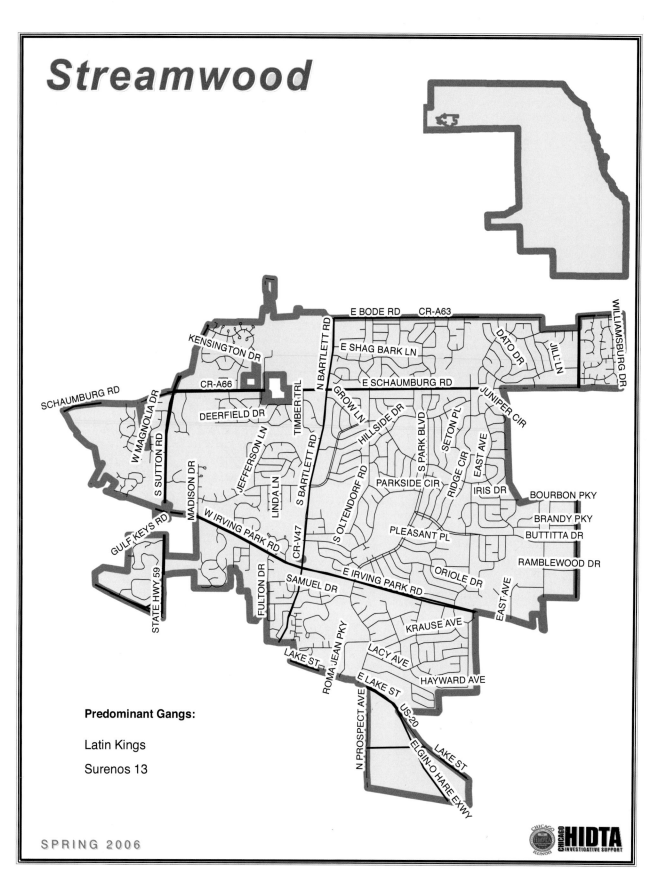

Streamwood

Section Three

Predominant Gangs:

Latin Kings

Surenos 13

SPRING 2006

CHICAGO HIDTA
INVESTIGATIVE SUPPORT

Please Note: The following map highlights only predominant gangs in the area noted. For a listing of gangs by suburb, see the Law Enforcement Directory on pages 246-262.

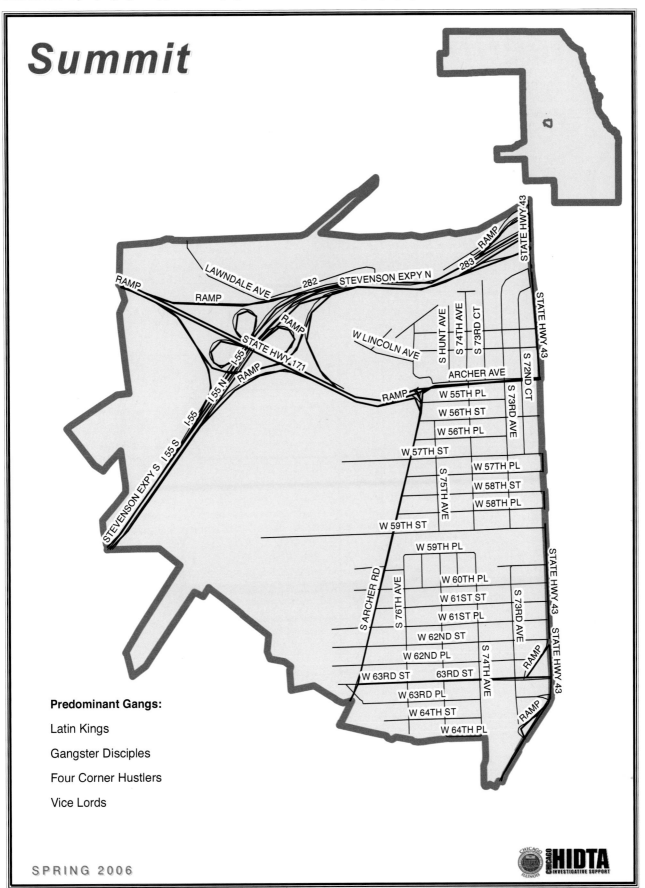

Summit

Predominant Gangs:

Latin Kings

Gangster Disciples

Four Corner Hustlers

Vice Lords

Section Three

CHICAGO HIDTA INVESTIGATIVE SUPPORT

Please Note: The following map highlights only predominant gangs in the area noted. For a listing of gangs by suburb, see the Law Enforcement Directory on pages 246-262

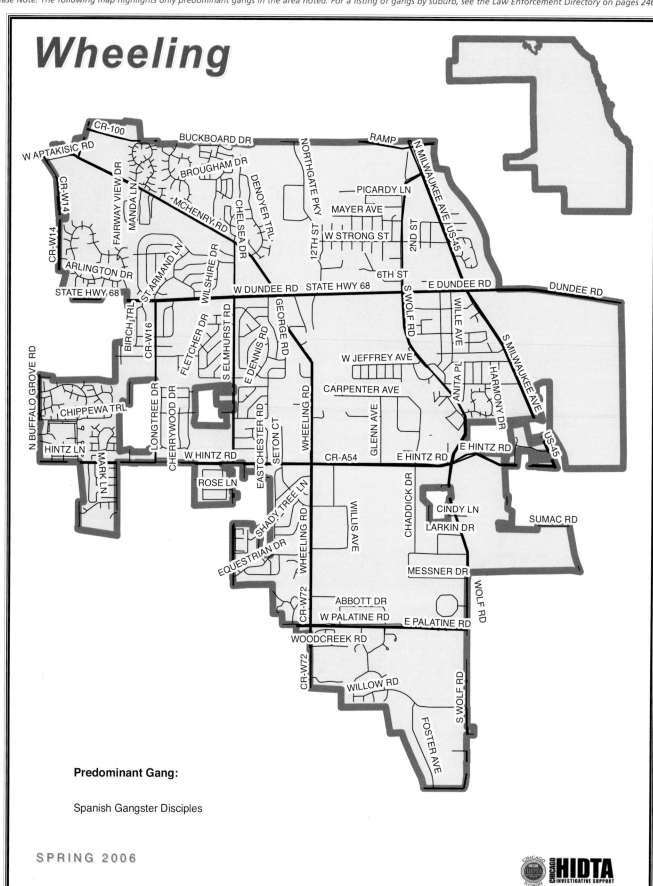

Wheeling

Predominant Gang:

Spanish Gangster Disciples

SPRING 2006

Section Three

Please Note: The following maps highlight only predominant gangs in the area noted. For a listing of gangs by suburb, see the Law Enforcement Directory on pages 246-262.

DuPage County

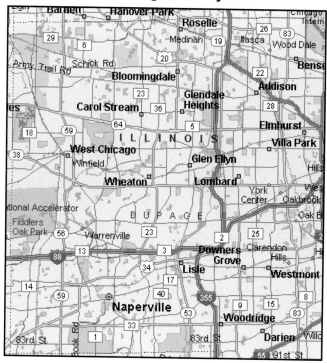

Predominant Gangs: Latin Kings, Gangster Disciples, Vice Lords, Sureno 13s, Satan Disciples, Latin Counts, Four Corner Hustlers, Nortenos 14, 18th Street Gang, Latin Dragons

Kane County

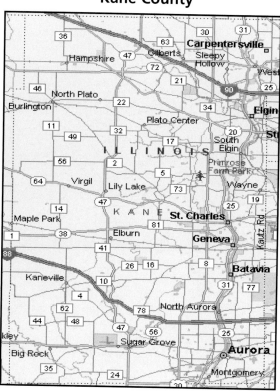

Predominant Gangs: Latin Kings, Latin Disciples, Gangster Disciples, Vice Lords, Maniac Latin Disciples, Ambrose, Deuces, Sureno 13s

Lake County

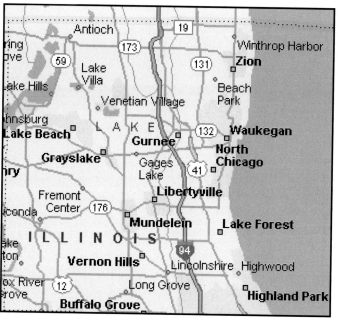

Predominant Gangs: Latin Kings, Maniac Latin Disciples, Gangster Disciples, Vice Lords, Aryan Nation, Four Corner Hustlers, Insane Deuces, Renegades, MS 13s, Sureno 13s

McHenry County

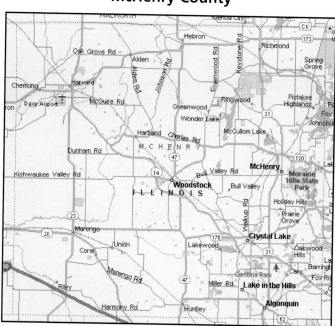

Predominant Gangs: Latin Kings, Latin Dragons, Gangster Disciples, Nortenos 14, Sureno 13s, Skin Heads, Outlaws Motorcycle Gang, Crossroads Motorcycle Gang, Sojourner Motorcycle Gang

SECTION 4

Gang Initiation, Identifiers, Slang and Media Influences

GANG INITIATION

In order to join a gang, a prospective member must participate in an initiation process. These acts of initiation vary from gang to gang. The process of initiation may include, but is not limited to, the following acts:

- attends meetings, pays dues and interacts with members to gain acceptance

- memorizes the code of conduct

- engages in a fight with one or more active members until he proves devotion and stamina by not backing down

- engages in an act of violence, such as a robbery or a drive-by shooting, to demonstrate his loyalty to the gang

- vandalizes property with gang graffiti

- commits burglary of a police officer's residence to steal firearms

- holds or conceals guns or narcotics for the gang

- sells drugs for the gang or serves as a lookout for police during drug transactions

- runs the gauntlet, while being beaten by members

- shoplifts

- commits criminal act and gets arrested

- if "flipping" membership from one gang to another gang, commits acts of violence against a member of their former gang

- "sexed in" for females wanting to join the gang, engages in sexual acts with several male gang members

- commits battery against a non-gang member

- candidate is chosen or sponsored by an established gang member

GANG IDENTIFIERS

Age

The estimated age of younger gang members is 13-15 years of age, while leaders or older gang members are generally between 25-30 years of age. Due to their dangerous lifestyle, many of the hard-core gang members die young or are incarcerated.

Graffiti

Ten years ago, graffiti was prevalent throughout the City. Gangs used graffiti to advertise gang affiliation, mark their territory and to show disrespect to rival gangs. Today, there is much less graffiti in the City as most gangs are more interested in remaining low key in order to make their drug sales. They do not want to draw attention to their illegal activities. Graffiti found today is more often created by the predominantly Hispanic gangs. In the suburbs, graffiti is still a significant gang activity.

See Graffiti Examples on pages 145-149.

Gang Colors, Clothing, Jewelry and Tattoos

Ten years ago, gang members could be easily identified by certain gang colors they would wear, jewelry worn to depict certain gang symbols, and the sports and other clothing worn with images similar to their gang monikers.

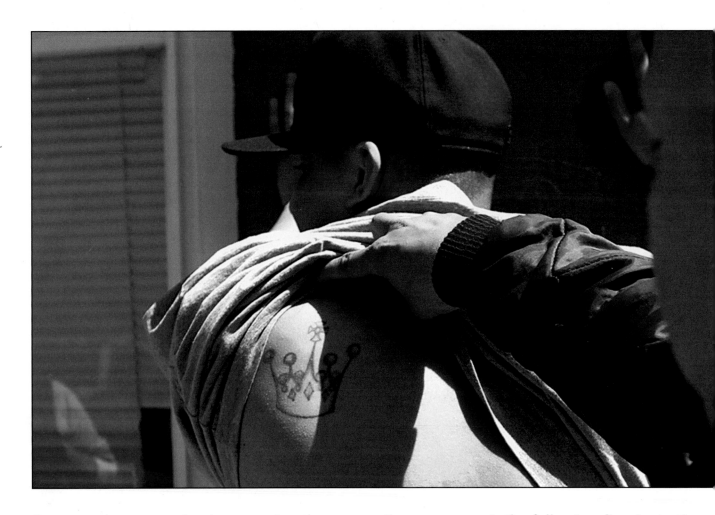

Gang members wanted to 'represent' to the world. Today, there is a trend to move away from gang identifiers so that 'gangbangers' are not so easily identified by police or rival gangs. Many gang members are wearing less obvious blue jeans and white t-shirts when out in public, saving their gang colors and jewelry for gang parties or more private events only.

Popular gang tattoos are, for many gang members, no longer placed where they are readily visible and might be placed, for example, under their shirt rather than on their face.

See Color Examples on pages 158-159.

See Tattoo Examples on pages 150-157.

Disguise

Gang members have been known to "disguise" themselves in rival gang colors when committing criminal acts in order to encourage police to suspect their enemies of the crime. This does not, however, appear to happen often.

Even more rare is the following disguise tactic: A West Chicago officer reported that, in his area, some male gang members were disguising themselves in female wigs during drive-by shootings, during other criminal activity or while driving through rival gang territory. This trend was not, however, reported by any other suburban police departments surveyed and thus, seems to be unique to those few individuals.

Gang Hand Signs

Gang hand signs have become a more important identifier to law enforcement since colors, tattoos and clothing are less obvious today.

Gang members generally use signs to identify themselves to fellow gang members, making hand signs that represent their own gang or that show disrespect to rival gangs. Hand signs may also symbolize a gang's location, such as a street corner.

See Hand Sign Examples on pages 160-161.

AMBROSE

ASHLAND VIKINGS

BISHOPS

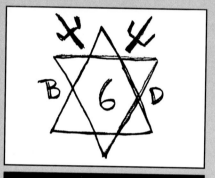

BLACK DISCIPLES

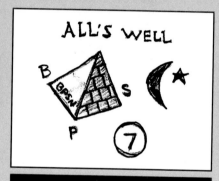

BLACK P-STONES

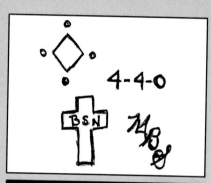

BLACK SOULS

BOSS PIMPS

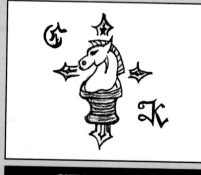

CITY KNIGHTS

CULLERTON DEUCES

FOUR CORNER HUSTLERS

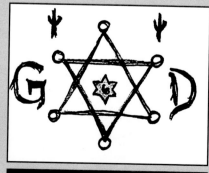

GANGSTER DISCIPLES

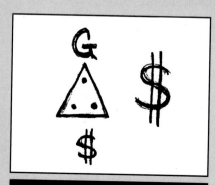

GANGSTER STONES

Section Four

Section Four

GAYLORDS

HARRISON GENTS

IMPERIAL GANGSTERS

INSANE C-NOTES

INSANE DEUCES

INSANE DRAGONS

INSANE LATIN BROTHERS

INSANE UNKNOWNS

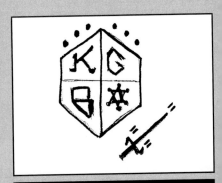

KRAZY GETDOWN BOYS

LA FAMILIA STONES

LA RAZA

LATIN COUNTS

LATIN DRAGONS

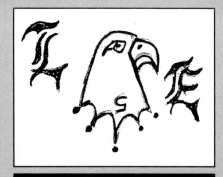

LATIN EAGLES

LATIN JIVERS

LATIN KINGS

LATIN LOVERS

LATIN PACHUCOS

LATIN SAINTS

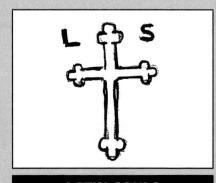

LATIN SOULS

LATIN STYLERS

MANIAC LATIN DISCIPLES

MICKEY COBRAS

MILWAUKEE KINGS

Section Four

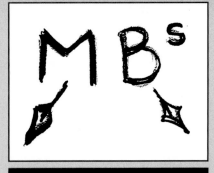

MORGAN BOYS

ORCHESTRA ALBANY

PARTY PEOPLE

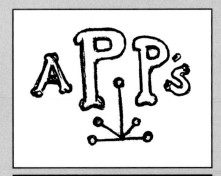

PARTY PLAYERS

POPES

RACINE BOYS

SATAN DISCIPLES

SIMON CITY ROYALS

SIN CITY BOYS

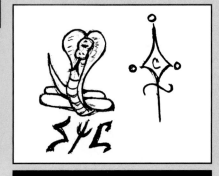

SPANISH COBRAS

SPANISH GANGSTER DISCIPLES

SPANISH LORDS

Section Four

SURENO 13S

TWO-SIXERS

TWO-TWO BOYS

VICE LORDS

YLO COBRAS

YLO DISCIPLES

Section Four

GANG TATTOOS

Source: Illinois Department of Corrections

AMBROSE

ASHLAND VIKINGS

BISHOPS

BLACK DISCIPLES

BLACK GANGSTER / LLL / NEW BREED

BLACK P STONE NATION / EL RUKN

GANG TATTOOS

Source: Illinois Department of Corrections

BLACK SOULS

C-NOTES

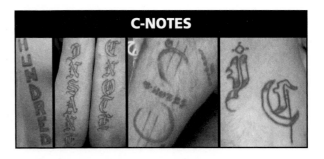

CAMPBELL BOYS (MANIAC & INSANE)

DRAGONS (INSANE, LATIN)

FOUR CORNER HUSTLERS

GANGSTER DISCIPLE NATION

GAYLORDS

GANG TATTOOS

Source: Illinois Department of Corrections

(ALMIGHTY) HARRISON GENTS

IMPERIAL GANGSTERS

INSANE (CULLERTON) DEUCES

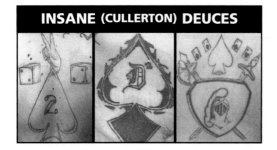

POPES (INSANE, ALMIGHTY)

INSANE UNKNOWNS

LA FAMILIA / PUERTO RICAN / FUTURE STONES

GANG TATTOOS

Source: Illinois Department of Corrections

LA RAZA

LATIN COUNTS

LATIN EAGLES

LATIN JIVERS

LATIN KINGS

LATIN LOVERS

GANG TATTOOS

Source: Illinois Department of Corrections

LATIN SAINTS

LATIN SOULS

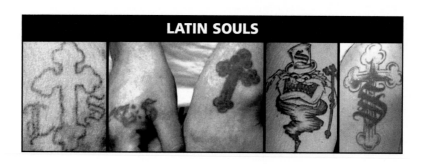

MANIAC LATIN DISCIPLES

MICKEY COBRAS

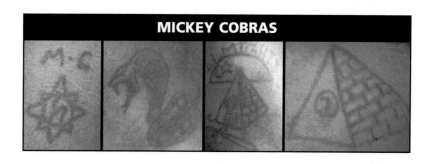

MILWAUKEE KINGS

GANG TATTOOS

Source: Illinois Department of Corrections

ORCHESTRA ALBANY

PARTY PEOPLE

PARTY PLAYERS

SATAN DISCIPLES

SIMON CITY ROYALS

Section Four

155

GANG TATTOOS

Source: Illinois Department of Corrections

(INSANE) SPANISH COBRAS

SPANISH GANGSTER DISCIPLES

TWO-SIX NATION

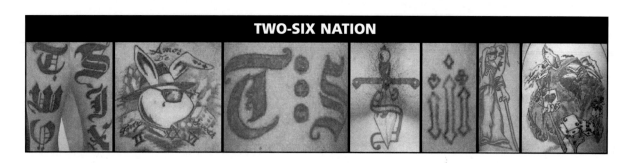

TWO-TWO BOY

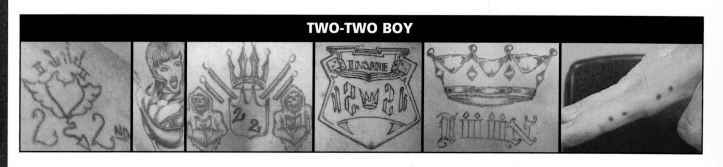

CONSERVATIVE VICE LORDS

CICERO INSANE VICE LORDS

GANG TATTOOS

Source: Illinois Department of Corrections

EBONY VICE LORDS

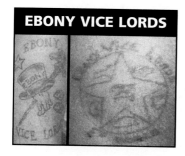

IMPERIAL INSANE VICE LORDS

INSANE VICE LORDS

MAFIA INSANE VICE LORDS

RENEGADE VICE LORDS

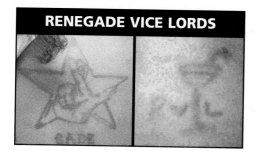

TRAVELER VICE LORDS

Sureno 13s Photos provided by the West Chicago Police Department.

SURENO 13S

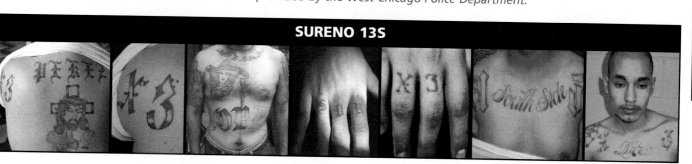

GANG COLORS

Source: *Chicago Police Department*

FOLKS ALLIANCE

AMBROSE

Black — Sky Blue

BLACK GANGSTERS
Black — Blue

CITY KNIGHTS
Black — Gray

GANGSTER DISCIPLES
Black — Blue

INSANE DEUCES

Black — Green

LATIN EAGLES
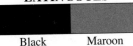
Black — Gray

LATIN SOULS
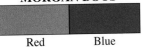
Black — Maroon

MORGAN BOYS

Red — Blue

PARTY PEOPLE

Black — White

SATAN DISCIPLES

Black — Yellow

SPANISH GANGSTER DISCIPLES

Black — Blue

TWO-TWO BOYS
Black — Blue

ASHLAND VIKINGS

Black — Green

BLACK SOULS

Black — White

C-NOTES
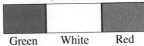
Green — White — Red

HARRISON GENTS

Black — Purple

INSANE DRAGONS
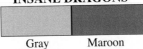
Gray — Maroon

LATIN JIVERS
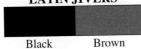
Black — Brown

MANIAC LATIN DISCIPLES

Black — Sky Blue

NEW BREED LLL

Black — Blue

POPES - INSANE

Black — White

SIMON CITY ROYALS

Blue — Black — Green

SURENO 13
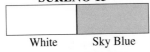
White — Sky Blue

Y.L.O. COBRAS

Black — Green

BLACK DISCIPLES

Black — Blue

CAMPBELL BOYS

Blue — Red

CULLERTON DEUCES

Black — Gray

IMPERIAL GANGSTERS

Black — Pink

LA RAZA
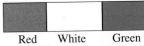
Red — White — Green

LATIN LOVERS
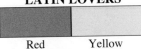
Red — Yellow

MILWAUKEE KINGS
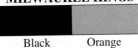
Black — Orange

ORCHESTRA ALBANY

Brown — Black — Yellow

RACINE BOYS

Sky Blue — Blue

SPANISH COBRAS

Black — Green

TWO - SIX

Black — Tan

Y.L.O. DISCIPLES

Black — Sky Blue

2006

Source: Chicago Police Department

PEOPLE ALLIANCE

BISHOPS

| Black | Copper |

CONSERVATIVE VICE LORDS*

| Black | Red |

GANGSTER STONES

| Black | Red |

INSANE UNKNOWNS

| Black | White |

LATIN COUNTS

| Black | Red |

LATIN SAINTS

| Black | Blue |

MICKEY COBRA STONES

| Green | Black | Red |

POPES - ALMIGHTY

| Black | Blue |

SPANISH VICE LORDS*

| Black | Gold |

UNDERTAKER VICE LORDS*

| Black | Gold |

BLACK P STONES

| Red | Black | Green |

EL RUKNS

| Red | Black | Green |

GAYLORDS

| Black | Sky Blue |

LA FAMILIA STONES

| Black | Orange |

LATIN DRAGONS

| Black | White |

LATIN STYLERS

| Gray | Maroon |

PACHUCOS

| Black | White |

RENEGADE VICE LORDS*

| Black | Gold |

TITANIC P STONES

| Red | Black | Green |

UNKNOWN VICE LORDS*

| Black | Gold |

CICERO INSANE VICE LORDS*

| Black | Gold |

FOUR CORNER HUSTLERS*

| Black | Red |

IMPERIAL INSANE VICE LORDS*

| Black | Gold |

LATIN BROTHERS ORG.

| Black | Purple |

LATIN KINGS

| Black | Gold |

MAFIA INSANE VICE LORDS*

| Black | Gold |

PARTY PLAYERS

| White | Maroon |

SPANISH LORDS

| Black | Red |

TRAVELING VICE LORDS*

| Black | Gold |

VICE LORDS*

| Black | Gold |

Section Four

Vice Lords: Red or Gold and Black

Chicago Police Department
Philip J. Cline
Superintendent of Police

Bureau of Strategic Deployment
Deployment Operations Center
Gang Analytical Program

2006

GANG HAND SIGNS

Source: Illinois Department of Corrections

AMBROSE

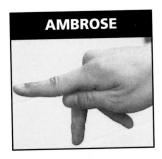

BISHOPS

BLACK DISCIPLES

BLACK GANGSTER LLL/NEW BREED

BLACK P STONES

BLACK SOULS

C-NOTES

CAMPBELL BOYS (MANIAC & INSANE)

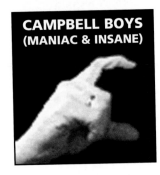

DRAGONS (INSANE, LATIN)

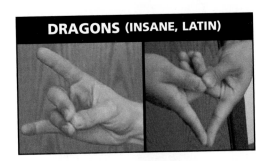

GANGSTER DISCIPLE NATION

GAYLORDS

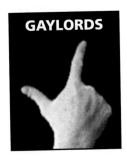

(ALMIGHTY) HARRISON GENTS

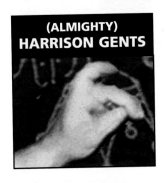

IMPERIAL GANGSTERS

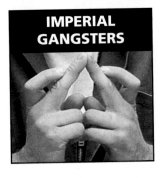

POPES (INSANE, ALMIGHTY)

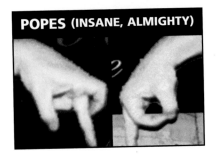

INSANE UNKNOWNS

LA RAZA

LATIN COUNTS

Section Four

Source: Illinois Department of Corrections

LATIN EAGLES

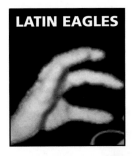

LATIN KINGS

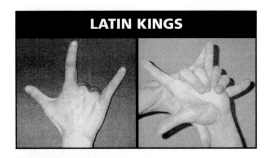

LATIN SAINTS

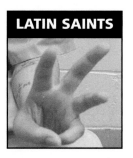

LATIN SOULS

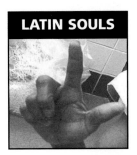

MANIAC LATIN DISCIPLES

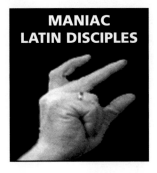

ORCHESTRA ALBANY

PARTY PEOPLE

PARTY PLAYERS

SATAN DISCIPLES

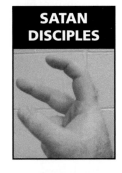

SIMON CITY ROYALS

(INSANE) SPANISH COBRAS

SPANISH GANGSTER DISCIPLES

TWO-SIX NATION

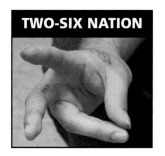

Section Four

GANG SLANG

Slang or the language used by gangs originates on the street. New words or expressions are constantly being cultivated and added to this growing vocabulary. Street jargon represents other common words or phrases in our everyday language. These expressions allow gang members to converse among themselves, while preventing "outsiders" from understanding this communication. This method may be either written or oral.

As gang members are confined to jail or sentenced to prison, street terms or expressions are used and added to or combined with jail or prison slang. Eventually, when gang members are released back into society, they take back to the street an expanded vocabulary.

The language of the street is dynamic in nature since it is constantly being revised and amended. Words or expressions of today may be obsolete or outdated tomorrow.

GLOSSARY OF GANG TERMS

Source: Chicago Police Department

(insert name) rots: deceased rival gang member "rots in hell" (appears in graffiti)

187: to kill someone, California penal code for murder, appears in Black P Stone graffiti

24-24: dope spot open for business twenty-four hours a day

24-7: twenty-four hours a day, seven days a week

7-7: dope spot open for business seven days a week

8-ball: eighth of an ounce of cocaine or heroin

AK: AK47 assault rifle

Angel dust: PCP

Anniversary roll: an attack on a rival gang (usually a drive-by shooting) to commemorate the anniversary of the death of a slain gang leader

AR: AR15 assault rifle

audi: Cook County Juvenile Center

baby teeth: crack cocaine

bag: small packet of narcotics

bag up: package bags of narcotics for street sale

bang: gang bang, being involved in gang activity

banger: gang banger, gang member

beef: complaint, ongoing dispute

bend the block: drive around the block

bill: gram of heroin or $100

bird: kilogram of cocaine

bishop: rank in gang

blade: knife

blow: heroin

blue coat, blue boy: uniformed police officer

blunt: reefer, large hand rolled marijuana cigarette

B.O.: burn out, sold out of dope, need another pack

bogart: to con or trick

bogus: fake, phony or counterfeit

bolt or break: run

boy: heroin

breakdown: shotgun

brick: kilogram of cocaine

bricks: term used by the Blackstones to put down the Gangster Disciples

bring lunch: bring narcotics

bud: marijuana

bumpin titties: to fight with

bunnies or bunny: put down of Two Six members, who use the rabbit head as a gang symbol

burbs: suburbs

burn bag: bogus narcotics (look-a-like-drugs)

burn out: cloned cellular phone

bust, bust a cap: shoot or fire a gun

C: Spanish Cobra gang member or Conservative Vice Lord gang member

cabbage: cash money

call the shots: give the orders

candy: $10 bag of cocaine

cap: to shoot at

catch a V: punishment for breaking gang rule or code of silence

caught a case: arrested for criminal offense

cellie: person who shares cell with another inmate

chief: gang leader, someone that "calls the shots"

chrome: marijuana

claim: announce your gang affiliation, represent

"Come get some!": challenge to a fight by rival gang

cop: buy dope

county: Cook County Jail

crib: house or apartment

crossed out: eliminated from the gang

crown: Latin King gang member

cut house: location where dope is weighed and packaged

cuz: cousin, close friend

D(s): Disciple gang member(s)

deck: street location where drugs are sold

deep: many, i.e. riding three deep

demos: $10 bag of heroin

deuce five: .25 caliber automatic

deucey deuce: .22 caliber handgun

deuce and a half: .25 semi-automatic

dime: $10 bag of narcotics or cannabis

dis, dis'n: disrespect, show disrespect for someone, putdown

dissed out: given disrespect or no respect

dome shot: shot to the head, execution style

don: leader of the New Breed

donkey donuts: putdown of Gangster Disciples

double deuce: .22 caliber gun

Double I: Imperial Insane Vice Lords

drive-by: shooting from a passing vehicle

drop a dime: to inform on someone

drop the flag: to leave the gang

dubs: $20 bags of heroin

egg: ounce of cocaine

elite: rank in the Vice Lord hierarchy

ends: money

enforcer: gang member who punishes violating members

false flagging: representing oneself as a rival gang member

FBI: police, plainclothes police officers

field marshall: rank in the Black Gangster hierarchy

Five-O: police

flake: nerd or geek

flake: cocaine

flip: change gang allegiance, testifying against fellow gang member

forks: (pitchforks) Disciple gang members

four five: .45 caliber handgun

four four: .44 caliber handgun

G: Gangster Disciple gang member

game: criminal activity

gang banger: member of a gang

gang bang: fight a rival gang member, participate in gang activity

gangsta: gang member

gangsta rap: music of the 1990s that extols the gang lifestyle

gapped up: armed with handguns

gaps: guns

gat: gun

gauge: shotgun

get down: fight

get free: get high from drugs

girl: cocaine

"got you faded": "I'm going to kill you"

governor: rank in gang

gump: homosexual

gunned up: armed with handguns

gunner: shooter from the gang

half bird: half kilo of cocaine

happy stick: marijuana cigarette laced with PCP

heads up: to fight someone one on one

heat up: draw attention to

hit ya: call you later

hit: attack on rival gang member

hoe: put down of a moe (Black P Stone or Blackstone)

holdin: carrying narcotics or weapons

homeboy: friend from the neighborhood, fellow gang member

homie: friend from the neighborhood

hood: neighborhood

hoodie: hooded sweatshirt

hook up: to meet up with

hooks: Vice Lord gang member

hornets: Robert Horner CHA housing project

house arrest: home confinement (ordered by the court) or staying off the street (gang term)

in the wind: on the run, on the move

inca: leader in Latin King hierarchy

jammy: dope spot

jets: housing projects

joint: hand rolled marijuana cigarette

juice: power or influence

junior: new gang member, young gang member

K: kilogram of cocaine

key: kilogram of cocaine or heroin

kickin': hanging out with, relaxing, "chillin"

kick back: hang out, relax

kite: a letter (written correspondence)

kite in the wind: a letter sent or received by an inmate

(insert gang name) Killer: shouted by rivals when attacking or disrespecting gang i.e.., King Killer

(insert gang name) Love: shouted by members of gang during an attack on a rival gang i.e.., King Love

knock him out the box: to kill someone

las: whimp or whiner

leaf: marijuana cigarette saturated with PCP

lick: quantity (bags) of narcotics packaged for street sale

lieutenant: rank in gang

lock down: increased security within the prison system, inmates confined to cells

mac: mac 10 machine pistol

marshall: rank in Black Gangster hierarchy

midget: young gang member

minister: rank in Black Disciple hierarchy

missile: handgun

mob: the gang

mufti: enforcer within the Blackstones hierarchy

mule: person that transports narcotics or guns

moe: Black P Stone member

narc, narcos: plainclothes police officer(s)

nation: the gang, gang membership

nation days: drug profits from one day a month are set aside for bond money and attorney fees for gang members with criminal cases

nickel: $5 bag of narcotics or cannabis

nine: 9mm handgun

neutron: neutral, person not associating with a street gang

O.G.: original gangster (older gang member)

old girl or O.G.: mother

on deck: on the dope spot selling narcotics

on the square: on the dope spot selling narcotics

on paper: on probation or parole

on the pipe: person that smokes crack cocaine

on the line: work selling dope on the street for a drug operation

onion: one ounce of cocaine

OZ: ounce of cocaine

package: quantity of narcotics

pack: quantity of narcotics, individually packaged for street sale

pack man or pack runner: individual that delivers pack to dope spot

paper: cash money

paying tribute: giving a certain percentage or fixed amount from drug profits to incarcerated leaders

payback: retaliation for gang violence (shooting or murder)

peel a cap: fire a gun

pee wee: new gang member, young gang member

PHD: pumpkin head deluxe (see pumpkin head)

piece: handgun, firearm

pipe: gun

pitch: sell drugs

pop a cap: shoot a gun, fire a shot

powder: powder cocaine

power: rank or control within a gang

pot: marijuana

prince: rank in Black P Stones or Black Gangster hierarchy

product: narcotics sold on the street

pumpkin head: beating of gang member as the result of committing a violation

punk, punk ass: coward

raid: search warrant

rank: hold position or status within the gang

rap: talk

rat partner: close friend

reds: red bricked buildings in Cabrini-Green, currently influenced by Gangster Disciples

regent: rank in Gangster Disciple hierarchy

renegade: splinter group from original gang

rep: reputation

represent: identifying oneself as a gang member

ride: car

ride with: to associate with a particular gang

RIP: rest in peace (appears in graffiti or tattoos to honor slain leaders or members)

rip: to steal, "rip off"

rock house: location where rock cocaine is cooked up or sold from

rocks: crack or rock cocaine

roll: drive-by shooting, attack rival gang in retaliation

rules: controls gang, controls certain neighborhood

run the gauntlet: initiation (beating) of prospective gang members or used as a form of violation

runs it: controls gang, controls a certain area

safe house: dwelling that does not contain narcotics or weapons, location where individuals can feel "safe"

section: faction of the gang that congregates in a certain area

security: lookouts for police at dope spots

serve: sell drugs

set: party or a particular gang

sexed in: female performs sex acts with males in order to be accepted into the gang

shake house: location where dope is weighed or packaged

shank: knife

shanked: knifed

sherm sticks: marijuana cigarettes laced with PCP

shooter: gang member that will shoot or has shot at rivals

shortie: new gang member, young gang member

shorty: police

slab: kilogram of cocaine or heroin

slick boys: plainclothes police officers

slinging rocks: selling rock cocaine

smoke some dope: smoke rock cocaine

smoke: reefer, marijuana or cannabis

snakes: members of the Cobras

snitch: informant

snort: ingest cocaine or heroin through the nasal cavity

soldier: foot soldier, gang member without rank

solid: term used by members of the Four Corner Hustlers and Traveling Vice Lords meaning together or united

spot: street location where drugs are sold from

stack up: save up (money)

stank 'em: kill 'em

stash: hidden money or narcotics

stash house: residence where money, narcotics or firearms are hidden

steel: handguns

static: conflict

stole on me: hit me, punched me

stone: Black P Stone, Cobra Stone, Gangster Stone or La Familia Stone members

straight: alright, good

straight up: that's the truth

strap: gun

street tax: monies paid by drug dealers to the gang in order to work a certain area

strip: where the gang hangs out or sells dope

strips: bags or narcotics taped to adhesive strip for street sale

strong: many, a lot of

sweat: interrogate

swords: guns

tac: PCP

take out the game: to kill someone

take out the box: to kill someone

tall: numerous, a lot of, i.e.. tall Folks

tar: black tar Mexican heroin

tatts: tattoos

tec: tec 9 machine pistol

the joint: the penitentiary

the law: the police

the man: the police, the system

the mob: the gang, Gangster Disciples

three eight: .38 caliber handgun

throw: to sell drugs

throw down: challenge

tic: PCP

tip: area for selling street narcotics

tollie: toluene, clear solvent soaked in rag and inhaled to get high

tollie head: person who gets high on tollie

toos: tattoos

toot: cocaine

trap: secret compartment in vehicle to conceal drugs, large amounts of money or guns

trap car: vehicle installed with secret compartment to conceal drugs, large amounts of money

trey eight: .38 caliber handgun

tribute: monies paid to incarcerated gang leaders from narcotic sales

trick: informant

trim: female companionship

trim: beat up

tune up: beat up

turf: geographical area controlled by gang

turn: to sell drugs to

turnkey: lockup keeper, jailer

twisters: door keys

two deep: riding two people in a vehicle

three deep: riding three people in a vehicle

undercover: living in or traveling through rival gang territory

universal: rank in Vice Lord hierarchy

violation: punishment for breaking gang rule or code of conduct

V'd out: violated out of a gang, usually by beating

weed: marijuana, cannabis

weight: large quantity of narcotics

whack: attack or kill

"What you be about?": "What gang do you belong to?"

"What up?": greeting among fellow gang members, or can be constructed as a challenge to rivals

whites: white bricked buildings in Cabrini-Green, influenced by the Gangster Disciples

wickey stick: marijuana cigarette laced with PCP

wire up: apprise or inform

work the spot: sell narcotics or provide security at drug location

work: drug stash, quantity of narcotics ready for street sale

young blood: new gang member or young gang member

"You straight?": "You selling drugs?"

x'ed out: eliminated from the gang

Gang Behavior and The Media

Children and adolescents may be drawn to gangs because of a need to belong to a group where it is commonly believed that there is power in being different or better than others. The gang offers an alternative life style where the gang can control its own world and make life meaningful and thrilling.

Do members of youth gangs play out their aggressiveness and violence after viewing a gang-related film? Films involving gangs and violence have existed since the late 20s, and have become increasingly more liberal in their depiction of violence.

Even in the late 20s, the debate arose as to whether crime and gangster films causes youth to commit crimes and acts of violence.

Cited in an early study by Frederick Thrasher, *The Gang: A Study of 1,313 Gangs in Chicago*, one gang member, when asked why he committed crimes, explains that "it looked so easy in the movies, and we thought we could get away with it, too."

Delinquent behavior may be partially the result of what is exciting and stimulating through film. The film itself may be seeking a greater underlying meaning, and in fact, attempting to demonstrate that gang violence leads to consequences such as long-term incarceration or death. The child or adolescent that views the film, though, may not necessarily perceive the underlying meaning. He or she may only see the thrill of being part of the action, banding together with a group coming from similar backgrounds and feelings of rage, distress and alienation from society. The violent scenes in the film become the focus and the appeal, the deeper meaning lost.

The film *Colors*, a gang-related movie, has had an impact on adolescent gang members. The Bloods and the CRIPS, two rival gangs, are introduced to the general populace where they may have not even known these gangs existed. Although many police and gang experts say that the movie does not provide an accurate picture of gang life, to gang members, their life style has been glorified. Since the release of this film depicting gang activity in Los Angeles, membership in the CRIPS has increased significantly in St. Louis.

Rap music has become an avenue for gangs to glorify gang violence under the guise that it is a depiction of what is "real." Several rappers have come out of the area of Atlantic Drive, a street in Compton (Los Angeles area) known for narcotics and gang activity. Gangster rap has become mainstream to many children and adolescents who idolize the talk, the dress, and the hard-life reality that offsets gang members coming from the CRIPS and the Bloods or from society at large. The influence of gangster rap appears to have encouraged gang membership or, at least, increased in youth the desire to be like a 'gang member' by glorifying defiance and rage toward police, identifying drugs and violence with freedom and individuality, and demeaning education.

One incident which captured significant media attention is the shooting and murder of rapper Tupac Shakur, where a key suspect, a known CRIPS leader, has been alleged to have ordered the hit on Shakur. The actual four in the white Cadillac that perpetrated the drive-by shooting,

Memorial to a slain gang member.

may not be perceived by gang members as murderers, but may be glorified by CRIP gang members as those who protect what is real to them, their pride and their identification with power in a world manufactured by images of defiance and violence.

Gangsta rappers have become self-proclaimed reporters of lyrics reflecting the anger and violence of urban youth. Although the lyrics in themselves do not cause the acts of violence, they certainly reinforce the images as badges to be worn by those who repeatedly sing and believe in their messages. The lyrics often praise anarchy, loyalty to the gang without regard for human beings or authorities outside the gang's culture and beliefs.

According to the testimony of the American Psychiatric Association on the Effects of Violent and Demeaning Musical Lyrics on our Nation's Youth presented by the APA's Deputy Medical Director Roberts T.M. Phillips, M.D., Ph.D., to the Senate Subcommittee on Juvenile Justice (02-23-94), violent and sexually explicit lyrics and images foster violent behavior:

167

"Numerous studies have clearly established the relationship between actual exposure to violence and its negative consequences on normal childhood development. A substantial body of research has also demonstrated the association of violent or aggressive behaviors with repeated exposure to televised violence. Simply put, the more violent programming children view, the greater is the risk they will behave violently or aggressively."

Gang-like activity has also been glorified in video games, such as in the popular *Grand Theft Auto*, which allows players to create gang-like activity, identify with the `shooter' who gets points for the murder and killing of gang member opponents, and is awarded for successfully completing a crime. The game provides stimulation to the thrill seeking player, but it also promotes and glorifies gang-like activity as a commonplace norm where enemies are lurking in every corner of every day life and society.

The restrictions for buying these games are limited; though many of the sites will ask for the purchaser's age, there is no practical way of preventing a child or adolescent familiar with computers and Internet usage from using a borrowed or stolen credit card to purchase the game. Games such as *Grand Theft Auto* allow for the continuous and repetitious access to a game that encourages the child or adolescent to build a mental world of violence. The action and images are attractive to players because they mimic the films, gangster rap music and promotion of violent characters that are glorified because of their unusual appearance and behavior.

According to Dr. Craig A. Anderson, in Violent Video Games, Myths, Facts, and Unanswered Questions, (*Science Directorate*, October 2003, 16:5), when including all relevant empirical studies using sound analytical techniques related to behavior science, violent video games have been demonstrated to be associated with increased aggressive behavior and increased physiological arousal, as evidenced in experimental studies. Children and young adults, when continually exposed to violent images, especially when little direction is supplied toward their moral edification, can be influenced by the images they perceive to the extent that there is an increase in feelings of violence and related behavior.

There is no doubt that gang life and gang violence has spread from urban cities into numerous suburban areas, and that violent acts are committed. If the violent images in music, movies and video games do not directly cause this expansion, they certainly cannot be contributing positively toward preventing the expansion.

SECTION 5

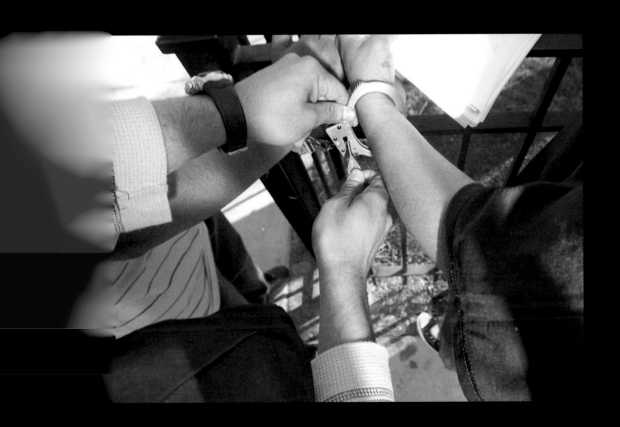

Gang Crimes
and Economics

THE COST TO LAW ENFORCEMENT

Police officers put their lives on the line every day. Only a few examples, in one month alone, of the gang violence directed toward Chicago law enforcement are illustrated here:

On **FEBRUARY 5, 2005,** a Chicago police officer en route to work in his vehicle was struck in the rear. The officer confronted the driver of the striking vehicle and was repeatedly struck in the head and face and knocked to the ground by known Gangster Disciples.

On **FEBRUARY 11, 2005**, members of the Two-Six Street Gang opened fire on several Chicago Police officers.

On **FEBRUARY 18, 2005,** a self-admitted member of the Latin Kings attempted to murder an off-duty Chicago Police officer by firing a shot at the officer. The offender attempted to shoot the officer when the officer responded to sounds of gunfire and observed the offender holding a gun. The officer was wearing his badge and had identified himself as police.

On **FEBRUARY 22, 2005,** members of the Four Corner Hustlers made death threats to a hospitalized Chicago Police Officer.

CHICAGO POLICE DEPARTMENT CRIME DATA

REPORTED INDEX CRIMES

(Please note that for most index crimes, gang-affiliation is not tracked.)

The Chicago Police Department provided statistics reflecting overall reported crimes and gang-related crimes for calendar years 2004 and 2005. The numbers reflect only crimes reported, without taking into account any follow-up investigation that may have later revealed that the incident was actually gang- related. It is important to note that not all of the crimes reported actually occurred. Further investigations by the detective division may have revealed some incidents were not bona-fide due to false reports, improper classification, incidents occurring outside the City, etc.

Crimes recorded as gang-related are entirely dependent on how the victim reports the incident to the preliminary investigator. Mere gang member involvement does not automatically indicate a gang-related crime as not all incidents are gang motivated. Follow-up investigations may later reveal that a crime was gang-related, but unlike homicides, other crimes are not tracked and later categorized and identified as gang-related.

The statistics indicate a small percentage of gang-related batteries and assaults. One would think that those statistics would have higher numbers. Gang drive-by shootings in the past have involved vehicles stolen by gang members, but the statistics indicate there were no gang-related motor vehicle thefts. This is a situation in which gang involvement could not be proven and was not documented during the preliminary reporting stage. Logistically, tracking and re-categorizing certain crimes as gang-related after follow-up investigations were conducted would be a major task for any police department dealing with populations the size of Chicago. The narcotic statistics are a good indicator of gang involvement. This is based on the fact that almost all narcotic incidents involve an immediate investigation and arrest.

CITY OF CHICAGO — INDEX CRIME
JANUARY-DECEMBER 2005

(City of Chicago Index Crime Down 6.7% from 2004)

Crime	Jan-Dec 2004	Jan-Dec 2005	% Change
Murder	448	446	-0.4%
Criminal Sexual Assault	1,757	1,618	-7.9%
Robbery	15,965	15,961	0.0%
Aggravated Assault	7,290	6,680	-8.4%
Aggravated Battery	11,530	11,254	-2.4%
Burglary	24,542	25,298	3.1%
Theft	94,651	83,235	-12.1%
Motor Vehicle Theft	22,788	22,491	-1.3%
Arson	772	683	-11.5%
Violent	36,990	35,960	-2.8%
Property	42,753	131,707	-7.7%
TOTAL	179,743	167,667	-6.7%

Index Crime Comparison

- Total index incidents down 6.7% compared to Jan-Dec 2004.
  - Total index incidents down in 23 of 25 districts.
  - Violent index incidents down in 15 of 25 districts.

Source: Chicago Police Department

CHICAGO POLICE DEPARTMENT — ASSET FORFEITURE UNIT
JANUARY-DECEMBER 2005

- A total of 7,444 cases were processed by the Asset Forfeiture Unit. The total amount of United States Currency involved in these cases was $17,283,177.45.

- A total of 8,842 vehicles were seized for the year. Of these, 509 vehicles (21 of which contained traps/hidden compartments) were forwarded to the Cook County State's Attorney's Office for forfeiture. The remaining 8,333 vehicles were cleared for disposition through the Chicago Department of Revenue.

- The Asset Forfeiture Unit conducted four (4) vehicle auctions in which 280 vehicles were sold, yielding gross sales in the amount of $373,300.00.

CHICAGO POLICE DEPARTMENT
OVERALL REPORTED CRIMES
Versus GANG RELATED CRIMES

Yearly Statistics	2004	Gang-04	2005	Gang-05
Criminal Sexual Assault	1,889	15	1,782	2
Robbery	16,466	179	16,419	117
Battery	87,652	1,390	84,132	935
Reckless Conduct	1,099	119	1,332	113
Assault	28,997	523	27,094	372
Stalking	465	3	420	1
Burglary	24,735	31	25,564	23
Theft	96,118	87	84,976	49
Motor Vehicle Theft	26,533	0	25,447	0
Arson	811	11	710	9
Deceptive Practice	14,301	16	14,032	13
Criminal Damage	53,528	459	54,569	479
Criminal Trespass	15,977	154	16,655	134
Weapons Violations	4,360	282	4,146	202
Prostitution	7,502	34	6,114	32
Obscenity	13	1	20	0
Sex Offense	1,994	3	1,889	2
Gambling	1,125	142	1,078	221
Animal Fighting	73	1	68	0
Ritualism	1	0	1	0
Offense Involving Children	4,452	6	3,964	2
Kidnapping	626	5	496	2
Narcotics	58,336	9,179	57,493	9,966
Liquor Violations	988	208	1,003	183
Public Peace Violations	1,440	15	1,446	22
Intimidation	379	22	280	18
Interfere with Public Official	541	10	614	5
Other Offenses	31,248	117	29,536	87
Public Indecency	9	0	4	0

CHICAGO POLICE DEPARMENT REPORT
CHICAGO GANG-MOTIVATED MURDERS
BY DISTRICT — YEAR 2005

District	Total	Percent
01	0	0.0%
02	7	4.2%
03	9	5.4%
04	8	4.8%
05	14	8.4%
06	11	6.6%
07	7	4.2%
08	20	12.0%
09	13	7.8%
10	13	7.8%
11	7	4.2%
12	5	3.0%
13	0	0.0%
14	7	4.2%
15	6	3.6%
16	1	0.6%
17	1	0.6%
18	5	3.0%
19	4	2.4%
20	1	0.6%
21	5	3.0%
22	1	0.6%
23	0	0.0%
24	3	1.8%
25	19	11.4%
Total	**167**	**100.0%**

CHICAGO GANG-MOTIVATED MURDERS BY DISTRICT – YEAR 2005

District 01 – 0%
District 02 – 4.2%
District 03 – 5.4%
District 04 – 4.8%
District 05 – 8.4%
District 06 – 6.6%
District 07 – 4.2%
District 08 – 12.0%
District 09 – 7.8%
District 10 – 7.8%
District 11 – 4.2%
District 12 – 3.0%
District 13 – 0.0%
District 14 – 4.2%
District 15 – 3.6%
District 16 – 0.6%
District 17 – 0.6%
District 18 – 3.0%
District 19 – 2.4%
District 20 – 0.6%
District 21 – 3.0%
District 22 – 0.6%
District 23 – 0.0%
District 24 – 1.8%
District 25 – 11.4%

0   5   10   15   20
PERCENT

Source: CPD Detective Division Homicide Database query on Feb. 17, 2006.

Note: The totals reflect the district in which the victim's body was located.

Note: All gang-motivated murder data provided pertain to murders with the following motive types: Street Gang Altercation, Gangland Narcotics, and Narcotics Territorial.

CHICAGO GANG-MOTIVATED MURDERS BY LOCATION — YEAR 2005

Location	Total	Percent
CHA Property	7	4.2%
Private Residential Property	13	7.8%
Alley	7	4.2%
Street	90	53.9%
Automobile	35	21.0%
Miscellaneous Outdoor Locations	12	7.2%
Commercial Location	3	1.8%
Total	167	100.0%

"RIP (Rest In Peace) BAG" is painted on the door in memory of a gang member who has been killed.

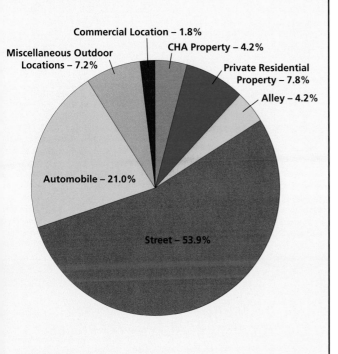

Source: CPD Detective Division Homicide Database query on Feb. 10, 2006.

Note: Location Type refers to the location where the body was found. This may or may not be the location where the murder occurred.

Note: Private Residential Property includes the following residential categories: Apartment, Hallway, House, Vestibule, Gangway, Porch, and Yard.

Note: Miscellaneous Outdoor Locations include the following categories: School Yard, Park Property, Parking Lot, and Vacant Lot.

Note: Commercial Locations include the following categories: Restaurant, Retail Store, and Gas Station.

CHICAGO GANG-MOTIVATED MURDERS BY WEAPON — YEAR 2005

Weapon Type	Total	Percent
Bludgeon/Club	3	1.8%
Firearm	158	94.6%
Stabbing/Cutting Instrument	3	1.8%
Burn	1	0.6%
Other	2	1.2%
Total	167	100.0%

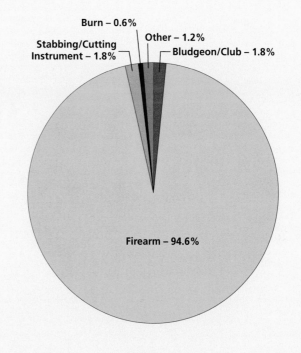

Source: CPD Detective Division Homicide Database query on Feb. 10, 2006.

Section Five

175

CHICAGO GANG-MOTIVATED MURDERS VICTIM DEMOGRAPHICS — YEAR 2005

Demographic Category	Total	Percent
Victim Sex		
Male	160	95.8%
Female	7	4.2%
Victim Race/Ethnicity		
Caucasian	4	2.4%
African American	114	68.3%
Hispanic	48	28.7%
Other	1	0.6%
Victim Age Group		
0-12	0	0.0%
13-16	9	5.4%
17-19	34	20.4%
20-24	56	33.5%
25-29	37	22.2%
30-34	12	7.2%
35-39	6	3.6%
40-49	6	3.6%
50+	7	4.2%

Source: CPD Detective Division Homicide Database query on Feb. 17, 2006.

CHICAGO GANG-MOTIVATED MURDERS OFFENDER DEMOGRAPHICS — YEAR 2005

Demographic Category	Total	Percent
Offender Sex		
Male	82	100%
Female	0	0.0%
Offender Race/Ethnicity		
Caucasian	2	2.4%
African American	50	61.0%
Hispanic	29	35.4%
Other	1	1.2%
Offender Age Group		
0-12	0	0.0%
13-16	7	8.5%
17-19	26	31.7%
20-24	26	31.7%
25-29	15	18.3%
30-34	4	4.9%
35-39	2	2.4%
40-49	1	1.2%
50+	0	0.0%
Missing	1	1.2%

Source: CPD Detective Division Homicide Database query on Feb. 17, 2006.

Note: For the following reasons, offender demographic totals do not equal the number of gang-motivated murders that occurred during Year 2005: (1) offender information is only available when the Chicago Police Department Detective Division clears the murder, (2) some murders involve multiple offenders, and (3) some murders by a single offender involve multiple victims. For murders occurring in Year 2005, the CPD Detective Division Homicide Database includes demographic information on 82 offenders in cleared cases.

FIREARM RECOVERIES, AGGRAVATED BATTERY WITH FIREARM CITY OF CHICAGO — YEAR 2005

of Aggravated Battery w/Firearm 1,655

Firearm Recoveries 9,856

Source: Aggravated Battery w/Firearm, CHRISD query on Feb. 17, 2006.

Aggravated Battery w/Firearm UCR codes 041A, 041B, 0450, 0451, 0480, 0481.

Firearm Recoveries, Forensic Services Division.

MURDER CLEARANCES CITY OF CHICAGO — YEAR 2005

Crimes can be cleared through an arrest or through exceptional means, including having an offender who is known but dead or one that is not available for arrest (i.e. out of the country).

of 2005 Murders Cleared in 2005 or 2006 446

of 2005 Murders Not Cleared 197

% Cleared 44.1%

Source: CPD Detective Division Homicide Database query on Feb. 22, 2006.

Just a few are noted here from a one month period.
(stories condensed)

4 arrested after shootout Chicago Sun-Times
(2-25-06): Four teens were arrested near Currie High School following a shoot out between rival gangs. At about 3:15 p.m. a fight broke out between 30 youths, some armed with guns and baseball bats. Shots were fired at 51st and Pulaski — near the Orange Line entrance. No one was injured. Two 17-year olds and two 18-year olds were charged with misdemeanor reckless conduct.

Father, 2 of his kids, shot Chicago Tribune
(2-23-06): The woman held her boyfriend as he lay bleeding on the ground near his car, unaware that bullets had passed through his body and struck two of the couple's children in the back seat. "Internal strife" in the Mickey Cobras gang may have led to the shooting, Supt. Philip Cline said. Freeman has ties to the Mickey Cobras, Cline said, and the area around Fuller Park is a traditional stronghold of the South Side-based gang.

Police say mall beating gang-related Daily Herald
(2-21-06): Three people attacked two victims with baseball bats in what Vernon Hills police say was a gang-related beating in the Westfield Shoppingtown Hawthorn parking lot.

19 arrested in school brawl Chicago Sun-Times
(2-4-06): Nineteen students were arrested at Chicago Vocational Career Academy after a pulled fire alarm allowed a fight that started inside the school to escalate into "a melee" outside the building, authorities said. "I want to transfer," a student said. "It's an interruption to education. And most of the fights are just over gangs." A teacher from another South Side high school said post-fire-alarm fights are a nagging problem at his school, at CVS and at least one other South Side school. "Students pull fire alarms to get people outside so they can fight them," said the teacher.

Cops suspect gang battle in shooting of 3 students
Chicago Sun-Times **(2-1-06):** Gang graffiti may have sparked a shooting at a food mart near Schurz High School that has left three of its students injured, police said. Police said members of one gang were spraying graffiti on the wall of a building in the moments leading up to the shooting... "I didn't know what to do," said one student, 14, who was getting off the bus when the shooting happened. "I was shocked. I saw kids running out of alleys."

HOMICIDE

The Chicago Police Department reports that 37% of 2005 murders were gang-related (where motive was determined). During 2005, 94% of all gang murders involved a firearm. In 25 Chicago Police Districts, during 2005, there were 446 murders with an average of 17 murders per district. In the past two years, Chicago has seen an impressive and significant 25% drop in homicides.

Survey results showed 15 homicides reported in the suburbs. (See Section Three.)

ILLEGAL SOCIAL CLUBS

Chicago Police Commanders have expressed concern over the growing violence occurring in gang-run illegal "social clubs." These clubs serve liquor, but have no liquor license. Englewood recently reported a murder occurring at a local "social club." The City of Chicago is working to secure these illegal locations so that no one is able to enter.

CRIMINAL SEXUAL ASSAULT

Eighty-two suburban police department surveys reported a combined nine cases of gang-related sexual assault. Although law enforcement sources note that gang-involved individuals may commit sexual assault, it is generally not a gang-initiated crime.

ROBBERY, BURGLARY AND THEFT

According to Chicago police sources, most gang-related cases involve home invasions on dope dealers. Eighty-two suburban police departments reported a combined total of 33 gang-related robberies, 38 gang-related thefts and 36 gang-related burglaries. Generally, these crimes are not recorded as to whether the crime is gang-related or not.

AGGRAVATED ASSAULT & BATTERY

Aggravated Assault/Battery is the intentional causing of serious bodily harm or attempt to cause serious bodily harm, or threat to serious bodily injury or death. It includes attempted murder. There are numerous aggravated assaults and aggravated batteries related to gang involvement, with many going unreported since the assault is often a situation where one gang member shoots another gang member. Law enforcement does not code these crimes as to whether it is gang-related or not, so precise numbers are not available.

MOTOR VEHICLE THEFT

Mainly occurring in predominantly Hispanic gang areas, motor vehicle theft is common. Gang members steal mostly vans, use the van for "ride by" shootings and then dump the vehicle. Again, these crimes are not recorded as to whether they are gang-related or not.

ARSON

Site of a Gang Bombing in Chicago.

Gang bombing and/or arson are not very prevalent in the Chicago area, but have occurred periodically over the past few years. On March 3, 2005, a 13-year old, a 17-year old and a 21-year old were charged with aggravated arson in a Rockford, Illinois home fire-bombing. People in the home got out unharmed, but the house was a total loss. Rockford detectives suspected the fire was gang-related. The 21-year old was also charged with earlier fire-bombings.

Also, on March 22, 2005, a Chicago gang member, Jacky Burks, was convicted of murder, aggravated arson and heinous battery charges. Burks had thrown a Molotov cocktail through a West Side home's living room window in March 2001, killing a 4-year old boy. Two other family members were severely burned.

CRIME GUNS AND GUN TRAFFICKING

Approximately 9,800 firearms were recovered by Chicago Police in 2005.

It is a misconception that crime guns are generally purchased illegally. In fact, the majority of crime guns in Illinois have initially been purchased through legal means. Street gangs secure the guns in a number of ways. Someone who meets the eligibility requirements for gun purchase (a straw purchaser) may have a drug or other debt to the gang, and thus is called upon to purchase weapons for the gang to pay off their debt. Girlfriends very often work as the straw purchaser for their gang boyfriends. In other cases, straw purchasing rings are established where a ring of five or ten people may purchase guns, provide them to a ring leader who may or may not be a gang member, and then the gang will illegally purchase multiple guns from the ring leader. At times, a gang will trade Chicago quality heroin or cocaine to drug distributors in other states in return for guns.

Street gang members generally use cheaper guns, such as a High Point or Davis at their drug sites since police are more likely to show up and confiscate these weapons. It is the middle and top level leaders that often have more expensive weapons such as the MAC-11, AK-47 or TEC-9. Police note that a few gang members may even carry weapons (guns or knives) that are disguised as cell phones.

If it is proven that a buyer has made three illegal transfers, it is possible that the buyer will be charged with gun running. Working with the Department of Alcohol Tobacco Firearms and Explosives (ATF), Chicago Police trace all crime guns recovered through an on-line process — the F-TIP System, which is unique to Illinois. This system allows the police to trace the gun to its original purchaser, while also providing the number of legally purchased weapons by this owner. If multiple crime guns are traced to one purchaser, that person may be suspected of gun running and the Federal Firearms Licensed Dealer (FFL) may be suspected of illegal firearms trafficking.

GUN TRAFFICKING CASE EXAMPLE

A Memphis, Tennessee woman, Tamiko Holloman, allegedly bought as many as 50 to 60 guns at pawn shops in Memphis on behalf of a convicted felon with ties to Chicago gang members. The felon then sold them in bulk to members of the Gangster Disciples and the Vice Lords in Chicago. At least seven of the guns were recovered by Chicago Police, including one used to commit a carjacking and two in the possession of convicted felons.

Interestingly enough, even though the F-TIP System is available to them, suburban police departments do not always take advantage of it. Suburban departments can submit a faxed or 'hard trace' to ATF or they can use the newly formed, more efficient E-TRACE system.

Many suburban police departments also refrain from using the ATF's national Integrated Ballistic Information System (IBIS), and they do not submit the firearms to the Illinois State Police Crime Lab for the ballistics test. Some recommend that an Illinois State Police portable unit be developed that would, in effect, bring IBIS technicians and equipment to department sites or an area site, but this approach may hinder the timeliness of getting the information into the system at the time the crime is committed. IBIS equipment allows firearms technicians to acquire digital images of the markings made by a firearm on bullets and cartridge casings; the images then undergo automated initial comparison. If a high-confidence candidate emerges, firearms examiners compare the original evidence to confirm a match, thereby allowing law enforcement to discover links between crimes more quickly, including links that would have been lost without the technology.

ATF strongly recommends that all law enforcement agencies utilize IBIS and the F-TIP system on ALL firearms (crime guns or those found in a yard, etc.), bullets and cartridge casings.

In past years, most crime guns were legally purchased in Illinois. However, in 2004, Chicago Police unofficially estimated that 65% of legally purchased crime guns had been purchased out of state, mostly from Indiana, Mississippi and Alabama. At one point, a gun shop in Riverdale, Illinois was rated number two in the country for the sale of guns recovered in criminal cases. However, tougher Illinois laws and local ordinances have been effective in reducing the sale of crime guns in our State. Some local ordinances, for example, restrict sellers by prohibiting the sale of guns to Chicago residents or by allowing the purchase of only one gun per month per person.

An estimated 80% of guns are legally purchased through permanent sites with Federal Firearms Licenses (FFLs) while 20% come from gun shows. FFLs may include gun shops, pawn shops or other locations licensed to sell guns.

ILLEGAL DRUG DISTRIBUTION

The illegal drug market in the United States is one of the most profitable in the world. Chicago is the major transportation hub and distribution center for illegal drugs throughout the Midwest due to its geographic location and multi-faceted transportation infrastructure. Chicago is the nation's largest trucking center and has the busiest rail yards, serving as the principle trans-shipment point for products shipped between Mexico and Canada, as well as the East and West coasts. Major drug trafficking groups, such as the Colombian, Mexican and Nigerian groups, handle wholesale distributions and major shipments of drugs to Chicago.

It is estimated that Chicago street gang narcotic sales is more than half a billion dollars a year. This kind of money would put a legitimate organization into the Fortune 500. The Chicago Police Department estimates that 68,000 gang members control Chicago's street level sales of narcotics.

Street corner drug sales are the financial backbone of Chicago gangs. Gangster Disciples, Vice Lords, Latin Kings, Black P Stones and Black Disciples control the distribution and retail sale of cocaine, heroin and marijuana in the Chicago area.

Gang involvement in drug trafficking ranges from street level sales to wholesale distribution. The entrepreneurial gang member will shift a retail drug trafficking operation into adjoining communities or states. Many suburban teenagers and young adults drive to Chicago to buy heroin and crack cocaine for their own use and to distribute it to their friends and associates.

Users travel from as far as southern Wisconsin or northwestern Indiana to purchase heroin at numerous open-air drug markets operated by street gangs on the west and south sides of Chicago.

In general, Chicago Police report that African American gangs are more likely to work in open air markets, while Hispanic gangs tend to make their deals by cell phone, setting up a designated street spot or indoor location to make the transaction with the customer.

Chicago Police Officer searches a vehicle for narcotics and weapons.

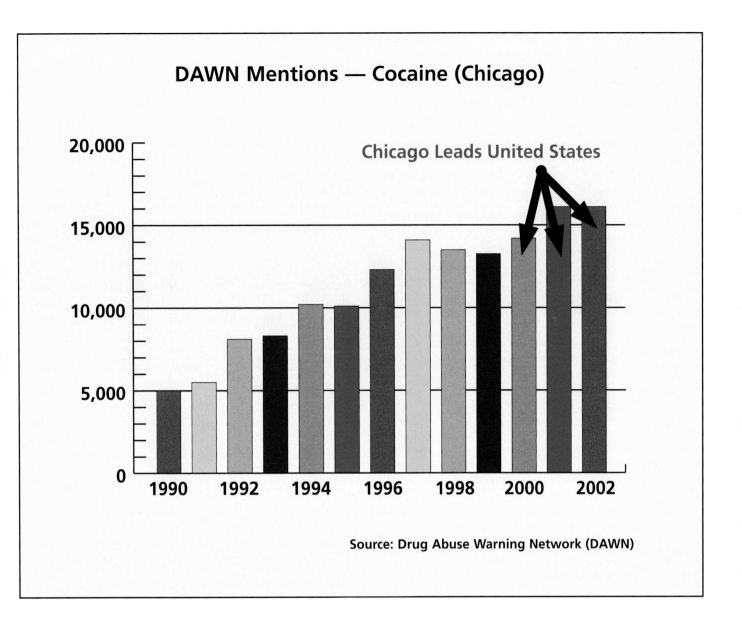

DAWN Mentions — Cocaine (Chicago)

Chicago Leads United States

Source: Drug Abuse Warning Network (DAWN)

Cocaine

Cocaine trafficking is run almost exclusively by Mexican organized crime. They transport large quantities of cocaine to Chicago from Houston, El Paso, Los Angeles, Arizona and Miami on a regular basis. Cocaine is delivered wholesale to the street gangs at a purity rate of about 98%. It is delivered in the form of Cocaine Hydrochloride — a powder form often referred to as "coke." Gangs then cut the cocaine to a purity rate of about 33% or less and sell it retail on the street either in its powder form that a user would sniff or snort or in the form of "crack." Gangs make "crack" by bringing the powder form back to its original base. A "crack" user would heat and smoke this form of cocaine. From Chicago, cocaine is distributed to cities such as Des Moines, Fort Wayne, Grand Rapids, Lexington, Columbus, Toledo, St. Paul and Milwaukee. Chicago also serves as a transshipment point for the Detroit distribution center. The level of violence associated with the trafficking of cocaine, especially crack, exceeds that of all other drugs and is largely due to the competition between street gangs over sales and distribution.

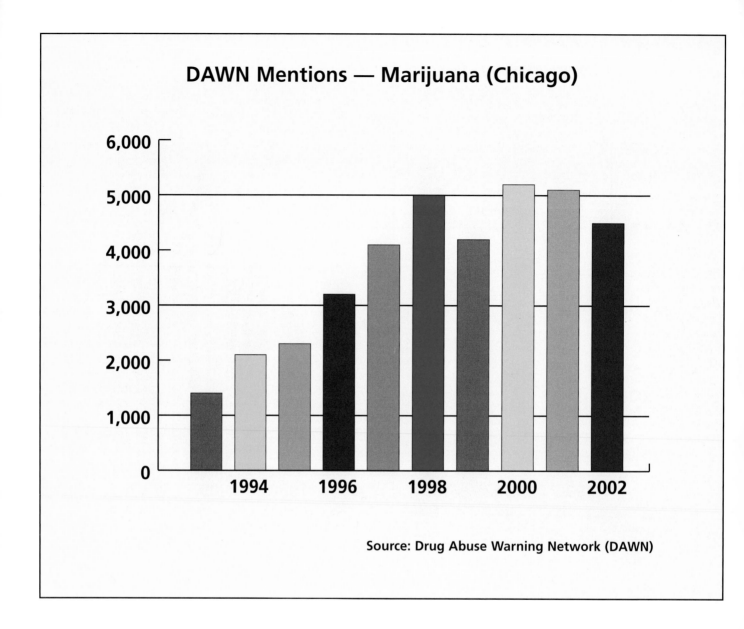

DAWN Mentions — Marijuana (Chicago)

Source: Drug Abuse Warning Network (DAWN)

Marijuana

Marijuana is the most widely available illegal drug in the United States. Marijuana available in Chicago is usually transported from southwestern states and Mexico. Mexican drug trafficking organizations and criminal groups are the primary transporters and wholesale distributors of the drug in Chicago. Chicago Police have seen an increase in marijuana street corner sales and an increase in local marijuana production cultivated both indoors and outdoors in recent years.

This woman tells police that she'd like to get out of "the life" and get help.

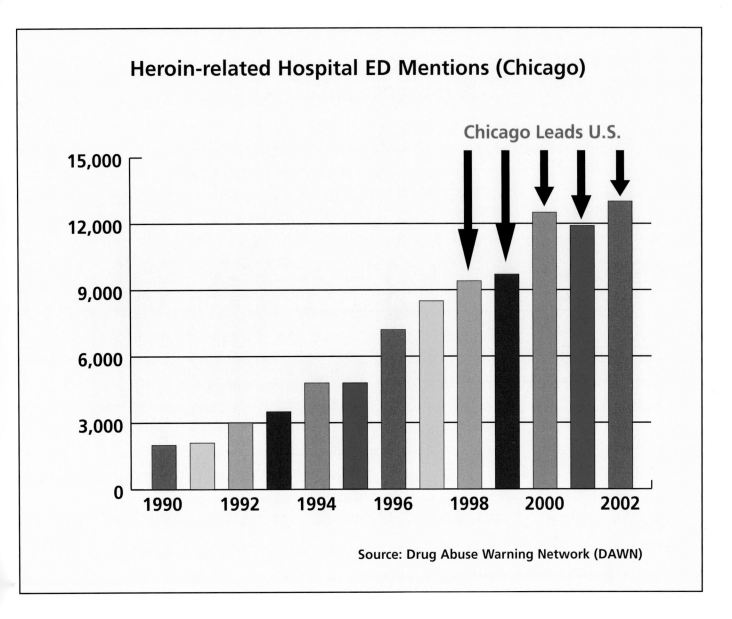

Heroin-related Hospital ED Mentions (Chicago)

Chicago Leads U.S.

Source: Drug Abuse Warning Network (DAWN)

Heroin

Heroin is the second greatest drug threat facing the United States. Heroin distribution and abuse occur at high levels in Chicago, and traffickers use the City as a distribution hub for supplying other markets throughout the Midwest. Chicago is unique among American cities in that heroin from all four source areas is available on a regular basis. According to DEA's Domestic Monitor Program, most of the heroin available at the retail level in Chicago originates in South America.

However, analysis of seizures and investigative activity reveal that heroin from other sources— Mexico, Southwest Asia and Southeast Asia— continues to be available in the City. Over the past decade, the increased competition among multiple sources of supply has increased the supply, lowered the cost and increased the purity of heroin available on the streets. At the wholesale level, the purity of heroin in Chicago typically ranges between 50 and 90 percent. Using primarily diphenhydramine, heroin is cut to a purity of between 15 and 20 percent for

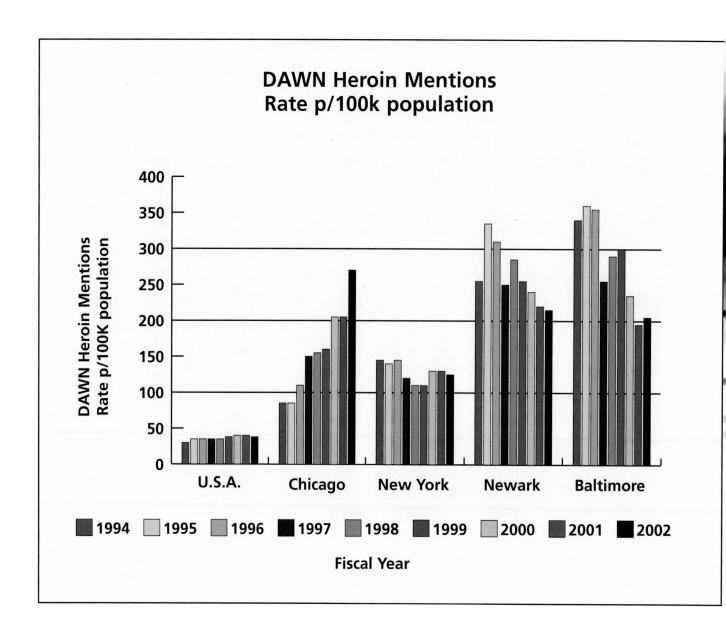

DAWN Heroin Mentions
Rate p/100k population

Legend: 1994, 1995, 1996, 1997, 1998, 1999, 2000, 2001, 2002

Fiscal Year

individual retail sales. On the westside of Chicago, this product is then sold retail on the streets by the Gangster Disciples, Vice Lords and Mickey Cobras. Traffickers distribute heroin from Chicago throughout Illinois and to other states including Indiana, Iowa, Michigan, Minnesota, Missouri, New York, Ohio, Tennessee and Wisconsin. Law enforcement officials in Cleveland, Dayton, Pittsburgh and St. Louis report that Chicago is a source for heroin available in their jurisdictions. Pure heroin is a fine white powder, but because of impurities left from the manufacturing process or the presence of additives, it can also appear tan, gray, pink or even black in color. Injection is the most practical and efficient way to administer low-purity heroin, but it can also be sniffed or smoked.

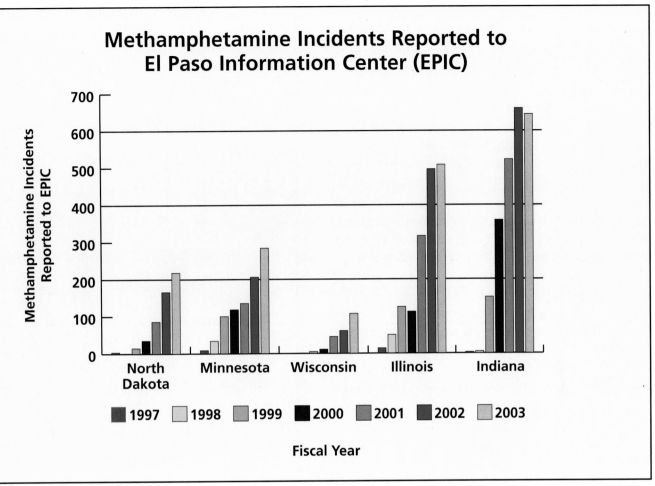

Methamphetamine Incidents Reported to El Paso Information Center (EPIC)

Methamphetamine Incidents Reported to EPIC

North Dakota · Minnesota · Wisconsin · Illinois · Indiana

■ 1997 □ 1998 ■ 1999 ■ 2000 ■ 2001 ■ 2002 □ 2003

Fiscal Year

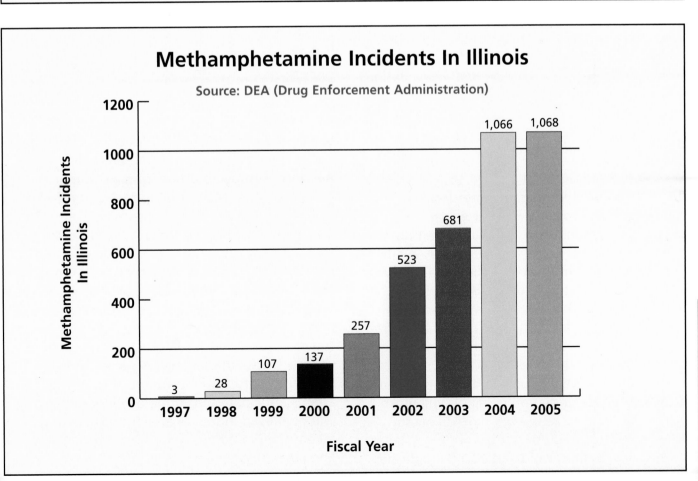

Methamphetamine Incidents In Illinois

Source: DEA (Drug Enforcement Administration)

Methamphetamine Incidents In Illinois

Fiscal Year	Incidents
1997	3
1998	28
1999	107
2000	137
2001	257
2002	523
2003	681
2004	1,066
2005	1,068

Fiscal Year

Section Five

Methamphetamine (Meth)

Meth is the third largest drug threat in the United States. Meth trafficking in Chicago changed dramatically in the mid-1990s when Mexican drug cartels started operating super labs. This resulted in a significant increase in the supply of the drug. Before the Mexican super-labs, independent labs, including labs run by biker gangs, maintained control of the market. Today, independent labs continue to operate on a smaller scale. There is concern that, although not yet a major problem in Chicago, Meth, generally distributed wholesale in 5, 10 or 20 pound loads, could continue to grow in popularity because it is cheaper and produces a longer effect than crack cocaine. Chicago Police report an increase in Meth use, distribution and in the number of labs operating in the City. Based on its availability and severe physiological effects, the violence associated with meth trafficking and use is also increasing. Currently, Chicago is more involved in wholesale distribution of Meth, acting more as a transportation hub than the end drop-off point for the drug. Hells Angels and Outlaw biker gangs are active in both midlevel wholesale and retail distribution in Illinois, while Hispanic gangs, such as the Latin Kings, are involved in midlevel wholesale distribution to several states in the Great Lakes area. Law enforcement investigations into Chicago based Asian street gangs revealed that these gangs were heavily involved in major financial crimes resulting from the use and distribution of crystal meth. (See Case Example on page 192.)

Retail sales currently do not come close to competing with cocaine and heroin sales in Chicago. Communities in rural areas that do not have cocaine and heroin supplies readily available are probably the most at risk of having a serious Meth problem since Meth is fairly simple to make on the local level. Besides the dangers linked to the use and distribution of this drug, it is important to note that Meth labs produce poisonous gas and five to seven pounds of toxic waste for every pound of meth produced. Recently passed legislation in Illinois will make it more difficult to secure the ingredients for making meth by requiring retail outlets, such as drug stores, to place cold and allergy medicines that contain pseudoephedrine from an easily accessible location to a more secure location. Pseudoephedrine is an ingredient used in the production of meth.

Open Air Markets

CASE EXAMPLE

The Gangster Disciples, one of the largest street gangs, is also one of the most successful due to its corporate-like structure. The GDs operated one of the largest gang-run narcotics networks, if not the largest, that stretched into 35 states with drug sales over $100 million dollars a year. In the 1980s, when crack-cocaine began flooding into Chicago, the lucrative drug trade emerged as the gang's priority. The GDs refined their organization to run a citywide network of dope dealing franchises. They bought drugs from the Colombian cartels in 100 to 200 kilo shipments. They then distributed them down the ranks, and profits and street taxes were sent back to the gang leadership. The GD drug trade is efficient and their 24-hour open-air drug markets remain pretty much intact today.

Shutting down the open-air drug markets is the key in bringing down an organized narcotics gang network. Removing drugs from a community greatly reduces the homicide rate and other violent crimes. The Chicago Police Narcotic & Gang Intelligence Section (NAGIS) is very successful in targeting narcotics locations with street corner conspiracy cases. Once an open air drug market has been shut down by NAGIS, the area is saturated by uniformed patrol officers. This high visibility police presence prevents another group from taking over the drug spot. This technique has proven to be very successful in Chicago. So successful, in fact, that Drug Enforcement Administration (DEA) agents anticipate that some of these markets will be moved indoors—a sales milieu that is inherently more dangerous for both customers and law enforcement.

Unexpected Alliances

Law enforcement constantly attempts to dismantle gangs by attacking the leadership, which causes internal top level member disputes in a struggle for power. Police and prosecutors view these struggles as a weakness. One sign that the discipline and leadership is breaking down is that gang members have begun to put aside the alliance to their gang if they can make more money. Today, unlike in years past, gangs will rent out "drug distribution" street corners and public housing buildings to rival gangs to make more money.

Young gang members on the street no longer are taught the gang laws, such as not using addictive drugs. Prison is now where members learn the rules. Gang leaders say that if their organizations are to survive, members must once again know and follow the rules. Greed, in the form of drug money, continues to compromise the gangs' written ideals of unity.

Drug-related Violence

Most law enforcement agencies in Illinois cite the violent crime associated with gang-related drug trafficking as the most serious criminal threat to the State. Violent crime associated with street gangs, while declining in some major urban areas like Chicago, is increasing in suburban and rural areas as these gangs expand their drug markets and rivals fight for drug distribution territory.

Gang Communications

In the City and the suburbs, gangs use the Internet and rely heavily on cell phones and text messaging when trafficking narcotics. Gangs will sometimes use "throw-away" cell phones that are sold with a certain number of hours of use. Rather than add minutes to the phones, gang users will throw it out and buy another phone.

One officer noted that police should be aware that gang members using cell phones with camera capabilities may try to provoke officers in order to photograph them in a harmful light.

Gangs also have websites with encrypted codes that allow them to discuss their activities and announce narcotic locations. A source of information from within the Latin King street gang revealed to the Cook County Sheriff's Police Gangs Crime Unit that members of this gang could log onto a website, enter a password and have access to information regarding narcotics sales. Activities are also discussed in Internet chat rooms.

Law enforcement is facing new challenges because of wireless technology and many believe new legislation must be passed in regards to court overhears for police to be successful in future narcotic investigations involving these technologies.

The Black Disciples went high-tech, pirated a legitimate Christian radio station and used it to advertise locations to purchase narcotics.

Other means of communication include fax, e-mails, party lines and two-way radios.

Marketing Narcotics

Chicago gangs have utilized interesting ways to market their drugs, including passing out business cards. The cards include the dealer's street name, the type of drugs sold by the gang and the location.

Another marketing tool is very similar to that used by a grocery store. When a new drug spot opens up, dealers will hand out free samples hoping to attract repeat customers. The samples are not always lower grade dope, but at times consist of a very pure quality heroin. Emergency rooms have found themselves treating as many as ten heroin overdose victims who all received free dope from the same location.

Another technique dealers are using to increase profits is to have their customers cash forged checks in exchange for drugs. The dealers will round up a group of buyers who have legitimate IDs and hand each one of them a forged check, usually in the thousand dollar range. The gang will then drive these buyers to a bank or currency exchange, where they are instructed to cash the forged checks. If they are successful, the buyer will keep some of the proceeds, enabling them to pay for their drugs and turn the rest of the money over to the gang.

EXAMPLES OF CHICAGO POLICE OPERATIONS TARGETING ILLEGAL DRUGS

NOTE: *In 2005, Chicago Police shut down 53 open air drug markets and charged 735 drug dealers.*

January 30, 2006

"Operation Northern Pike," targeted an open-air market in Edgewater that was run by several gangs, including the Gangster Disciples, Mickey Cobras, Vice Lords and Black P Stones. Twelve gang members were charged.

January 6, 2006

In *"Operation Triggerfish"*, Chicago Police charged 20 Gangster Disciples with running a drug market at the Dearborn Homes. Cocaine and white heroin were sold 24 hours a day, seven days a week, generating an estimated $10,000 in daily revenue for the gang. Police made 19 undercover drug purchases and recovered $16,000 in crack cocaine and heroin, $4,800 in cash and one gun.

December 20, 2005

In *"Operation Dorado,"* police arrested two high-ranking members, both so-called "governors" of the Maniac Latin Disciples. They were charged with criminal drug conspiracy. Police said they ran a crew that sold crack and powder cocaine, ecstacy and marijuana on the northwest side. A dozen others were also charged in the investigation. Police made 18 undercover drug purchases and recovered $17,000 in ecstacy, powder and crack cocaine, $4,034 in cash, four vehicles and two handguns.

"Operation Clownfish" resulted in charges against 14 members of the Conservative Vice Lords street gang. Police seized $7,000 in illegal drugs and $11,685 in cash.

December 16, 2005

"Operation Zebra Shark" charged 15 Gangster Disciples members with running an open air drug market in the Auburn area. Officers conducted 17 drug purchases and seized nearly 50 grams of cocaine. More than $1,000 in cash and four vehicles were also seized. One of the offenders was also charged with the armed robbery of a high school student.

December 9, 2005

"Operation Blue Shark" charged a West Side street boss of the Dirty Unknown Vice Lords of running an open-air drug market and with dog fighting and cruelty to animals. Nine others were also taken into custody. Police seized $9,000 in illegal drugs, $776 in cash and one vehicle.

"Operation Squirrelfish" targeted an open-air drug market run by a faction of the Black P Stones street gang. In this operation, 13 individuals were charged. Police seized $14,000 in illegal drugs, $1,700 in cash and two handguns.

November 18, 2005

"Operation King Snapper" targeted drug sales in a five block area on the north side. Police said the drug market, run by the Gangster Disciples, operated within 1,000 feet of a church and two schools. Thirteen gang members were charged in the three month undercover operation.

November 7, 2005

Chicago Police charged two men after discovering more than $15 million (101 bricks) in cocaine at a northwest Chicago residence. Police also charged one of the individuals with failure to register a firearm after finding four guns in his home.

MORTGAGE AND REAL ESTATE FRAUD

Due to the rapid decline in mortgage interest rates and the booming housing market in recent years, financial institutions and lenders have let their guard down in the area of due diligence and quality control on loan applications. This created an atmosphere and environment for mortgage fraud to be perpetrated. Mortgage fraud is on the rise and all indications show that it is growing. Inner city street gangs that survive on drug trafficking have transcended into the white collar crime arena. "It's the new street hustle," said a convicted drug dealer and self-admitted Gangster Disciple gang member.

One recent Chicago Vice Lord case involved 80 million dollars in fraudulent mortgage activity. A Black Disciple case revealed $70 million in mortgage fraud.

Chicago Police report that there are a number of known Chicago gang members who own their own mortgage companies in order to perpetrate fraud or money laundering activities. Cook County Sheriff's Police report that *a common tactic used to launder illicit drug profits in the suburban Cook County area is mortgage fraud.* Thus, this is a problem in both the City and its suburbs.

Mortgage Fraud in its simplest definition is the collaboration of co-conspirators, such as mortgage brokers, appraisers, real estate agents, title company agents, buyers, sellers, and attorneys, to orchestrate a theft by means of fraud, forgery and deception.

Every fradulent mortgage that is originated will contain some form of misrepresentation or material misstatement to deceive the financial institution such as an inflated appraised value, a fictitious employer, false income and W-2s, phony pay check stubs or a nominee who is purchasing the property for another.

Examples of Mortgage Fraud include but are not limited to:

PROPERTY FLIPPING — a nominee will purchase a foreclosed or dilapidated piece of property for a discounted price. This property will be sold to another nominee for an inflated appraised value. The real owner will take the proceeds check from the closing and have the nominee endorse it. The owner then deposits the check in his own account. Both loan applications for the nominee buyers were fraudulent and will contain some or all the material misstatements mentioned above.

NOMINEE PURCHASERS — an individual will purchase a piece of property for another using his or her own credit history. The individual who cannot purchase the property is some-one who does not have a legitimate source of income but has the money to pay for a mortgage payment. This money is usually gained through some form of illegal activity.

TWO SETS OF SETTLEMENT STATEMENTS — this form of fraud is more difficult to perpe-trate. The sellers will have the utmost trust and confidence in the real estate agent or mortgage broker. The property is purchased using a nominee buyer for an agreed price. The loan application goes to the lender for an inflated amount. The loan is approved and, at the closing, the sellers will sign one set of closing statements reflecting their agreed price. This is usually under the direction of the closing agent, who is a co-conspirator, or the mortgage broker and real estate agent they put their trust in. Sellers need not be represented by an attorney when selling their own property. The other set of closing statements and the excess proceeds check is forged by the co-conspirators.

Recent legislation requires that loan originators must be licensed through the state. This legisla-tion is an important deterrent to mortgage fraud.

Illustration of a Complex Mortgage Fraud Scheme

Drug dealer Tony wants to buy a home. He has never maintained legitimate employment, has no credit history and lots of illegally gained cash. Tony goes to a friend, Billy, who is a mortgage broker. Billy agrees to assist Tony in finding a straw purchaser for the purchase of Tony's house. Tony pays Billy $5,000 for his assistance.

Billy finds John, a friend of a friend who has good credit. Billy explains to John that he will be paid $5,000 cash for the use of his credit in obtaining a mortgage for a home purchase. John is told that the real purchaser has bad credit and cannot get a loan.

Billy sells John a home purchased recently, in another associate's name, Jane, for $100,000. Jane was paid $2,500 for the use of her credit to purchase the home. Jane's application contained false information.

Billy has a friend conduct an appraisal for Jane's property. Billy pays the appraiser $5,000 and requests a value of $200,000.

Billy has John sign a blank loan application and he himself fills in the employer, monthly income and assets sections of the form. Billy then locates a lender who is willing to fund the full $200,000 purchase price of the home for John. The lender requires pay stubs, W-2 forms and bank account information, which Billy creates on his computer and faxes to the institution.

Billy collects $8,000 cash from Tony and has John deposit the funds into his bank account.

Several weeks later, an hour before the scheduled closing, Tony gives John $13,000 cash. Tony and Billy drive John to a bank where he is instructed to obtain a cashier's check for $13,000 made payable to the title company. The funds are to be used for the buyer's closing costs.

At the closing, Billy signs all of the seller paperwork for Jane. Billy also takes the $100,000 (equity) check made payable to Jane and eventually deposits the funds into his personal bank account. John is given possession of the home and signs all of the necessary paperwork for the purchase. The monthly mortgage payment is $2,000.

Every month Tony gives John $2,000. John deposits the money and sends off a check to the lender.

Two years later, a search warrant is executed at the home. Tony is arrested and stops providing the $2,000 to John. During the search, the closing documents are recovered. The property goes into foreclosure. The lender is only able to sell the home for $150,000.

Note: Individuals who agree to become the "straw purchaser" because they believe it will result in "easy money" often do not understand that they may later find themselves owing capital gains taxes and more when the property is sold.

KEY DOCUMENTS NEEDED TO DETECT MORTGAGE FRAUD

1. The RESPA or Closing Statement:

This document will show the flow of money, outlining the disbursements from escrow (i.e. who is getting money at closing, who is getting paid off, what liens are being satisfied.) The mortgage brokers fee is also reflected on the closing statement as well as the down payment from the borrower. This document will reflect any monies being transferred to other parties who are not principals to the transaction. Observe if there are any liens being paid off that were recorded a short time before closing.

2. The Loan Application or the 1003:

The 1003 contains the borrower's signature and may have false information regarding employment, income, credit worthiness and other assets or real estate held. This loan application will also contain the loan officer's signature along with all the other disclosures signed and dated by the borrower. Does the borrower show assets or real estate owned? How much credit card debt is reflected on the mortgage application? Large amounts or debt would mean the income of the borrower has to be proportional to their debt to qualify for the loan. Look at the purpose of the loan. Is it a purchase or a refinance? If a purchase, did the buyer indicate that they would occupy the property or was it an investment? If a refinance, when was the property first purchased and what was that amount?

3. The Title Report:

The original title report will contain information on the chain of title. It will reflect who holds liens on the property and how old they are. It will show transfers and what kind of deed was conveyed. Are there payoffs on the RESPA that are not consistent with those being shown on the preliminary title report? Also, the sale price of the most recent sale should be indicated on the title report. If this was less than six months previous and the new price seems inflated, this is a good indication you may be dealing with a nominee and an inflated appraised value. Was anyone recently quit claimed onto the title?

4. The Loan submission form or 1008:

This form acts as a summary as it indicates what the parties' expectations were at the time of the loan application. This is the form the mortgage wholesaler or end lender will receive from the mortgage broker. Observe whether there were any changes in the loan amount or income amount from the original application or 1003.

5. The appraisal:

The appraisal should be included in the complete loan package submitted to the lender. The appraisal will show what properties were used as comparables to the subject. The appraiser's signature and license number will appear on the report. This report can be reviewed to verify how the appraiser arrived at the value of the subject property. Information provided on the appraisal report for the comparable properties will need to be visually inspected. Lenders have no quality control on the appraisal—they have to trust and go with the values indicated on the report.

IDENTITY THEFT, COUNTERFEITING AND CYBERCRIME

In 2004, it was estimated that yearly illegal proceeds generated from computer-related crimes surpassed illegal drug sales. Some estimate that the yearly cost of Cybercrime is well over $100 billion, with no sign of slowing down. However, the gang's primary source of income is still derived from narcotics trafficking. Current gang involvement in high tech crime is somewhat limited and any involvement usually involves the outside expertise of a trusted associate. Experts believe that gang involvement may increase in the future, particularly if narcotics sales decrease as a result of law enforcement efforts or increased competition from rival gangs.

An estimated 10 million Americans are identity theft victims each year. Fake IDs ("Mica"-Spanish slang for laminated ID cards) and other counterfeit documents like insurance cards and social security cards are prevalent in Chicago's Little Village area along 26th Street. The Latin Kings control most of these operations and collect "street tax" from numerous fraudulent ID sellers. Chicago Police investigations have resulted in arrests and confiscation of millions of dollars of contraband. Through their investigations, officers learned the Latin Kings were extorting $3,000-$6,000 per month from crews selling fraudulent identification. Local, state and federal law enforcement agencies have been successful in shutting down numerous operations, but due to great demand and huge profits, new operations constantly open up.

One well respected Chicago area video producer who has interviewed many Latin King members stated that Latin King members told him that they have received orders for false identification from overseas and they fill these orders through the mail. This could be a serious homeland security concern.

The majority of fake IDs are being sold to immigrants wishing to secure employment and to minors for illegal liquor purchases. Another use is for the cashing of forged checks. The Latin Kings have been known to target Mexican immigrants through intimidation, recruiting the immigrants at bus stops. Immigrants are promised IDs and social security cards for employment, but only after they agree to cash forged checks. Refusal could result in the threat of bodily harm.

Larger street gangs, like the BDs, GDs, and Vice Lords who run open air drug markets, have been known to recruit entire groups of drug buyers at a single dope spot to cash forged checks. The gang will verify that the buyer has a legitimate ID and promise them a percentage of the proceeds once they cash the check. The checks are either stolen or computer generated by a gang member with computer skills.

Another seemingly non-ending counterfeit product being sold in Little Village and in various flea markets across Chicago is illegal music CDs and movie DVDs. This type of counterfeiting is known as IP (Intellectual Property) piracy and costs U.S. businesses upwards of $250 billion a year while robbing the nation of hundreds of thousands of jobs and as much as a billion dollars a year in lost tax revenues. The Latin Kings have limited involvement, but nonetheless, profits are generated and funneled to the gang.

CHECK FRAUD CASE EXAMPLE:

In the 1990s, an Asian Chicago street gang named the Scorpians were heavily involved in check forgery. Certain gang members were highly educated in computer technology. They started out using computer generated checks, but became more sophisticated after learning how to wash checks. This process made it more difficult for banks and lending institutions to immediately detect fraud. The gang would recruit associates with legitimate bank accounts to cash the forged checks. The proceeds funded an international crystal methamphetamine drug ring. The forged check operation defrauded banks out of millions of dollars, before the FBI, U.S. Postal Inspectional Services, and Chicago Police Department shut down the operation.

Telemarketing Fraud is also a concern. Gang members have been able to secure positions with telemarketing firms. The gang members take these jobs for the larger payoff of conning unsuspecting individuals out of their money and stealing their identity (e.g., credit card information).

DOG FIGHTING AND ANIMAL CRUELTY

The Chicago Crime Commission acknowledges the link between animal cruelty and human violence, and is particularly concerned about dog fighting, which is often-times street gang related and thus, also linked to guns and narcotics.

During the 2002 calendar year, court advocates following animal cruelty and dog fighting cases in Chicago recorded 51 juvenile arrests out of 169 arrests known to them. Of 114 misdemeanor cruelty arrests, 21 were juveniles; of 55 felony arrests, 30 were juveniles.

Pit bulls are often purchased, bred or stolen by those interested in dog fighting.

The Chicago Crime Commission's RAV2 Program (Reduce Animal Violence, Reduce All Violence) is working to:

■ train and motivate *all* law enforcement professionals to use **animal abuse search warrants** and dog fighting statutes. This may result in the arrest of violent offenders, the recovery of guns and narcotics and the enforcement of other laws, in addition to the recovery of abused animals.

■ train law enforcement and criminal justice professionals to use the new **animal fighting forfeiture law**, which provides that money, vehicles, houses and other real property, can be seized and forfeited upon conviction of dog fighting. As a consequence, offenders may lose their property, thus evicting the criminal element (gangs, guns, drugs) from that location.

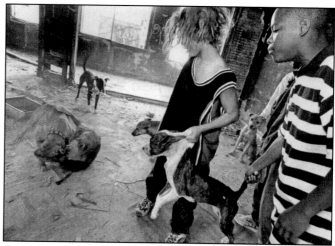

Photo by: Brenda Ann Kenneally, SABA

Young children are witnesses or even participants in Chicago area dog fighting, an extremely violent activity often resulting in the death of one or both animals. Children placed in this environment are learning that this casual destruction of life is acceptable entertainment.

When used appropriately, new animal cruelty legislation will work as a unique tool for curbing gang activity, drug dealing and gun violence.

In 2004, approximately 52% of the Chicago Police Animal Abuse Control Team's arrests, resulting from search warrants executed on the basis of dog fighting or animal cruelty information, included gun or drug charges as well.

MONEY LAUNDERING

Photo provided by Lake County Sheriff's Office.

In Chicago, some of the most common methods for gang money laundering involve real estate transactions, the music industry, night clubs and lounges, beauty and barber shops, cell phone stores, hand car wash facilities and clothing shops. Cook County Sheriff's Police report that suburban gangs also invest profits from drug sales in legitimate businesses in an attempt to launder the money. Suburban businesses some-times used to launder the illicit profits include car washes, beauty salons, taverns and restaurants.

The U.S. Attorney's Office also notes that real estate and mortgage fraud have become popular money laundering activities. They estimate that the Black Disciples, as an example, launder 1.5 million dollars per month.

TERRORISM

There is little, if any, valid evidence currently link-ing the Chicago area street gangs with terrorist activity. There are rumors that the MS13 (Mara Salvatrucha) street gang may be working with al Qaeda to bring terrorists across the Mexican/ United States border, but the FBI has stated that this link to al Qaeda has never been substantiated.

Still, it is in our best interest to pay attention to the possibility of street gangs linking with terrorists. In the 1980s, Libya was willing to pay 2.5 million dollars to Chicago's El Rukn street

gang to commit acts of terror. An investigation revealed that the El Rukn gang bought a LAWS rocket from an undercover ATF agent. The plan was to bomb government buildings. Also, several members of the Black P Stones/El Rukns follow a strict Islamic (Sunni Muslim) code. Following the attacks on 9-11, the FBI classified the gang as a "terrorist threat." Given their history and strict Islamic beliefs, their activities are monitored closely.

In the mid-1990s, a Chicago Four Corner Hustler leader, Angelo Roberts, was so upset about effective policing initiatives cutting into the gang's drug operations that he told a Chicago Police informant that he wanted to acquire missiles and automatic weapons to blow up the Kedzie and Harrison police district building and wage a war against police. Although Roberts did not show up for the deal — an undercover operation of the Chicago Police and Alcohol Tobacco Firearms & Explosives (ATF) — the Four Corner Hustlers traded a large sum of money and cocaine for an M72A2 Laws anti-tank rocket. Later, police found Roberts murdered.

The making of false identity cards, green cards, passports and driver's licenses is an active business of today's Latin Kings. The Latin Kings, in a 1999 investigation, were shown to be heavily involved in the selling of false identity paperwork to illegal aliens. This may make the Latin Kings a viable threat since terrorist organizations are looking to provide their members with the means to move about freely in U.S. society.

Jose Padilla, also known as Abdullah al-Muhajir, arrested in 2002 in a suspected al-Qaeda plot to explode a radioactive "dirty bomb" in the U.S., was a former Chicago Latin King. A BBC News, June 11, 2002 story, Profile: Jose Padilla, notes that although his juvenile record is sealed, Jose "was alleged to have been implicated in a Chicago gangland murder when he was 13" and "some reports say he converted to Islam while in jail." He was not a Chicago resident when arrested in the dirty bomb case; however, it does beg the question as to whether those looking to get involved in street gang life for reasons such as a sense of belonging or respect, or for monetary gain might also feel that terrorist groups would meet their needs as well.

On January 27, 2006, the Sun-Times reported in the article "Gang member charged in terrorism hoax" that a gang member from Northlake named Gilbert Romero was charged with two counts of making false statements and one count of reporting a hoax terrorism threat. According to the article,

"Romero told agents that "Individual A" was organizing a terrorist attack against the United States and recruiting people to join in, the indictment said. The attack on a Chicago company headquarters — which the feds won't name — would feature a truck loaded with 55-gallon drums of ammonium nitrate and diesel fuel, Romero told agents, the indictment said. The bomb would be detonated with a cellular telephone call...Romero told agents that "Individual B" used to live on a farm and knew how to make a bomb in a car using brake fluid and chlorine tablets and would give Romero those materials in exchange for drugs. Romero's gang would provide AK-47 and MAC-10 machine guns to shoot any police officers that interfered with the plan, he told agents, according to the indictment. He said the operation would be financed by proceeds from a pending medical malpractice lawsuit involving Romero's mother or by holding currency exchange or jewelry store owners hostage to extort ransom money from their families, the indictment said."

Although, according to the indictment, the story above is untrue, it is frightening that such a detailed plan could enter the mind of any gang member.

HUMAN TRAFFICKING AND PROSTITUTION

The formal definition of Human Trafficking is: the recruitment, transportation, transfer, harbouring or receipt of persons, by means of the threat or use of force or other forms of coercion, of abduction, of fraud, of deception, of the abuse of power or from a position of vunerability or of the giving or receiving of payments or benefits to achieve the consent of a person having control over another person, for the purpose of exploitation. For these purposes, exploitation is the prostitution of others or other forms of sexual exploitation, forced labor or services, slavery or practices similar to slavery, servitude or the removal of organs. Victims are often women and children.

Salvador A. Cicero-Dominguez notes in his research paper, <u>Assessing the US-Mexico fight against Human Trafficking and Smuggling: Unitended results of the U.S. immigration policy</u>, that trafficking is second only to drug trafficking as a criminal enterprise and is often tied to illegal arms sales. Victims are lured by the prospect of a well-paid job as domestic servants, factory workers or waitresses. They are often recruited, especially women and children, through fake advertisements, mail-order brides catalogues and through casual aquaintances. Promises of modeling careers, tourism, and educational studies are only a few of the means that are used to manipulate victims into the trafficking industry. Women and girls are typically forced to work as prostitutes. Cicero-Dominguez also notes that the "Country Reports on Human Rights Practices 2004" indicates that the corrupt police (in Mexico) sometimes violated the rights of undocumented immigrants. Futhermore, migrants who transited Chiapas, Mexico complained of the double dangers of extortion by the authorities and robbery and killings by the organized street gangs (such as Mara Salvatruchas – MS13s).

Street gangs in the Chicago area have, over the past ten years, become more and more "all about the money" and there is a great deal of money to be made in the trafficking industry. Sureno 13s have a significant presence in the Chicago suburbs and the MS13 street gangs have only just begun to form in Chicago suburban areas. Both of these extremely violent street gangs are directly tied to Mexican organized crime operations involved in human trafficking. It is the opinion of the Chicago Crime Commission that street gangs directly tied to these Mexican organized crime groups should be closely monitored in order to prevent their possible future interest in becoming part of this lucrative criminal enterprise of modern day slavery.

Finally, it is important to emphasize that, at this time, there appears to be no known direct connection between Chicago area gangs and human trafficking.

SECTION 6

Prison, Parole and Probation

GANGS IN THE PRISON SYSTEM

Illinois Department of Corrections Overview

The concept of Security Threat Groups (STG) and their activities is not new to IDOC. The purpose, objectives and techniques of Security Threat Groups remain virtually static; however the players periodically change. IDOC also monitors non-traditional Security Threat Groups, such as groups that have ties to terrorist organizations, extremist organizations or organizations sympathetic to extremist views.

It is the policy of the Illinois Department of Corrections to maintain a safe and secure operation of its institutions, to provide a safe and secure environment for staff and offenders and to ensure public safety. Ordinarily, these goals are accomplished through routine security procedures. In some cases, however, the security threat posed by an offender or group cannot be adequately managed by routine security procedures. In these cases, such groups may be actively managed through the use of the authorized confidential security initiatives established by the agency.

In order to enforce security policies, the Illinois Department of Corrections created a Central Intelligence (Gang) Unit under the supervision of the Director. This unit has been specifically designed to gather information regarding the offender gang population, monitor the activities of gangs and prevent the furtherance of gang activities.

Communicating From Prison

Incarcerated leaders of the most organized street gangs are still able to control outside gang activities from within their prison cells. Top leaders are usually serving life or multiple life sentences without the possibility of parole. They find ways of transmitting and receiving gang activity reports, requests and orders. They communicate from prison to prison and from prison to the streets and vice versa. Isolating a gang leader in solitary confinement does not always restrict gang communication. They employ a multitude of innovative techniques to communicate with each other. They bribe prison guards and even subpoena each other to appear at their court hearings. Once in court, they give hand signals or speak in code. Messages can be written in exotic languages and tiny script called micro-writing. They sometimes write and distribute letters to each other in a form of invisible ink made with their own urine. Messages, drugs and money are also smuggled into prison through the gang's network of family and friends. In early 2006, a firearm was smuggled into a local prison. If a certain gang member is being paroled, he will be presented with all kinds of messages, phone numbers, contacts, hit lists and more. Imprisoned leaders select certain trusted gang members prior to their parole and train them to control and manage the gang's narcotics network and territories. This ensures that revenue is generated for the organization in prison. Gang members in prison are taught techniques in perfecting crimes and even how to disarm law enforcement personnel. This information then gets passed on to the gang members on the street.

Aryan Brotherhood

Photo provided by Lake County Sheriff's Office.

One of the most violent prison gangs is the Aryan Brotherhood (AB), a white supremacist organization. According to the FBI, AB members make up less than one tenth of one percent of the nation's inmate population, but they are

NEW TREND

More often today than ten years ago, gang members are being tried federally and sent to federal penitentiaries. This has proven to be an effective approach to lowering homicide rates in Chicago; however, this may also create a more wide spread national gang problem. Gang members in federal facilities have access to criminals from throughout the nation who have likely committed more serious crimes. For instance, a gang member may interact with a financial crime expert or a high level major drug dealer, basically providing a more sophisticated "crime education system" for the gang.

responsible for 18% of all prison murders. The AB was founded in 1964 at the San Quentin Maximum Security Prison. In 1981, two incarcerated members of the AB brutally killed the leader of the D.C. Blacks in the federal prison in Marion, Illinois. The AB gang has chapters in almost every major state and federal prison in the country. Estimates of membership and associates exceeds 15,000 both in and out of prison. According to an FBI report, one of the AB practices is known as "polishing the rock." This simply means "the rule of thumb" is that once on the streets, one must take care of his brothers that are still inside. The penalty for not doing so is death.

Probation/Parole: Recommended Gang Specific Conditions to Prevent Further Gang Involvement

Source: Michael P. Coghlan, former DeKalb County State's Attorney

The probation order offers a unique opportunity that provides an excuse to quit the gang, and many young people are looking for an excuse to do just that. Probation can help people to leave the danger zone if the right conditions are written in the probation order.

- ■ Talk to the parents to secure a list of friends for the no contact list, a list of locations (get names and addresses), and for any recommendations they may have for conditions of probation.

- ■ Talk to the judge and tell the judge exactly what to say to the probationer. The judge needs your input. "We want to help you... You put yourself on probation..."

■ Use the following wording:

"Probationer must comply with the following conditions, in addition to other conditions imposed by law and the probation officer."

"No contact with individuals who are involved with gang activity and/or drug abuse."

"For purposes of this probation order, you are required to follow the definitions provided in this court order."

Delinquent Group (GANG definition): three or more individuals who associate and/or identify with each other, and have as a primary purpose the planning, threat, attempt or commission of criminal, delinquent or illegal acts.

"No public display of tattoos."

"No clothes, jewelry, signs or symbols commonly identified with a gang."

"You must carry a valid state-issued picture identification card with you at all times while on probation."

"Do not appear in court unless you are a witness or a party to a case scheduled in court at the time you appear in the courtroom."

"Fully cooperate with all police and probation requests for testing your blood, breath or urine for alcohol or other drugs."

"Fully cooperate with all police and probation officer requests to search and/or seize your person, property, residence, vehicle or other places and things in your possession or control."

"You are not to be present at any of the following locations:"

1)

2)

"No voluntary contact with the following individuals:"

1)

2)

"No voluntary contact with any other individual who was or may be a witness against you, except that your attorney may interview or cause to be interviewed any individual who may assist with your defense."

Other conditions...

"Witness intimidation is a criminal offense and a violation of probation."

Secure signature of probationer. "I have read the foregoing conditions of probation and I agree to follow all the above conditions, in addition to other conditions of probation set by the court and probation officer."

SECTION 7

GANGS IN SCHOOLS

Chicago Public Schools & Gangs

The Chicago Public School system consists of 613 schools. In September 2004, there were over 426,000 students enrolled in Chicago public schools. The school system also employs almost 46,000 people. The Chicago Police Department's database is able to separate most incidents occurring on school property. It should be noted that certain incidents may have occurred on school grounds, but did not involve students or school employees. This would include incidents that occurred on school property when the schools were closed. Statistics provided by the Chicago Police Department show a relatively small percentage of gang-related reported crimes compared to the overall reported crime that occurred on school grounds. A reasonable explanation for this could be that the victim rarely reported the incident as gang-related or the investigator did not classify the incident as gang-related.

CPS students enjoy physical education class.

The Chicago Police Department works very closely with the public schools to curb gang activity. The 25 police districts assign officers to work inside most high schools and detail marked police patrol vehicles to monitor schools within their districts during student arrival and dismissal times. It is not unusual to see anywhere from 5 to 10 district police cars parked around a public high school during dismissals.

At times, not even the strong police presence can prevent gang violence. Gang disruptions are usually instigated by juvenile members or "shorties." The shorties know that, if they are arrested for minor infractions, police can only keep them in custody for a short period of time before releasing them to a parent or legal guardian. Consequences of minor offenses, and at times major offenses, do not deter a young person from conducting gang crimes. Gang fights or even gang-related shootings are not unusual with police parked right around the corner.

EXCERPT INTERVIEW FROM THE CHILDREN IN ORGANIZED ARMED VIOLENCE STUDY, INSTITUTIONAL GANGS AND VIOLENCE IN CHICAGO

by Dr. John M. Hagedorn, University of Illinois-Chicago, Great Cities Institute

Dr. Hagedorn interviewed a number of gang members for this research paper. The following is an interview with one of the Chicago gang members **(GM)** from the report:

GM: My job, all the little kids, was to go to school, to the high school with guns already. Our first gun was a .38. We was to go and pick them up from school everyday.

Q: When you said pick them up, what, your job was to bring the guns or?

GM: Bring the guns to school and wait for them (older gang member) to get out. And we were the security if anybody tries to do something, we were there as protection, because they had to walk far to get back to the neighborhood.

Q: So, you would come with the guns and give them to the older guys?

GM: No, I would just keep them on us, we'd keep them on us, because they was like, you're still young, we're going to end up in the county jail, but you'd just go to the juvenile thing so that was the chances we were taking at that time. That's when I got to hold my first gun, when I was twelve years old.

Q: When you were twelve years old?

GM: Right.

The Chicago Public Schools (CPS) forward all school-related gang intelligence to the Chicago Police Department Deployment Operations Center (DOC). Information is provided by the Chicago Public Schools Bureau of Safety and Security and from all school officers. At the DOC, the information is analyzed and then related to gang intelligence. According to the CPS Bureau of Safety and Security, CPD Patrol and CPS Security problem solving deployments are made as a result of this intelligence, and high level coordination is achieved during regular, Friday afternoon DOC meetings at CPD headquarters. Other jurisdictions surrounding Chicago participate in the DOC meetings as well, and have access to intelligence via the I-CLEAR crime information system. Durbak believes that along with the critical addition of I-CLEAR, the CPD's DOC is "the greatest and most effective improvement instituted by the Chicago Police Department to battle street gang crime."

The Chicago Crime Commission recommends that suburban jurisdictions take advantage of the I-CLEAR system when possible and work closely with the Chicago Police DOC. The Chicago Public Schools Director of Safety and Security also suggested that organized forums for Chicagoland School Resource Officers could be a medium for information exchange and the sharing of best practices.

School Statistics Provided By The Chicago Police Department

Please note: The following charts represent crime on school property, including crimes occurring at times and days when students are not in school. The Chicago Public Schools provided information, based on a query of the Chicago Police Clear System, on the crimes occurring between 7:00 a.m. – 7:00 p.m. and excluding weekends. Using this criteria, the total 2005 reported crimes were 12,690 and 13,119 in 2004. These numbers more closely reflect the crime totals for crimes occurring during school hours. Additionally, the Chicago Police Department "Juvenile Justice" bulletin, Vol. 2, Issue 2, notes that "educational property" was the location for arrest for 26.5% of juveniles arrested during 2004.

OVERALL REPORTED CRIMES ON CHICAGO PUBLIC SCHOOL PROPERTY

Yearly Statistics	2004	2005
Homicide	3	1
Criminal Sexual Assault	28	24
Robbery	147	170
Battery	5,671	5,523
Public Peace	58	67
Assault	2,574	2,367
Stalking	8	2
Burglary	259	255
Theft	2,236	2,292
Motor Vehicle Theft	49	46
Arson	30	20
Deceptive Practice	86	67
Criminal Damage	1,168	1,173
Criminal Trespass	632	608
Weapons Violations	560	515
Prostitution	1	1
Obscenity	2	1
Sex Offense	141	125
Gambling	25	20
Offense Involving Children	107	106
Kidnapping	15	11
Narcotics	927	840
Liquor Violations	32	28
Public Peace Violations	268	242
Intimidation	24	22
Interfere with Public Official	-	10
Other Offenses	154	129
Totals:	15,205	14,665

It is highly recommended that suburban schools within a reasonable geographic area strengthen their gang intelligence through greater shared communication (organized task forces) amongst school unit officers.

Chicago Police Prevention Programs In Schools

D.A.R.E. — the Chicago Police (School Visitation Section) teach this curriculum that is designed to encourage youth to make good decisions, resist peer pressure and understand the consequences of participating in criminal activities. The curriculum consists of 10 weeks of instruction given by a uniformed police officer.

G.R.E.A.T. — Chicago Police provide classroom instruction for school-age children and a wide range of community-based activities that result in the young people developing the necessary life skills and the sense of competency, usefulness and personal empowerment they need to avoid involvement in youth violence and criminal activity.

Youth Alternatives to Gangs and Drugs Program — This program, offered by the Chicago Police Preventive Programs North and South, provides the following programs for youth:

- How to avoid gangs

- Learning to be confident in yourself

- Choosing Friends (qualities to look for in a friend)

- What to do when confronted by gangs for recruitment

Youth Gangs In Schools

According to the Office of Juvenile Justice and Delinquency Prevention's *Youth Gangs in Schools* report,

"Youth gangs are linked with serious crime problems in elementary and secondary schools in the United States. A report issued by the U.S. Department of Education and Justice (Chandler, K.A., Chapman, C.D., Rand, M.R., and Taylor, B.M. 1998. *Students' Report of School Crime: 1989 and 1995*) found that the percentage of students reporting the presence of gangs at school nearly doubled between 1989 and 1995. This report also found a strong correlation between the presence of gangs and both guns and drugs in school. Higher percentages of students

This girl's black eye was given to her by her gang boyfriend.

REPORTED CRIME ON CHICAGO PUBLIC SCHOOL PROPERTY — REPORTED AS GANG RELATED

Yearly Statistics	2004	2005
Robbery	4	2
Battery	57	67
Assault	36	25
Burglary	-	1
Theft	2	-
Criminal Damage	21	15
Criminal Trespass	10	8
Weapons Violations/Firearms	1	2
Sex Offense	-	1
Offense Involving Children	-	1
Gambling	4	3
Narcotics	74	78
Liquor Violations	1	2
Public Peace Violations	1	6
Intimidation	2	3
Other Offense	1	3
Total:	**214**	**217**

Suburban schools must also be highly alert to infiltrating gang activity. In December 2005, a 27 year-old Evanston elementary school janitor was sentenced to five years in prison for dealing crack cocaine on school grounds. Working with gang members, he endangered children by storing drugs at Lincolnwood Elementary School. He also allowed drug dealers on school property after hours.

reported knowing a student who brought a gun to school when gangs were present at the school (25 percent) than when gangs were not present (8 percent). Students who reported that drugs (marijuana, cocaine, crack or uppers/downers) were readily available at school were much more likely to report gangs at their school (35 percent) than those who said that no drugs were available (14 percent). The presence of gangs more than doubled the likelihood of violent victimization at school (nearly 8 percent, compared to 3 percent)."

The Chicago Crime Commission's highly evaluated Community Youth Program, piloted in Chicago, showed that of 100 first time juvenile offenders, over 60 % were arrested the first time during school on school grounds...thus educators must seriously consider effective strategies for halting a student's progress down this unhealthy path, which may be part of or could lead to gang involvement.

The ERIC Clearinghouse on Urban Education *Gangs In Schools — ERIC Digest 99* notes four factors primary in the formation of juvenile gangs. Briefly, they include:

■ Youth experience a sense of alienation and powerlessness because of a lack of traditional support structures, such as family and school.

■ Gang membership give a youth the sense of belonging and becomes a major sense of identity for its members. Membership affords a youth a sense of power and control, and gang activities become an outlet for their anger.

■ The control of turf is essential to the well-being of the gang, which often will use force to control both its territory and members.

■ Recruitment of new members and expansion of territory are essential if a gang is to remain strong and powerful.

In responding to the problem, educators should develop programs appropriate to their area that have been professionally evaluated and proven effective. The ERIC Digest 99 recommends effective interventions as a basis for developing a comprehensive, school-wide strategy:

■ Target students vunerable to gang recruitment for special assistance, particularly through the use of peer counselors and support groups. Mentoring, conflict resolution programs and tutoring can be effective.

■ Establish moral and ethical education, values clarification and conflict resolution as important components of the school curriculum.

■ Create an inviting school climate where every student feels welcome.

■ Educate all school staff about gangs and how to respond to them.

■ Offer special programs for parents on gangs and how to deal with them as a parent. Present the information in a culturally sensitive way.

■ Monitor youths who are not enrolled in school but "hang out" on or near school property.

■ Offer educational programs for students about gangs, their destructiveness and how to avoid being drawn into them, preferably in small groups where they can express their feelings comfortably.

■ Provide regular opportunities for students individually and/or in small groups to discuss their experiences in school and make future plans that offer hope and personal rewards.

In considering the factors leading to gang involvement, it is also important to note that according to a high level Chicago Police official, in predominantly African American gangs, recruitment of young people into the gang by older gang members seems to be down, with the real lure for joining the gang being drugs and money. Thus, school leaders may want to address strategies for counteracting these lures, such as drug prevention education, the creation of meaningful after-school and summer job opportunities for youth and strong career preparation programs.

Early Intervention: The Community Youth Program

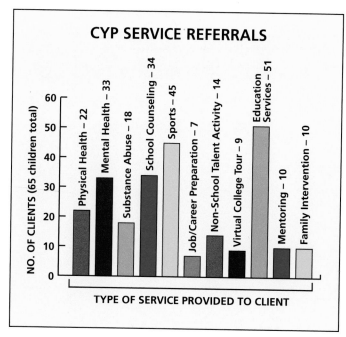

CYP SERVICE REFERRALS

NO. OF CLIENTS (65 children total)

- Physical Health – 22
- Mental Health – 33
- Substance Abuse – 18
- School Counseling – 34
- Sports – 45
- Job/Career Preparation – 7
- Non-School Talent Activity – 14
- Virtual College Tour – 9
- Education Services – 51
- Mentoring – 10
- Family Intervention – 10

TYPE OF SERVICE PROVIDED TO CLIENT

Chicago Crime Commission
Community Youth Pilot Program (CYP)

The CYP is an intensive, professionally evaluated, assessment-service demonstration program. It served first time juvenile offenders ages 9-16 in the south side communities of Chicago. One hundred police-intake and 20 school-intake children participated in the pilot.

Participating children received:

- an assigned case manager
- 3 hours of community work service
- health assessments and services
- educational assessments and services
- talent assessments and services; and
- a 3 hour parenting skills workshop (for parents of participating children)

The CYP **Process Evaluation**, completed by the Institute For Juvenile Research, noted the following:

In general, the comments from the families, staff and police were very positive. There is a lot of hope for the program and a lot of recognition for the work the case managers put in.

Program strengths included: 1) the breadth of the assessments provided; 2) the level of attention provided to each case; 3) the dedication of the staff; and 4) the flexibility of the program to adapt to problems when they arise.

In 2005, a formal **Outcomes Evaluation** was initiated and will be completed in Fall 2006. To give a more comprehensive idea of the data collected, consider that for each participant, over 500 pieces of information were entered.

As part of a preliminary evaluation of the effectiveness of the Community Youth Program, analysis focused on whether participants displayed improved psychological and physical functioning, as measured by the Child Health Questionnaire, when exiting the program versus when they entered the program. There was statistically significant improvement in scores on three of these subscales: social limitations (emotional and behavior), family activities and mental health.

CHQ SUBSCALES DISPLAYING IMPROVED FUNCTIONING

Subscale	Mean at Baseline	Mean at Exit
Social limitations – Emotion	81.75	93.33
Social limitations – Behavior	84.67	94.00
Family activities	68.26	84.01
Mental health	72.40	77.22

Findings of the Process and Outcomes Evaluations have and will be used by the Chicago Police as they work to implement a new **Juvenile Intervention and Support Center** — a screening/service center for juvenile offenders. In addition, the final report will be available to leaders from the Chicago Public Schools, the Department of Children and Family Services, state and local juvenile justice councils, numerous area service providers, and the public so that troubled youth can be better served.

SECTION 8

Gang Links to Other Organized Crime Groups, Politics, the Military and Criminal Justice Fields

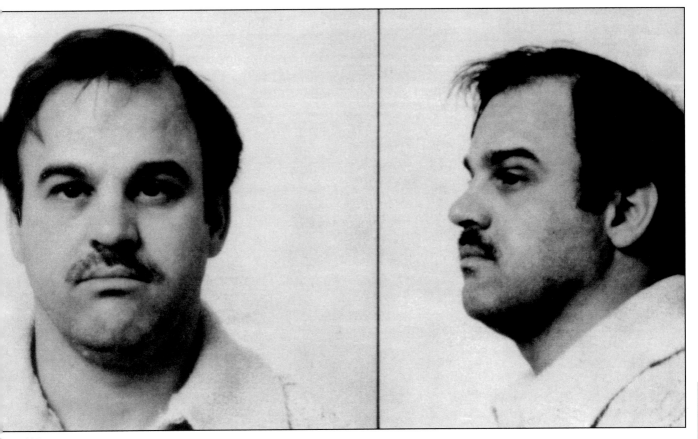

Ronald Jarrett

GANG LINKS TO TRADITIONAL AND OTHER ORGANIZED CRIME GROUPS

There is little definitive evidence linking street gangs to other organized crime groups; however, there are identified possible and known connections.

La Cosa Nostra (LCN)

The LCN's Grand Avenue Crew is alleged to be using street gang members to commit high line thefts in the suburbs, targeting jewelry, expensive automobiles and restaurant owners who may have a lot of cash in their homes. Some law enforcement experts believe these rumors to be false as the LCN, for theft of high line items, usually prefer to hire thieves with more expertise than the street gangs would provide.

It is also rumored that the street gangs may have made some sort of arrangement with the Taylor Street Crew to sell drugs in LCN territory in exchange for keeping all other street gang activity out of their way.

As traditional organized crime crews do not want to be in the public eye, it is possible that they may look to street gangs to carry out their "hits."

It is suspected, but not known for sure, that street gang members may have been hired to kill Ronald Jarrett of the Mafia's 26th Street Crew. He was shot and killed outside his Bridgeport home. Jarrett was a juice collector for money owed for gambling, cartage thief, and burglarly and spent a large part of his adult life in prison.

Steve Wambir, in his Chicago Sun-Times article *Mob's latest trend: farming out hits to gangbangers* (October 19, 2005), explains a case involving a west suburban bookie who was furious with a rival bookie for backing out of a deal:

> "In the 1995 case involving the furious suburban bookie, one of the alleged gang members involved owed the bookmaker money, so the bookmaker urged the gang member to rob the rival bookie. The gang member then could pay off his debt and keep whatever else he

could steal from the rival bookie's Glen Ellyn home, authories said. The west suburban bookie told the gang member what day would be best — a day when the target would be sure to have tens of thousands of dollars in cash on hand. And it was always understood, investigators say, that the rival bookie was to be killed — not just robbed. The hit fell apart when the DuPage County Sheriff's Police were tipped off to it. FBI and DuPage investigators caught the gang member and two fellow gang members outside the rival bookie's Glen Ellyn home as they tried to break in. A fourth escaped into the woods. While the three gang members were convicted of armed violence and burglary, investigators were never able to put together a good enough case to charge the bookmaker who set the crime in motion. But they were able to save a life."

In the same Sun-Times article, Warmbir also noted, "Mancari, who has alleged mob ties, was accused in February of reaching out to an associate in the El Rukn street gang to bump off a witness in the murder case against him. Unfortunately for Mancari, an FBI informant was in the same room when Mancari called a mobster associate from Cook County Jail to discuss the hit."

It is also possible that street gangs may fence their own stolen proceeds through La Cosa Nostra (LCN) operated businesses.

Colombian Jewelry Theft Ring

Irving Gonzalez of the La Familia Stones street gang was convicted for running a jewelry theft in an almost identical fashion to that of the Colombian Jewelry Theft Ring. The set up is one where the perpetrators, in two cars, wait at 5 S. Wabash for jewelry salesmen to exit the location. One perpetrator will signal to his partners in the other car when someone is a good target. When the valet brings the saleman's car around, the perpetrators puncture the car's tire. When the salesman's car finally stops a while later, they offer assistance to the salesman, and then proceed to steal the jewelry from the car.

Mexican Mafia

East Los Angeles Hispanics formed the Mexican Mafia, aka "LA EME" or "EME," during the late 1950s in the California Department of Corrections Penal System at Duele Vocational Institution in Tracy, California. The motivation for its origination was to form a "Gang of Gangs" that would supplant traditional territorial gangs once outside the prison. According to the FBI, it was organized along the lines of the old Sicilian Mafia with strict rules governing its members and for the primary purpose of establishing a well-organized criminal enterprise to further gang goals. Gang crimes include the control of heroin trafficking, drug rip-offs, human trafficking (possibly including prostitution), business robberies, gambling, extortion and even contract murders. EME does not hesitate to kill off competitors and have gone so far as to arrange for wholesale assaults on sheriff's deputies and inmates in Los Angeles County Jail to get their way. Members are traditionally from Southern California, but they have been increasing their presence elsewhere with all members abiding by the "blood in, blood out" code of honor. They are mentioned here because of their affiliation with MS 13 and Sureno 13s street gangs.

Mexican Cartels and Organized Crime

The Drug Enforcement Administration noted that there are four major illegal drug cartels in Mexico. They also explained that the term "Mexican Organized Crime" includes any organized crime organization that is primarily run by those of Mexican decent. Thus, the Mexican Mafia and Mexican Cartels would be considered Mexican Organized Crime. Many gangs have relationships with Mexican Cartels, as well as drug cartels in Colombia and Southeast and Southwest Asia.

GANGS IN POLITICS AND CRIMINAL JUSTICE FIELDS

Street gangs seeking clout and influence through the political arena is nothing new. Ultimately, such endeavors allow for more sophisticated and efficient operations. What makes this a favorable undertaking on their part, but equally difficult for law enforcement to track, are court rulings prohibiting surveillance or compiling dossiers on anyone connected to a political organization.

Past examples of gangs in politics include:

■ In March 1985, a State of Illinois charter was issued for the Unknown Conservative Vice Lords (UCVL). The group was set up as a non-profit voters' league with the name United Concerned Voters' League.

■ In 1992, while in prison, Larry Hoover of the Black Gangster Disciples created the 21st Century Voices of Total Empowerment (21st Century V.O.T.E.) as a local organization that also campaigned (unsuccessfully) for his parole in 1993. 21st Century V.O.T.E paraded the causes of disadvantaged African American youth while campaigning for solutions to the urban problems of drugs, unemployment, violence and homelessness. They managed to gain the attention of a few prominent politicians and community leaders. In 1994, Wallace "Gator" Bradley, a Hoover supporter (also described as a BGD enforcer) and member of V.O.T.E., was selected by Jesse Jackson to meet with President Bill Clinton on urban issues. He told the President he was there on behalf of the Better Growth and Development organization (BGD), which some members later claimed was simply a new name for the Black Gangster Disciples. Later, Wallace Bradley ran for alderman of the 3rd Ward (unsuccessfully). Few in law enforcement believed they were sincere in their efforts, noting that the Black Gangster Disciples were (and are still) heavily into the narcotics trade and remain one of the most virulent gangs on the street.

■ In 1996, Terry Young of the Traveling Vice Lords ran and was elected 2nd Ward Republican Committeeman.

■ Research conducted by the National Gang Crime Research Center in 1996 showed that 15% of the Gangster Disciple membership claimed to have worked for a politician. (80% said the gang leader asked them to do so, 18% said the politician initiated the action.)

■ The Chicago Sun-Times reported on December 26, 2002, that in the upcoming primaries then, of the City's 50 wards, gang-bangers worked as volunteers in 10 of the City's 50 ward elections. They also noted that back in the 1994 mayoral contest, when candidate Joe Gardner kicked off his campaign to unseat Mayor Daley, his rally was packed with gang-bangers.

■ Chicago Tribune and Sun-Times articles dated June 21, 2005 reported the plan and model for the redevelopment of the old Cabrini-Green housing site as part of a federal consent decree between Cabrini residents and the Chicago Housing Authority. According to the plan, one-third of the profits, possibly several million dollars by one estimate, will benefit those residents in the form of services. One of those pictured reviewing the model was Kelvin Cannon, president of the Cabrini Local Advisory Council. Police have identified Cannon as a former member of the Gangster Disciples, and a convicted felon with 9 prior arrests. The public should be aware of a convicted felon and identified Gangster Disciple having involvement in making decisions concerning these funds.

■ The Cook County State's Attorney's Office reported to the Chicago Crime Commission that gang members have made attempts to infiltrate the Cook County Clerk's Office and the Cook County Department of Corrections. According to the Cook County Sheriff's Office, gang members have also tried to gain employment as police officers and other related positions. The College of DuPage reported that gang members have been taking criminal justice classes at the College.

■ According to Steve Macko, ERRI Crime Analyst, in his article "Gangbanger Cops", in a three year span in the mid-1990s, the Chicago Police Department forced 15 officers to resign, charged them with gang-related crimes or investigated them for membership in a street gang.

IN THE NEWS...
Gangs in the Military

The following are excerpts from news stories:

Gangs claim their turf in Iraq
Chicago Sun-Times (5-1-06)

The Gangster Disciples, Latin Kings and Vice Lords were born decades ago in Chicago's most violent neighborhoods. Now, their gang graffiti is showing up 6,400 miles away in one of the world's most dangerous neighborhoods — Iraq...

"I have identified 320 soldiers as gang members from April 2002 to present," said Scott Barfield, a Defense Department gang detective at Fort Lewis in Washington state. "I think that's the tip of the iceberg."

Of paramount concern is whether gang-affiliated soldiers' training will make them deadly urban warriors when they return to civilian life and if some are using their access to military equipment to supply gangs at home, said Barfield and other experts...

Barfield said gangs are encouraging their members to join the military to learn urban warfare techniques they can teach when they go back to their neighborhoods. "Gang members are telling us in the interviews that their gang is putting them in," he said...

A law enforcement source in Chicago said police see some evidence of soldiers working with gangs here. Police recently stopped a vehicle and found 10 military flak jackets inside. A gang member in the vehicle told investigators his brother was a Marine and sent the jackets home, the source said.

Troops do double duty in gangs
Chicago Sun-Times (5-15-06)

Army soldiers who belong to the Gangster Disciples have robbed people to raise money for the gang, orchestrated drug and gun deals, and even killed two people after gang members were kicked out of a bar...

In 1996, the feds targeted a gun-and-drug operation involving Porter (a retired Army sergeant from Chicago) and 25 other Gangster Disciples, including Gerald Ivey — an active duty sergeant at Fort Carson — as well as other soldiers and civilians, officials said...

The crew bought cocaine and marijuana in El Paso, Texas, Exploiting Ivey's past contacts at nearby Fort Bliss, Thomasson (assistant special agent in charge of ATF's Seattle field division) said. They'd purchase marijuana for about $300 a pound in Texas and sell it for $1,200 a pound in Gary, Ind., which was Ivey's hometown.

Ivey also shipped guns back to Gary... ATF foiled a plan by Ivey to send fully automatic machine guns back to the Chicago area, Thomasson said.

In 1999, a Fort Hood soldier, Spec. Jacqueline Billings of Milwaukee, was identified by military prosecutors as the "governor" of a 40-member faction of the Gangster Disciples — many of whom were soldiers... She was sentenced to 27 years of confinement...

In July 1997, Billings allegedly ordered a hit on a club owner after she and other gang members were thrown out...Two Fort Hood soldiers in the Gangster Disciples bungled the job, killing two of the club's employees but not the owner... She was acquitted for murder but found guilty of battery. She was also convicted for her role in the robbery of a $15,000 Cartier watch and $2,500 in Cash in August 1997.

SECTION 9

Other Organized Crime Groups

OTHER ORGANIZED CRIME GROUPS

While this report focuses on the street gang activity in the Chicago metropolitan area, it is important to briefly note that there are other organized crime groups operating in and around the Chicago area that are not addressed comprehensively in this report, but are still worthy of attention. Some of these groups are noted here.

MOTORCYCLE GANGS

Outlaws Motorcycle Clubs and the Hell's Angels are involved primarily in the dealing of Meth, but have also been active in prostitution and the theft of motorcycles. There is a rivalry between these two groups, and with the Outlaws recent opening of a new clubhouse in Rockford, that has traditionally been Hell's Angel territory, there is an expectation that violence may erupt between these two gangs. It is also worth keeping an eye on possible rivalries that might form between biker gangs and street gangs if street gangs decide to infiltrate the Meth distribution networks that are currently controlled by these biker gangs. In late 2005 and early 2006, the Illinois Department of Corrections Intelligence Units intercepted outgoing and incoming mail from documented Chicago street gang leaders and members of various motorcycle clubs. Members of these gangs generally wear a full patch symbol on their clothing and women often carry the weapons.

Outlaws Motorcycle Clubs

The Outlaws M.C. (Motorcycle Clubs) have 38 support gangs in and around the Chicago area, including, but not limited to, the Legacy M.C., Fugarwe Tribe M.C., Madmen M.C., Brothers Rising M.C., Brothers M.C., Teamster Horsemen M.C. and others.

There are fourteen known clubhouses in Illinois and four clubhouses in the Chicagoland area:

3745 W. Division, Chicago, IL.
2601 W. 25th Street, Chicago, IL.
959 Grace Street, Elgin, IL.
818 Mulberry St., Rockford, IL (new location)

Hell's Angels

The Hell's Angels have 18 support gangs in and around the Chicago area, including but not limited to, the 100 MPD Club, Mad Dogs M.C., Iron Sleds, 10% Brotherhood M.C. and others. The Hell's Angels, originally a West Coast group, merged with the Hell's Henchmen to form the current gang. The Hell's Angels are responsible for setting off a car bomb known to be the fourth largest bomb ever to go off in the United States.

There are three known clubhouses in Illinois and two clubhouses in the Chicagoland area:

15609 S. Halsted, Harvey, IL
1109 Rock Street, Rockford, IL

ORGANIZED CRIME GROUPS

The Mafia, La Cosa Nostra or The Outfit

It must be constantly repeated that, although there is a common and dangerous misconception that organized crime is no longer a problem nationally or in the Chicago area, nothing could be further from the truth. The traditional "mob" is still a great danger to our society and the other ethnic organized crime groups are willing to develop alliances with the Chicago "Outfit" in order to thrive. The Outfit has always been able to adapt to any condition in order to survive and the current hierarchy is fully capable of

adjusting to handle any crisis. The 2005 indict-ments of fourteen subjects returned in the "Family Secrets" case were described by the United States Attorney (USA) Patrick J. Fitzgerald as a "hit on the mob", but did not represent an elimination of the Chicago Outfit. The prosecution charged the Outfit as a criminal enterprise and the evidence to be introduced is expected to provide proof regarding eighteen murders, including the 1986 deaths of Anthony and Michael Spilotro. This indictment obtained by USA Fitzgerald represents a major effort against the Outfit, but by no means will it result in the mob being out of business. Those in the hierarchy will still be able to plan and coordinate with younger un-indicted members and associates to ensure the continuation of the Outfit. While the "vice" businesses of illegal gambling, "juice" loans, prostitution and narcotics still remain the largest sources of income for the mob, they have moved increasingly into "legitimate" businesses

to insulate themselves from interference. Those businesses include bars, restaurants, construction, trucking companies, labor racketeering and any business where cash is the preferred form of payment.

With regard to labor racketeering, the federal government has conducted several initiatives to combat organized crime influence and control of labor unions. One investigation in the 1980's was code-named "Unirac" and targeted the International Longshoremen's Association. That investigation proved the involvement of members of the Genovese and Gambino Family members in the union activities in the ports on the east coast of the U.S. Many believed that this prosecution ended the threat of organized crime involvement in the union or the U.S. ports. But then, last year, the U.S. Department of Justice again filed suit asking for federal court takeover of the International Longshoremen's

Association because of racketeering activities of members of the Genovese and Gambino Family members in the union in the ports on the east coast of the U.S. The civil suit accused the union of being a "vehicle for organized crime" on the waterfront from Florida to Maine. The Chairman of the New York Homeland Security Committee warned that terrorists would seek to exploit that situation. Amid heightened concern for port security this threat cannot be ignored and provides proof that organized crime has not and does not cease to be a danger to our security.

Asian Organized Crime Groups

Asian organized crime groups have been involved in murder, extortion, kidnapping, gambling, fraud, counterfeiting, prostitution, weapons trafficking, drug trafficking, money laundering, alien smuggling and armed home invasions. A complex and fluid relationship exists between the Triads, Tongs, street gangs and American-Chinese organized crime groups.

Eastern European Organized Crime Travelers

The Travelers commit crimes that include ruse entry, burglary, home invasion, store diversion, home repair schemes, insurance fraud, fortune telling scams, welfare fraud, credit card and check fraud, shoplifting and the pigeon drop.

Nigerian Organized Crime

Nigerian groups are active in drug trafficking, money laundering, check fraud, credit card fraud, advance fee fraud, financial fraud, identification fraud, mail order scams and telemarketing scams.

Polish Organized Crime

Polish groups are known to have been involved in auto theft, insurance scams, drug smuggling, counterfeiting, bank fraud, money laundering, robbery, forgery, bombings and extortion.

Russian Organized Crime

Russian Organized Crime includes extortion, bribery, fuel tax scams, kidnapping, murder, auto theft, racketeering, money laundering, nuclear weapons trafficking, drug trafficking, healthcare fraud, insurance fraud, telecommunications fraud, credit card fraud, prostitution, weapons trafficking and counterfeiting.

Yugoslavian, Albanian, Croatian, Serbian Organized Crime Crews

These crews have been involved in commercial burglary, counterfeit indentification, narcotics trafficking, arson for profit, extortion and money laundering.

WHITE SUPREMACISTS

Ku Klux Klan

The Ku Klux Klan is the oldest of American hate groups. Although African Americans have typically been the Klan's primary target, it has also attacked Jews, immigrants, homosexuals and, until recently, Catholics. Two chapters have been identified in Illinois.

Aryan Nation

The Aryan Nation is also a white supremacist group. (See Section Six.)

SECTION 10

Law Enforcement
Strategies and Response

LAW ENFORCEMENT AND CRIMINAL JUSTICE RESPONSE

Chicago Police Department Violence Reduction Initiatives

Deployment Operations Center (DOC): The backbone of all the Chicago Police Department's efforts, DOC analyzes crime incidents in real time and makes deployment recommendations based on data, intelligence and information from the community.

Targeted Response Unit: A unit of highly professional and proactive officers are deployed to high crime areas to conduct aggressive, visible patrols focusing on guns, narcotics and stolen vehicles.

Area Narcotics Enforcement Teams: District gang teams work under the direction of the Area Deputy Chief within their areas to arrest street narcotics dealers.

CAGE Unit: Officers trace guns and go after offenders who illegally sell guns to criminals.

Operation Double Play: Officers arrest the street drug dealers, then pose as dealers to arrest and seize the vehicles of customers who come into the community to buy drugs.

Operation Closed Market: Two hundred officers that usually perform administrative duties are deployed in the midst of open air drug markets to disrupt, disturb and dislocate the people who run open-air drug markets.

Operation Disruption: Chicago Police utilize 30 high visibility surveillance cameras (pods) to prevent violence before it occurs. Pods, marked with flashing blue lights and the CPD logo, are mounted on City light poles and are equipped with the ability to capture criminal activity blocks away. The goal is to create a visible crime deterrent in high crime areas.

Operation Spring Cleaning: The Chicago Police launched Operation Spring Cleaning in 2004. It is a closely coordinated effort involving multiple City departments and partnering with law enforcement agencies to focus on reducing crime, disrupting narcotics sales and delivering City services during Spring break. This targeted and intense program occurs within an approximate 10 day span.

CPD Juvenile Intervention and Support Center
Under a multi-agency approach to juvenile crime and delinquency, the Chicago Police Department has begun to implement and test its most comprehensive juvenile intervention model. Participating with the CPD are the Cook County State's Attorney's Office, Probation Department, Juvenile Court, the Chicago Department of Children and Family Services, Chicago Public Schools, the Illinois Department of Children and Family Services, as well as other governmental and civic organizations. The foundation of this intervention model focuses on the creation of Chicago's first Juvenile Intervention and Support Center (JISC). The JISC is located at 3900 S. California Avenue and provides police and social service intervention services for CPD Districts 2, 7, 8, 9, 10 and 21. The central purpose of the JISC is to reduce juvenile crime and recidivism.

The Juvenile Intervention and Support Center:

- Provides more effective coordination of the activities and services of police, prosecutors, social workers and probation officers, and improves the efficiency of juvenile offender processing.

- Enhances case management for juvenile offenders requiring these services.

- Improves the quality and coordination of service provider referrals.

- Expands the availability and use of conferencing, peer juries and other victim-participant diversion options.

- Expands the involvement of schools, health care and other key social service partners in addressing the problems of juvenile crime.

- Fosters the development of improved and expanded juvenile offender prevention and intervention services.

- Reduces the amount of juvenile crime in the communities serviced and recidivism rates of juvenile arrestees served through the JISC.

- Dramatically reduces the number of juveniles that are vulnerable to criminal gang recruitment.

Chicago's Drug and Gang House Ordinance

This ordinance, 8-4-090 of the Municiple Code of Chicago, "Drug and gang houses, houses of prostitution and other disorderly houses," provides, in laymen's terms, that when there are two or more offenses of any nature upon a particular premise within a six month period, or any one felony offense, the premise shall be deemed a "public nuisance." Once so declared, an owner must take appropriate abatement measures; failure to do so may result in fine, incarceration or forfeiture of property. Generally speaking, these cases are resolved by agreement and do not end up in court. Property owners may be faced with fines related to the criminal activity itself (usually narcotics sales), which usually range from $3,000 - $6,000 per criminal activity cited, and with fines of $200 – $500 per day per building code violation. As there may be multiple building code violations, fines can quickly add up to thousands of dollars — often the maximum, which is $50,000. Owners will sometimes pay agreed upon fines and sell the property or they may agree to evict the criminal element from the premises, while making required repairs or adding security measures. In the end, the goal is to stabilize the property and surrounding community and eliminate the criminal activity in and surrounding it. Crime breeding properties are most often identified by 25 Chicago Police street corner conspiracy teams who work undercover to target illegal drug sales and other criminal activity occurring at the properties. Once evidence is secured through the work of these teams, the Chicago Police Drug and Gang House Enforcement Unit will take over from there, working with the court and the property owners to successfully resolve the case.

In 2004, the ordinance resulted in:

- 293 criminal counts and 739 building code violations

- targeting 65 properties in 22 street corner conspiracies

- filing 45 cases

- 20 agreed orders with 9 of those orders including complete vacates of the properties

- 4 forced sales

- $19,400 in fines. The goal is to stabilize the area, therefore the priority is usually the sale of a property to a more capable owner or to create an order with measures that change the way the old owner manages the property.

- $55,700 in default judgments. These defaults are applied to properties as liens or to owners as garnishments.

BEFORE   *AFTER*

CASE EXAMPLE: 846 N. Drake

Operation Closed Shop was a ten month undercover operation conducted by the Chicago Police Department's Narcotics and Gang Investigations Section (NAGIS). The investigation focused on heroin trafficking by the Four Corner Hustler street gang on the west side of Chicago. One of several locations involved in the operation, targeted by NAGIS' Drug and Gang House Prosecution Unit, was that of 846 N. Drake.

This single family brick house was owned and occupied by a family, whose members, on five different occasions, sold narcotics to undercover officers. In addition, nine other narcotics arrests occurred at the property during the time of the operation.

Upon completion of the operation, a case was filed under the city of Chicago's Drug and Gang House Ordinance, MCC 8-4-090. The case included the fourteen criminal counts and forty-four building code violations. Near the end of the operation, the family lost the property through foreclosure to Citigroup. Despite the foreclosure, the family continued to occupy the property without authorization. Under intense pressure from the City, Citigroup succeeded in completing an eviction of the family from the property.

One possible disposition in the adjudication of drug and gang house cases is the sale of a property to an approved non-profit organization. This is done through the Department of Housing.

Faced with this "inherited problem" and a maximum penalty of $50,000.00, Citigroup generously donated 846 N. Drake to Neighborhood Housing Services. The property has since been rehabbed completely and is now occupied by a Neighborhood Housing Services referred family.

METROPOLITAN ENFORCEMENT GROUPS (MEGS) STATISTICS FOR FY 2004
(7/1/2003 - 6/30/2004)

MEG	Weapons Seized	# of Drug Seizures	Street Value	Gang Arrests
DuMEG	23	194	$122,433,508	25
MANS	22	247	$25,179,249	51
KAMEG	53	280	$123,480	15
MEGLC	24	202	$23,523,087	74
MEGSI	51	358	$2,886,888	0
MCNEG	28	127	$102,764	23
QCMEG	5	73	$7,594,870	0
SIEG	48	186	$2,622,501	0
VMEG	21	84	$1,783,596	13
TOTAL	275	1,751	$186,249,943	201

Note: Gang Involvement is not always recorded.

Illinois Metropolitan Enforcement Groups

Metropolitan Enforcement Groups (MEGs), authorized by the Illinois General Assembly in 1977 under the Intergovernmental Drug Laws Enforcement Act (30 ILCS 715/6), are an important component in the collaborative effort to combat illegal drug traffic (and thus gangs) throughout Illinois. Illinois has nine MEG units covering 19 counties, with 21% of their personnel coming from the Illinois State Police and 79% from local and federal agencies. In FY 2004, the MEGs received 1.17 million in state grants (63% General Revenue Funds, 29 % Asset Forfeiture Funds and 8 % from the Drug Traffic Prevention Fund). The MEGs are:

- DuPage County Metropolitan Enforcement Group (DuMEG)

- Joliet Metropolitan Area Narcotics Squad (MANS)

- Kankakee Area Metrpolitan Enforcement Group (KAMEG)

- Metropolitan Enforcement Group of Lake County (MEGLC)

- Metropolitan Enforcment Group of Southwestern Illinois (MEGSI)

- Multi-County Narcotics Enforcement Group (MCNEG)

- Quad Cities Metropolitan Enforcement Group (QCMEG)

- Southern Illinois Enforcement Group (SIEG)

- Vermillion County Metropolitan Enforcement Group (VMEG)

INVESTIGATIVE HIGHLIGHT OF ONE ILLINOIS MEG:

VMEG agents participated in an Organized Crime Drug Enforcement Task Force (OCDETF) investigation with the Drug Enforcement Administration (DEA). This case resulted in the arrest of 4 principal targets in a cocaine distribution organization and the identification of additional targets. Confiscated items, estimated with a value of $434, 179, included 943 grams of cocaine, 982 grams of cannabis, 18 tablets of ecstasy, four vehicles, seven hand guns, $20,856 in U.S. Currency, $200 in counterfeit money and two computers. ISP Task Force Six, Bloomington Police Department, Normal Police Department and the Champaign U.S. Attorney's Office assisted in the investigation.

United State's Attorney – Northern District of Illinois

The U.S. Attorney's Office – Northern District of Illinois (U.S.A.O.) estimates that there are 13,000 police officers (with only a fraction working on gang cases) and about 60 federal agents working on gang cases versus the estimated 70,000 gang members operating in Chicago. The U.S.A.O. considers quality intelligence, coordination/communication, target prioritization and continuity to be key aspects to successful gang crime reduction strategies.

Cook County Law Enforcement Efforts

Cook County Sheriff's Police report these strategies as effective means for preventing and responding to gang activity: 1) street corner conspiracy cases; 2) gang saturation patrol in areas known for gang and narcotic activity; 3) reverse role drug operations; and 4) community awareness presentations to students and citizen groups.

The Cook County State's Attorney's Office suggested: 1) talking to parolees through the Project Safe Neighborhood model about increasing federal gun prosecution while at the same time offering services; and 2) Area Gang Strategy Meetings involving various federal agencies, assistant state's attorneys, assistant United States attorneys, and others, such as the Chicago Police Department, to coordinate strategies against the top 10 targets in an area creating the greatest violence problems.

Main 21 Initiative

Chicago Police Officers work with representatives from the U.S. Attorney's Office, State's Attorney's Office, Drug Enforcement Administration, Federal Bureau of Investigation, U. S. Department of Alcohol, Tobacco Firearms and Explosives, Illinois State Police, Illinois Department of Corrections, and the Cook County Sheriff's Office. The top 21 gang leaders are targeted through a multi-agency coordinated effort, with emphasis on those most involved with narcotics and violent activity.

Federal Bureau of Investigation

The FBI has established the National Gang Intelligence Center (NGIC) to stem the growth of gangs and related criminal activity in the United States. The NGIC, located in Washington, DC at the FBI Headquarters building, serves as an information hub for gang intelligence nation-wide. The NGIC uses an intelligence-driven approach, integrating the assets of the FBI and other federal, state and local law enforcement.

The mission of the NGIC is to support FBI Field Divisions and other law enforcement agencies through timely and accurate tactical and strategic analysis, focusing on the growth, migration, criminal activity and association of gangs.

The FBI Chicago Field Office focuses on long-term investigations designed to dismantle the infra-structure of Chicago's most violent street gangs through the multiple and simultaneous arrests of their leadership. This is accomplished through joint, multi-agency initiatives, such as the Safe Street Task Forces, which target gangs engaged in ongoing violent criminal activity.

Using federal Racketeer Influenced and Corrupt Organization (RICO) statutes, the Chicago Division and local law enforcement have worked together to successfully disrupt and dismantle entire gang factions by incarcerating their leadership, members and supporters. These joint investigations also focus on forfeiting gang members' assets and seizing their weapons, narcotics and narcotics proceeds, making it more difficult for any remaining or peripheral gang members to resume the gang's criminal activities.

In addition to these investigative activities, the Chicago Division's Field Intelligence Group (FIG) collects and processes intelligence on gang activity in order to identify current and emerging gang-related threats. That intelligence is then disseminated to both internal and external customers to facilitate a coordinated response by federal and local law enforcement agencies.

Project Safe Neighborhoods (PSN)

PSN is a highly effective, cooperative effort between federal, state and local law enforcement, and the Chicago Crime Commission (as Community Engagement Partner) that seeks stiff federal prison time for felons who are in possession of firearms and works with parolees on job training and education so they won't re-offend. There are also strong PSN media and juvenile programs in place. Pilot Chicago PSN areas showed a 38% drop in their homicide rates. Also, only 4 percent of parolees went back to prison for new crimes after attending PSN parolee meetings. But more than 22 percent of parolees from the same neighborhoods who did not attend those meetings wound up getting arrested again. For more information, visit the CCC-hosted PSN website at www.psnchicago.org.

Drug Enforcement Administration

DEA is mandated to target and disrupt the highest-level drug traffickers in the world. As a result, DEA investigates the primary sources of supply for the street gangs that distribute illegal drugs on the streets of Chicago. In fact, it is at this critical juncture—between the sources of supply and the street gangs— where investigations are most effective in disrupting drug distribution. For many years, DEA Chicago has been working aggressively with its law enforcement counter-

parts in targeting Chicago street gangs through a variety of initiatives, such as the Top 21 Initiative, and through the use of task forces. For example, DEA Chicago currently has dedicated four enforcement groups at the Chicago High Intensity Drug Trafficking Area (HIDTA) Task Force to target and dismantle both the highest-level drug traffickers in the street gangs and their sources of supply.

Section Ten

SECTION 11

Law Enforcement Suggestions and Areas For Further Study

LAW ENFORCEMENT AGENCIES SHARE THEIR SUGGESTIONS

- Use conspiracy charges when appropriate. Show gang relationships using gang enhancement laws.

- Work with Immigration and Customs Enforcement to remove illegal immigrant street gang members from the country, e.g. MS13s, 18th Street gang and Sureno 13s.

- Use local newspaper personal ads to learn gang members' personal relationships.

- Street Gangs and Social Network Analysis, (Andrew Papachristos, University of Chicago)

  Employ social network analysis which refers to an analytic approach that views the social world as patterns of regularities in relationships among individuals and groups — i.e., how people and groups are connected to each other and how these networks influence behavior. In short, this approach believes

that the structure of social networks influences all types of behaviors, including getting a job, voting, political decision making, disease transmission and group violence.

Social network analysis can be a useful tool for gang research and intelligence gathering. It can be used to "map":

- the social networks among gang members;

- patterns of gang violence;

- alliance structures; or

- cliques within larger groups.

- Recognize that girls and new recruits in the gang often carry the weapons or drugs. Drugs or weapons may even be hidden on babies or small children.

- Use confidential informants to make mass arrests.

- Secure information when on domestic violence calls, as a gang member's girlfriend often will have a wealth of information and may be willing to talk when just abused by her gang boyfriend.

- Be careful with whom secure information is shared. According to former DeKalb County State's Attorney Michael P. Coghlan, fifty-seven percent of gang members know someone in the criminal justice system (sibling or friend, etc.).

- Always ask an informant why they are willing to give the information they are providing. It is important to know this in order to validate the likelihood that the information is good.

GANGS, GUNS AND DRUGS: AREAS FOR FURTHER STUDY

Local, state and federal law enforcement agencies made a number of suggestions during our research interviews for increasing their effectiveness in dealing with criminal gang activity. The Chicago Crime Commission believes that these areas need further discussion and review before any recommendations can be made.

Homicide

- Las Vegas Police are able to secure immediate telephonic search and arrest warrants enabling them to act quickly in and around the crime scene to secure evidence. This is an option that Illinois policy makers should review and consider.

Narcotics

- Allow audio recording of all narcotics cases to be admissible in civil, criminal or administrative proceedings. Currently, recordings are not allowed into evidence unless an officer is killed or injured during the incident in question.

- Unlike Illinois, most states do not require law enforcement to get court approval to wear a wire, and when it is approved in Illinois it is only approved for a time period of 30 days. Extending the time period or eliminating the need for prior court approval all together should be considered.

Vehicles

- Noting that exceptions will have to be added, permit the seizure or impoundment of a vehicle for driving without a valid license or permit in effect.

- As occurs in New York, require that permanent license plates be issued right away, rather than issue temporary registration permits.

- Noting that exceptions will have to be considered and added: 1) require that anyone purchasing a license plate possess a valid driver's license; 2) require all registration of Illinois plates be linked to a VIN (vehicle identification number) that is acceptable to the National Crime Information Center; 3) ensure the integrity of the VIN reported and entered; and 4) require that VINs and license plate types match (truck, passenger, etc.).

- Noting that exceptions will have to be made, prohibit the possession of "jiggler keys" by anyone but licensed locksmiths, fleet owners, etc.

- Permit police, when writing multiple tickets, to write more than one charge on a ticket. Streamlining this process saves time and provides for increased officer safety as officers can not pay attention to the situation with the same focus while having to write up the multiple tickets.

- Increase awareness that, when law enforcement stops an individual in a rental car that is not registered in the individual's name, the rental car can be confiscated and immediately returned to the rental facility.

Weapons

- The use of tasers should be studied both in terms of law enforcement use and public use, as tasers may be used either as a weapon against police or citizens or as a less lethal tool for self-defense.

Victim – Witness

- Review the resources available in victim-witness relocation because, while funding has dwindled (according to law enforcement sources), intimidation and the paying off of witnesses has increased.

Chicago Crime Commission
Recommendations

GANGS, GUNS AND DRUGS: CHICAGO CRIME COMMISSION RECOMMENDED STRATEGIES, POLICY AND LEGISLATION

The Chicago Crime Commission recommends the following:

Homicide and Violence

- Mutual Combatants — Make aggravated unlawful use of a weapon a Class 2 felony if the person discharged the weapon and make aggravated unlawful use of a weapon by a felon a Class 1 felony if the felon discharged the weapon.

- Prohibit high-powered bullets which are often described as the "cop killer" bullets. Advertisers state that the bullets will defeat most body armor. Also, prohibit the FN's Five-seveN pistol, which will penetrate body armor.

Weapons

- Prohibit the purchase of more than one handgun per month.

- Extend the Assault Weapon ban. For a one-year period (September 13, 2004 — September 13, 2005) following the end of the ban, Chicago Police collected 413 assault weapons.

- Require gun dealer licensing through the state, which would provide more local oversight of these dealers.

- Ban .50 caliber sniper rifles, which are powerful enough to take down a commercial airliner.

- All police departments should take advantage of the ATF F-TIP System or E-TRACE System to trace all guns — crime guns and other found firearms.

- All police departments should take advantage of the ATF's National Integrated Ballistic Information Program (NIBIN), which deploys Integrated Ballistic Information System (IBIS) equipment into federal, state and local law enforcement agencies for use in imaging and comparing crime gun evidence. IBIS operates locally through the Illinois State Police Crime Lab.

- Gun show dealers and purchasers should be required to meet the same local, state or federal requirements as required for other legitimate gun dealer sites.

Criminal Justice

- Require DNA collection from all convicted felons.

- In cases where DNA is collected, require that DNA samples be collected and analyzed within 30 days of sentencing.

- Create a greater penalty for damaging City property used to combat crime, i.e. PODS (police cameras), police squad cars.

- Prohibit the posting of unauthorized personal information of criminal justice and law enforcement personnel, such as judges, police officers and prosecutors on the Internet.

- The Chicago Crime Commission and ATF should provide a forum for suburban police departments to work to form multi-agency gang task forces similar in nature to the Cook County area Main 21 Initiative. This initiative targets the gang members most involved with narcotics and violent activity through enhanced information sharing. With gang members operating more often in the suburbs, gang members may use any disconnect between agencies to their advantage.

- Strengthen penalties for making and selling false identifications.

- Provide means for law enforcement to secure a court ordered Emergency Pen Register in order to secure live time phone records. This would enable police to more quickly and effectively react to drug-related kidnappings and other cases.

Juvenile Justice & Early Intervention/Prevention

■ Support strong operations and sufficient funding for the juvenile corrections systems that was recently separated from the adult system.

■ Encourage public education on the wide range of mental health services to eliminate the common notion that receiving mental health services means that a person is "crazy." This common notion, held by many parents, often acts as an obstacle in securing aid for children who may need help in dealing with substance abuse, depression, behavior problems or other issues.

■ Encourage the financial support of substance abuse treatment programs that serve children. Most facilities only serve adults 18 and older.

■ Encourage non-profits and youth service systems to implement proven case management models for delinquent youth. These programs should assess health, education and social services needs and then link (not just refer) young people to appropriate services. The Chicago Crime Commission's Community Youth Program model is available upon request.

■ Encourage major youth service providers to test children for eye and hearing problems, as many children may miss their school-provided testing. The CCC's Community Youth Program found a significant number of the first time juvenile offenders in their program had eye or hearing problems that had not been identified or properly addressed.

Fight Crime: Invest In Kids Illinois

The Chicago Crime Commission endorses the following initiatives:

Fight Crime: Invest in Kids Illinois is an anti-crime organization made up of leading police chiefs, sheriffs, state's attorneys, crime victims and leaders of police officer organizations. It is a joint project of the Illinois Center for Violence Prevention and Fight Crime: Invest in Kids. The group recommends four steps for combating youth violence:

■ Assure all school-age children and teens access to after-school, weekend and summer youth development programs to shut down the "prime time for juvenile crime."

■ Assure all babies and preschool children access to early childhood care and school readiness programs proven to cut crime.

■ Help parents, early childhood caregivers and schools identify and assist troubled and disruptive children at an early age, and provide children and their parents the counseling and training that can help equip kids with the social emotional skills needed for success.

■ Prevent child abuse and neglect by a) providing resources and well-trained child protective services to safeguard endangered children and b) offering high-risk parents the in-home parent-coaching programs proven to cut in half abuse, neglect and subsequent teen delinquency.

Corporate and Business Community

■ Phone companies should, as part of their corporate giving strategies, detail at least one staff person to work with police.

■ Phone companies should stop selling 200 numbers. Buyers can then resell these numbers, making it difficult for police to find phone subscriber information for these numbers.

■ Encourage photo labs and stores to report to police criminal activity evidenced in photos.

■ Provide financial support to Project Safe Neighborhoods. Donations in support of the Community Engagement Plan for PSN can be made to the Chicago Crime Commission. (see page 267 for additional information). The PSN program has led to homicide drops of 38% in gang-ridden, pilot areas.

■ Encourage statutes that would end the use of telephone party lines for criminal gang activity.

■ Encourage radio and television companies to choose not to promote violent street gang-promoting music and visual scenes.

■ Encourage retail stores to choose not to sell video games that glorify criminal and gang activity.

■ Encourage business insurers to require or provide incentives for 24 hour businesses to have an exterior video surveillance system.

Parents, Schools and Communities

■ Encourage enhanced one-on-one adult support and supervision of children through relationships with mentors, faith community leaders, sports coaches, school counselors, etc. It is important to meet and know the adults who spend time with your child and secure a background check on these adults whenever possible to ensure the child's safety when with his or her mentor.

■ Like the Chicago Public Schools, suburban school security should work with their local police departments to explore the possibility of using the I-CLEAR crime information system for securing gang-related information.

■ If resources permit, schools should consider hiring a Community Liaison in order to link children with needed services not offered in the school itself.

■ See Section Seven: Gangs In Schools for additional assistance and information.

SECTION 13

Directories For Assistance

AVOIDING INVOLVEMENT OR GETTING OUT OF THE GANG

Young people are not the enemy. Our enemy is the criminal gang culture and life that takes hold of our youth and often leads to their injury, death or imprisonment. Too many children fall prey to the lure of gangs while looking for a sense of family, power, money, perceived safety, or some other need or want. Adults (and youth) can make a difference in their young lives, before or after a child has gotten involved with gang life. Young people, whether in school, at home, on the streets or in the correctional facilities can find positive opportunities and meaning in their lives if we: 1) provide effective and consistent caring; 2) provide meaningful and reasonable consequences for delinquency or serious crime; and 3) work to fill the most basic needs of young people — health, education, job opportunities and training, and social skills and services. All sectors of our community — youth groups, parents and caretakers, schools, the business sector, health facilities, law enforcement, criminal justice agencies, social service organizations, and the faith community — must work together to prevent, intervene and respond.

DIRECTORIES FOR ASSISTANCE & ACTION

Chicago Area Community and Youth Services

There are many agencies in the Chicago Metropolitan area that may provide the services a young person needs. The following is only a brief listing of some of these agencies.

Back of the Yards 773-523-4416
The Back of the Yards community is located on Chicago's Southwest Side, next to, or in "back of" the Union Stockyards, which operated from 1865 until 1965. The BYNC provides many programs and services to improve the quality of life for area residents including after-school tutoring, arts and crafts, and Mexican folkloric dance for students; a free shuttle bus service and home repair program for senior citizens; and an employment placement service, ESL, and GED classes for all area residents. The BYNC is also a leading economic development organization, creating thousands of new jobs by working with area industrial and retail businesses.

Boys and Girls Clubs of Chicago . . .312-235-8000
The mission of the Boys and Girls Clubs of Chicago is to inspire and enable all young people, especially those from disadvantaged circumstances, to realize their full potential as productive, responsible and caring citizens. They serve more than 17,500 young people per year after school and during the summer through 28 Clubs and 10 child care facilities throughout the Chicago area.

Bridge Youth and Family Services . .847-359-7490

B.U.I.L.D., Inc. 773-227-2880
Founded in 1969 as a gang intervention program working with teens in one Chicago neighborhood, BUILD now serves youth, ages 8 to 21, in eight communities with intervention, prevention, and college/career prep programs. In their rehabilitation program at the Detention Center, BUILD has an impact on youth throughout Cook County. BUILD also networks with agencies on a citywide basis and engages parents and others through a community outreach program that informs, supports and coordinates local adults in addressing gang and violence issues.

Chicago Area Project 312-663-3574
The Chicago Area Project was created in the 1930s by the sociologist Clifford R. Shaw to address the

problems of juvenile delinquency in some of the poorest communities in Chicago. The values and philosophy of CAP are centered around improving the quality of neighborhood life with a special focus on solving problems faced by young people and their families. Through its many affiliate programs, CAP provides direct services to diverse communities throughout Cook County. Through its community based affiliate organizations and special projects, the CAP staff collectively provides human and financial resources to its affiliates to promote leadership in youth, their parents and their entire community.

Chicago Park District 312-747-2200

Chicago Youth for Christ 630-588-0700
One CYC program, the MCYFC Juvenile Justice Ministry, is a mentoring program to teens in the criminal justice system and their peers in the community. Beginning with a moral and spiritual perspective, they seek to build into their lives a foundation for responsible family relationships, education and employment. The program cooperates with chaplains, probation and parole authorities and has had success in redirecting the lives of gang-involved young people.

**Latino Organization
of the Southwest** 773-925-0397

Lincoln's ChalleNGe Academy 800-851-2166
The purpose of the original Youth Challenge pilot program was to determine if life coping skills and employability of a high school dropout could be significantly improved through participation in a life skills program using a military model. Currently, 25 states are operating Youth Challenge Programs. Illinois has the largest program with an annual target of 800 graduates. Where traditional educational methods have failed, the Lincoln's ChalleNGe Academy has succeeded and proved to be a tremendous alternative for young people who have the ability to excel, but need an intensive, structured environment. The 8-core objectives for cadets attending the Academy are as follows: academic excellence; job skills; physical fitness; leadership/ followership; health, sex education & nutrition; life coping skills; responsible citizenship; and community service.

Metropolitan Family Services 312-986-4000

Northwest Youth Outreach 773-777-6377

Safer Foundation 312-922-2200
The mission of the Safer Foundation is to reduce recidivism by supporting, through a full spectrum of services, the efforts of former offenders, to become productive, law-abiding members of the community.

Southwest Youth Collaborative 773-476-3534
The Southwest Youth Collaborative (SWYC) is a community-based network of youth and community development organizations working together in five diverse neighborhoods on the southwest side of Chicago: Chicago Lawn, West Lawn, West Englewood, Gage Park and West Elsdon. Each year, SWYC enrolls approximately 400 youth in after-school and summer programs at three sites: SWYC Community Center at 6400 S. Kedzie, Greater Lawn Community Youth Network at 3500 W. 63rd Place, and Gage Park High School at 5630 S. Rockwell.

**Spectrum Youth and
Family Services** 847-884-6212

United Way – Suburban Chicago . . .312-242-2540

General Phone Numbers For Assistance

Bureau of Alcohol, Tobacco Firearms & Explosives (ATF)
Chicago Field Office 312-846-7200

Chicago Crime Commission 312-372-0101

City of Chicago
Graffiti Hotline/
Graffiti Blasters 312-744-1234

Mayor's Office of Inquiry
and Information 312-744-5000

Department of Human Services
24 Hour Help Line 312-744-5829
Chicago For Youth 312-744-3911
Teen Living/Shelter 773-548-4443

Chicago Police Department
Crack Hotline 800-CRACK 44
Preventive Program Division 312-745-5823
312-745-5838
Gun Workshops 312-745-5490
Anti-Gun Enforcement 877-CPD-GUNS
Gang Hotline 312-746-GANG
Report Crimes in Progress
in Chicago 911

Chicago Public Schools
Violence Prevention Hotline 888-881-0606
Crisis Intervention Hotline 773-553-4444
Gang Hotline 773-535-SAFE

Cook County Gang Hotline 773-890-3454

Cook County Sheriff's Office
Community Relations Unit 708-865-4776
Office of Preventive
Programs 708-974-6060
Police Department 708-865-4700
Gang Crime/Narcotics Unit 708-865-4745

Cook County State's Attorney's Office
Victim/Witness Assistance Unit . . .312-890-7200
Community Outreach 312-603-8710

Crime Stoppers 800-535-STOP

**Report Dog Fighting Tips
in Cook County** 800-535-STOP
(possible reward)

**Drug Addiction Crisis
& Referral Hotline** 800-758-5877

**Drug Enforcement Administration (DEA) –
Chicago Office** 312-353-7875

Federal Bureau of Investigations
Chicago Office 312-421-6700

Gang Outreach (Tattoo Removal) . .847-249-0558

HIDTA (Chicago) 312-603-8000

**Illinois Criminal Justice
Information Authority** 312-793-8550

**Illinois Department of Children
& Family Services**
Child Abuse Reporting Hotline . . .800-252-2873

**Illinois Department of Alcohol
and Substance Abuse** 312-814-3840

Illinois State Police
Public Information Office 217-782-6637

Marijuana Anonymous 800-766-6779

Narcotics Anonymous 818-773-9999

**National Alcohol and Substance
Abuse Information Center** 800-784-6776

**National Center for Victims
of Crime** 202-467-8700

National Cocaine Hotline 800-COCAINE

**National Crime Prevention
Council** 202-466-NCPC

National Drug Abuse Hotline 800-662-4357

**National Gang Crime
Research Center** 708-258-9111

National Runaway Switch Board . . .800-621-4000

National Treatment Referral 800-375-4577

**United State's Attorney's Office,
Northern District of Illinois** 312-353-5300

**U.S. Department of Education/
Schools Without Drugs** 800-624-0100

Law Enforcement Directory & Gang Listings by Suburb

No Survey was returned from this department.

*Addison Police Department
131 W. Lake Street
Addison, Illinois 60101
(630) 543-3080

Primary Area Gangs:	Emerging Gangs:
No response to survey	No response to survey

Algonquin Police Department
2200 Harnish Drive
Algonquin, Illinois 60102
(847) 658-4531

Primary Area Gangs:	Emerging Gangs:
Latin Kings	Sureno 13
Gangster Disciples	Skin Head
Vice Lords	Norteno 14
Simon City Royals	
Imperial Gangsters	
Skin Head	
Outlaws M.C.	
Spanish Gangster Disciples	
Norteno 14	
Future Stones	
Sureno 13	

Alsip Police Department
4500 W. 123rd Street
Alsip, Illinios 60658
(708) 385-6902

Primary Area Gangs:	Emerging Gangs:
Latin Kings	Satan Disciples
Gangster Disciples	
Satan Disciples	
Vice Lords	
Black Gangster Disciples	

Antioch Police
433 Orchard Street
Antioch, Ilinois 60002
(847) 395-8585

Primary Area Gangs:	Emerging Gangs:
None	None

Arlington Heights Police Department
33 S. Arlington Heights Road
Arlington Heights, Illinois 60005
(847) 368-5300

Primary Area Gangs:	Emerging Gangs:
Sureno 13	None
Latin Kings	
Spanish Gangster Disciples	
Gangster Disciples	

Bensenville Police Department
100 N. Church Rd.
Bensenville, Illinois 60106
(630) 350-3455

Primary Area Gangs:	Emerging Gangs:
Sureno 13	None
Latin Kings	
Insane Dragons	
Latin Counts	
Spanish Cobras	

Aurora Police Department
350 N. River Street
Aurora, Illinois 60506
(630) 859-1700

Primary Area Gangs:	Emerging Gangs:
Latin Kigs	Sureno 13
Vice Lords	
Gangster Disciples	
Insane Deuces	
Maniac Latin Disciples	
Sureno 13	
Ambrose	
Satan Disciples	
Latin Homeboys	

* Bannockburn Police Department
227 Telegraph Road
Bannockburn, Illinois 60015
(847) 945-2151

Primary Area Gangs:	Emerging Gangs:
No response to survey	No response to survey

* Barrington Hills Police Department
112 Algonquin Road
Barrington Hills, Illinois 60010
(847) 551-3006

Primary Area Gangs:	Emerging Gangs:
No response to survey	No response to survey

* Barrington Police Department
121 W. Station Street
Barrington, Illinois 60010
(847) 381-2141

Primary Area Gangs:	Emerging Gangs:
No response to survey	No response to survey

* Bartlett Police Department
228 S. Main Street
Bartlett, Illinois 60103
(630) 837-0846

Primary Area Gangs:	Emerging Gangs:
No response to survey	No response to survey

Batavia Police Department
100 N. Island Avenue
Batavia, Illinois 60510
(630) 879-2840

Primary Area Gangs:	Emerging Gangs:
No response to survey	No response to survey

Beecher Police Department
724 Penfield Street Box 1114
Beecher, Illinois 60401
(708) 946-6388

Primary Area Gangs:	Emerging Gangs:
No response to survey	No response to survey

Bellwood Police Department
3200 Washington Blvd.
Bellwood, Illinois 60104
(708) 547-3534

Primary Area Gangs:	Emerging Gangs:
No response to survey	No response to survey

Bensenville Police Department
100 N. Church Road
Bensenville, Illinois 60106
(630) 350-3455

Primary Area Gangs:	Emerging Gangs:
Sureno 13	Insane Dragons
Latin Kings	
Insane Dragons	
Latin Counts	
Spanish Cobras	

Berkley Police Department
5819 Electric Avenue
Berkley, Illinois 60163
(708) 449-8226

Primary Area Gangs:	Emerging Gangs:
Latin Kings	None
Disciples	
Vice Lords	
Four Corner Hustlers	

Berwyn Police Department
6401 W. 31st Street
Berwyn, Illinois 60402
(708) 795-5600

Primary Area Gangs:	Emerging Gangs:
Two-Sixers	4th Generation
Messiahs	
Latin Kings	
Pachucos	
Latin Counts	
12th Street Players	
4th Generation Messiahs	
Two-Two Boys	
Satan Disciples	
Insane Unknowns	
Maniac Latin Disciples	

Bloomingdale Police Department
201 S. Bloomingdale Road
Bloomingdale, Illinois 60108
(630) 529-9868

Primary Area Gangs:	Emerging Gangs:
Latin Kings	None
Gangster Disciples	

Blue Island Police Department
13031 S. Greenwood Ave.
Blue Island, Illinois 60406
(708) 597-8601

Primary Area Gangs:	Emerging Gangs:
No response to survey	No response to survey

Bolingbrook Police Department
375 W. Briarcliff
Bolingbrook, Illinois 60440
(630) 226-8600

Primary Area Gangs:	Emerging Gangs:
No response to survey	No response to survey

Braidwood Police Department
101 E. Main Street
Braidwood, Illinois 60408
(815) 458-2342

Primary Area Gangs:	Emerging Gangs:
No response to survey	No response to survey

Bridgeview Police Department
7500 S. Oketo Avenue
Bridgeview, Illinois 60455
(708) 458-2135

Primary Area Gangs:	Emerging Gangs:
No response to survey	No response to survey

Broadview Police Department
2350 S. 25th Avenue
Broadview, Illinois 60155
(708) 345-6550

Primary Area Gangs:
Vice Lords
Gangster Disciples

Emerging Gangs:
None

---

* Brookfield Police Department
8820 Brookfield Avenue
Brookfield, Illinois 60513
(708) 485-8131

Primary Area Gangs:
No response to survey

Emerging Gangs:
No response to survey

Buffalo Grove Police Department
46 Raupp Blvd.
Buffalo Grove, Illinois 60089
(847) 459-2560

Primary Area Gangs:
Latin Kings
Satan Gangster Disciples

Emerging Gangs:
None

Burbank Police Department
5650 W. 75th Place
Burbank, Illinois 60459
(708) 924-7300

Primary Area Gangs:
Ambrose
Satan Disciples
Latin Kings
Two-Sixers
Gangster Disciples
La Raza

Emerging Gangs:
Hells Angels
OutLaws

---

* Burnham Police Department
14450 Manistee Ave
Burnham, Illinois 60633
(708) 891-2122

Primary Area Gangs:
No response to survey

Emerging Gangs:
No response to survey

Burr Ridge Police Department
7660 County Line Road
Burr Ridge, Illinois 60521
(630) 323-8181

Primary Area Gangs:
None

Emerging Gangs:
None

---

* Calumet City Police Department
1200 Pulaski Road
Calumet City, Illinois 60409
(708) 868-2500

Primary Area Gangs:
No response to survey

Emerging Gangs:
No response to survey

Calumet Park Police Department
12409 S. Throop Street
Calumet Park, Illinois 60643
(708) 385-6863

Primary Area Gangs:
None

Emerging Gangs:
None

---

* Carol Stream Police Department
500 N. Gary Avenue
Carol Stream, Illinois, 60188
(630) 668-2167

Primary Area Gangs:
No response to survey

Emerging Gangs:
No response to survey

---

* Carpentersville Police Department
1200 L.W. Besinger Drive
Carpentersville, Illinois 60110
(847) 551-3481

Primary Area Gangs:
No response to survey

Emerging Gangs:
No response to survey

---

* Cary Police Department
255 Stonegate Road
Cary, Illinois 60013
(847) 639-2341

Primary Area Gangs:
No response to survey

Emerging Gangs:
No response to survey

---

* Channanhon Police Department
2441 West Eames
Channanhon, Illinois 60410
(815) 467-5152

Primary Area Gangs:
No response to survey

Emerging Gangs:
No response to survey

---

* Chicago Heights Police Department
1601 Halstead Street
Heights, Illinois 60411
(708) 756-6729

Primary Area Gangs:
No response to survey

Emerging Gangs:
No response to survey

---

* Chicago Ridge Police Department
10501 S. Oxford Avenue
Chicago Ridge, Illinois 60415
(708) 425-7831

Primary Area Gangs:
No response to survey

Emerging Gangs:
No response to survey

Cicero Police Department
4932 W. 25th Place
Cicero, Illinois 60650
(708) 652-2130

Primary Area Gangs:	Emerging Gangs:
Latin Kings	Sureno 13
Two-Sixers	4th Generation
Messiahs	
La Raza	
Satan Disciples	
Maniac Latin Disciples	
Gangster Disciples	
Insane Two-Two Boys	
Latin Counts	
Ashland Vikings	
Latin Angles	
Sureno 13	
4th Generation Messiahs	

* Clarendon Hills Police Department
201 Burlington
Clarendon Hills, Illinois 60514
(630) 323-2152

Primary Area Gangs:	Emerging Gangs:
No response to survey	No response to survey

Coal City Police Department
545 S. Broadway
Coal City, Illinois 60416
(815) 634-2341

Primary Area Gangs:	Emerging Gangs:
Latin Kings	None
Latin Counts	
Outlaws	
Vice Lords	

* College of Dupage Police Department
Department of Public Safety Lambert Road
Glen Ellyn, Illinois 60137
(630) 942-2000

Primary Area Gangs:	Emerging Gangs:
No response to survey	No response to survey

* Country Club Hills Police Department
3700 West 175th Place
Hills, Illinois 60478
(708) 798-3191

Primary Area Gangs:	Emerging Gangs:
No response to survey	No response to survey

Countryside Police Department
5550 East Ave.
Countryside, Illinois 60525
(708) 352-2171

Primary Area Gangs:	Emerging Gangs:
Latin Kings	None
Simon City Royals	

* Crest Hill Police Department
1610 Plainfield Road
Crest Hill, Illinois 60435
(815) 741-5111

Primary Area Gangs:	Emerging Gangs:
No response to survey	No response to survey

* Crestwood Police Department
13840 S. Cicero Ave
Crestwood, Illinois 60445
(708) 371-4800

Primary Area Gangs:	Emerging Gangs:
No response to survey	No response to survey

Crete Police Department
1370 Benton Street
Crete, Illinois 60417
(708) 672-0912

Primary Area Gangs:	Emerging Gangs:
Gangster Disciples	None
Latin Counts	
Latin Kings	
Vice Lords	
Four Corner Hustlers	

* Crystal Lake Police Department
100 West Municipal Complex Drive
Crystal Lake, Illinois 60014
(815) 459-2020

Primary Area Gangs:	Emerging Gangs:
No response to survey	No response to survey

* Darien Police Department
1702 Plainfield Road
Darien, Illinois 60561
(630) 970-3999

Primary Area Gangs:	Emerging Gangs:
No response to survey	No response to survey

Deerfield Police Department
850 Waukegan Road
Deerfield, Illinois 60015
(847) 945-8636

Primary Area Gangs:	Emerging Gangs:
Spanish Gangster Disciples	None
Latin Kings	
Vice Lords	
Black Pistons Nation	
Gangster Disciples	

DeKalb Police Department
200 S. 4th Street
DeKalb, Illinois 60115
(815) 748-8400

Primary Area Gangs:	Emerging Gangs:
Ambrose	Latin Saints
Latin Kings	
Latin Saints	
Insane Deuces	

* Des Plaines Police Department
1420 East Minor Street
Des Plaines, Illinois 60016
(847) 391-5400

Primary Area Gangs:	Emerging Gangs:
No response to survey	No response to survey

Dixmoor Police Department
170 W. 145th Street
Dixmoor, Illinois 60426
(708) 388-3340

Primary Area Gangs:	Emerging Gangs:
Gangster Disciples	Outlaw/Vice Lords
Vice Lords	
Latin Kings	
Satan Disciples	

* Dolton Police Department
4030 Park Ave
Dolton, Illinois 60419
(708) 847-2533

Primary Area Gangs:	Emerging Gangs:
No response to survey	No response to survey

Downers Grove Police Department
825 Burlington Avenue
Downers Grove, Illinois 60515
(630) 434-5695

Primary Area Gangs:	Emerging Gangs:
Insane Popes	None
Imperial Gangster	
Vice Lords	
Two-Six Boys	
Gangster Disciples	
Latin Kings	
Thirteens	

* East Dundee Police Department
120 Barington Ave
East Dundee, Illinois 60118
(847) 428-4034

Primary Area Gangs:	Emerging Gangs:
No response to survey	No response to survey

*East Hazel Crest Police Department
17223 S. Troop Street
Crest, Illinois 60429
(708) 798-2186

Primary Area Gangs:	Emerging Gangs:
No response to survey	No response to survey

Elburn Police Department
301 East North Street
Elburn, Illinois 60119
(630) 365 – 5070

Primary Area Gangs:	Emerging Gangs:
Latin Counts	None
Satan Disciples	

Elgin Police Department
151 Douglas Ave.
Elgin, Illinois 60120
(847) 289-2691

Primary Area Gangs:	Emerging Gangs:
Latin Kings	None
Fourteens	
Thirteens	
Maniac Latin Disciples	
Gangster Disciples	
Spanish Gangster Disciples	
Insance Deuces	
La Raza	
Spanish Cobras	
Vice Lords	

Elk Grove Police Department
901 Wellington Ave.
Elk Grove, Illinois 60007
(847) 357-4169

Primary Area Gangs:	Emerging Gangs:
Latin Kings	None
Two-Six Boys	
Gangster Disciples	

* Elmhurst Police Department
125 East First Street
Elmhurst, Illinois 60126
(630) 530-3050

Primary Area Gangs:	Emerging Gangs:
No response to survey	No response to survey

* Elmwood Park Police Department
11 Conti Parkway
Elmwood, Illinois 60635
(708) 453-2147

Primary Area Gangs:	Emerging Gangs:
No response to survey	No response to survey

Evanston Police Department
1454 Elmwood Ave.
Evanston, Illinois 60201
(847) 866-5048

Primary Area Gangs:	Emerging Gangs:
Gangster Disciples	Bloods
Black P Stones	
Latin Kings	
Vice Lords	
Four Corner Hustlers	
Bloods	

Evergreen Park Police Department
9420 S. Kedzie Ave
Evergreen Park, Illinois 60642
(708) 422-2142

Primary Area Gangs:	Emerging Gangs:
Gangster Disciples	None
Latin Kings	
Four Corner Hustlers	
Ambrose	
Satan Disciples	
Vice Lords	

Flossmoor Police Department
2800 Flossmoor Road
Flossmoor, Illinois 60422
(708) 957-4500

Primary Area Gangs:	Emerging Gangs:
Gangster Disciples	None
Latin Kings	
Black Disciples	
Four Corner Hustlers	

* Ford Heights Police Department
1343 Ellis Avenue
Ford Heights, Illinois 60411
(708) 758-3441

Primary Area Gangs:	Emerging Gangs:
No response to survey	No response to survey

* Forest Park Police Department
517 Des Plaines Avenue
Forest Park, Illinois 60130
(708) 366-2425

Primary Area Gangs:	Emerging Gangs:
No response to survey	No response to survey

* Forestview Police Department
7000 W. 46th Street
Forestview, Illinois 60402
(708) 788-0318

Primary Area Gangs:	Emerging Gangs:
No response to survey	No response to survey

* Fox Lake Police Department
301 S. Route 59
Fox Lake, Illinois 60020
(847) 587-3100

Primary Area Gangs:	Emerging Gangs:
No response to survey	No response to survey

* Fox River Grove Police Department
408 North West Highway
Fox River Grove, Illinois 60021
(847) 639-2411

Primary Area Gangs:	Emerging Gangs:
No response to survey	No response to survey

* Frankfort Police Department
14 S. Hickory Street
Frankfort, Illinois 60423
(815) 469-9435

Primary Area Gangs:	Emerging Gangs:
No response to survey	No response to survey

* Franklin Police Department
9545 West Belmont Avenue
Franklin Park, Illinois 60131
(847) 671-8200

Primary Area Gangs:	Emerging Gangs:
No response to survey	No response to survey

* Geneva Police Department
20 Police Plaza
Geneva, Illinois 60134
(630) 232-4736

Primary Area Gangs:	Emerging Gangs:
No response to survey	No response to survey

* Glen Ellyn Police Department
535 Duane Street
Glen Ellyn, Illinois 60137
(630) 469-1187

Primary Area Gangs:	Emerging Gangs:
No response to survey	No response to survey

*Glencoe Police Department
325 Hazel Avenue
Glencoe, Illinois 60022
(847) 835-4112

Primary Area Gangs:	Emerging Gangs:
No response to survey	No response to survey

Section Thirteen *(side tab)*

* Glendale Heights Police Department
300 Civic Center Plaza
Heights, Illinois 60139
(630) 260-6070

Primary Area Gangs:
No response to survey

Emerging Gangs:
No response to survey

* Glenview Police Department
1215 Waukegan Road
Glenview, Illinois 3082
(847) 729-5000

Primary Area Gangs:
No response to survey

Emerging Gangs:
No response to survey

* Glenwood Police Department
1 S. Rebecca
Glenwood, Illinois 60425
(708) 753-2420

Primary Area Gangs:
No response to survey

Emerging Gangs:
No response to survey

Grayslake Police Department
33 S. Whitney Street
Grayslake, Illinois 60030
(847) 223-2341

Primary Area Gangs:
Latin Kings
Sureno 13
Vice Lords
Gangster Disciples
Maniac Latin Disciples
Orchestra Albany
Bikers
Aryan Brothershood

Emerging Gangs:
None

* Gurnee Police Department
4587 Grand Avenue
Gurnee, Illinois 60031
(847) 244-8640

Primary Area Gangs:
No response to survey

Emerging Gangs:
No response to survey

Hanover Park Police Department
2121 W. Lake Street
Hanover Park, Illinois 60103
(630) 372-4400

Primary Area Gangs:
Latin Kings
Thirteens
La Raza
Gangster Disciples

Emerging Gangs:
None

Harvard Police Department
201 W. Front Street
Harvard, Illinois 60033
(815) 943-4431

Primary Area Gangs:
Latin Kings
Dragons
Sureno 13
Gangster Disciples
Norteno 14
Vice Lords

Emerging Gangs:
None

* Harvey Police Department
15301 S. Dixie Highway
Harvey, Illinois 60426
(708) 331-3030

Primary Area Gangs:
No response to survey

Emerging Gangs:
No response to survey

Harwood Heights Police Department
7300 W. Wilson
Harwood Heights, Illinois 60656
(708) 867-4353

Primary Area Gangs:
Latin Kings
Latin Pacnuces
Insane Deuces
Satan Disciples

Emerging Gangs:
Sureno 13

* Hawthorn Woods Police Department
2 Lagoon Drive
Woods, Illinois 60047
(847) 438-9050

Primary Area Gangs:
No response to survey

Emerging Gangs:
No response to survey

* Hazel Crest Police Department
3000 w 170th Place
Hazel Crest, Illinois 60429
(708) 335-9640

Primary Area Gangs:
No response to survey

Emerging Gangs:
No response to survey

* Hickory Hills Police Department
8652 W. 95th Street
Hickory Hills, Illinois 60457
(708) 598-4900

Primary Area Gangs:
No response to survey

Emerging Gangs:
No response to survey

Highland Park Police Department
1677 Old Deerfield Road
Highland Park, Illinois 60035
(847) 432-7730

Primary Area Gangs:
Spanish Gangster Disciples
Latin Kings
Sureno 13

Emerging Gangs:
Sureno 13

* Highwood Police Department
17 Highwood avenue
Highwood, Illinois 60040
(847) 432-2152

Primary Area Gangs:
No response to survey

Emerging Gangs:
No response to survey

* Hillside Police Department
30 N. Wolf Road
Hillside, Illinois 60162
(708) 449-8851

Primary Area Gangs:
No response to survey

Emerging Gangs:
No response to survey

Hinsdale Police Department
121 Symonds Drive
Hinsdale, Illinois 60521
(630) 789-7070

Primary Area Gangs:
Latin Kings
Black Gangster Disciples
Two-Sixers
Origional Crew

Emerging Gangs:
Original Crew

Hodgskins Police Department
6015 Lenz Avenue
Hodgskins, Illinois 60525
(708) 354-4623

Primary Area Gangs:
Latin Kings
Sureno 13

Emerging Gangs:
None

Hoffman Estates Police Department
1200 N. Gannon Drive
Hoffman Estates, Illinois 60195
(847) 882-1818

Primary Area Gangs:
Gangster Disciples
Black P Stone
Latin Counts
La Raza
Latin Kings
Two-Sixers
Vice Lords
Sureno 13
Spanish Cobras

Emerging Gangs:
Sureno 13

* Hometown Police Department
4331 South west Highway
Hometown, Illinois 60456
(708) 422-2188

Primary Area Gangs:
No response to survey

Emerging Gangs:
No response to survey

* Homewood Police Department
17950 Dixie Highway
Homewood, Illinois 60430
(708) 798-2131

Primary Area Gangs:
No response to survey

Emerging Gangs:
No response to survey

* Huntley Police Department
11704 Coral street
Huntley, Illinois 60142
(847) 669-2141

Primary Area Gangs:
No response to survey

Emerging Gangs:
No response to survey

* Island Lake Police Department
P.O. Box 450
Island Lake, Illinois 60042
(847) 526-2100

Primary Area Gangs:
No response to survey

Emerging Gangs:
No response to survey

* Itasca Police Department
411 N Prospect Avenue
Itasca, Illinois 60143
(630) 773-1004

Primary Area Gangs:
No response to survey

Emerging Gangs:
No response to survey

*Joliet Police Department
150 West Jefferson
Joliet, Illinois 60431
(815) 726-2491

Primary Area Gangs:
No response to survey

Emerging Gangs:
No response to survey

* Justice Police Department
7800 S. Archer Road
Justice, Illinois 60458
(708) 548-2191

Primary Area Gangs:
No response to survey

Emerging Gangs:
No response to survey

* Kenilworth Police Department

419 Richmond Road
Kenilworth, Illinois 60043
(847) 254-2141

Primary Area Gangs:
No response to survey

Emerging Gangs:
No response to survey

* Kildeer Police Department

22049 Chestnut Ridge Road
Killdeer, Illinois 3001
(847) 438-6010

Primary Area Gangs:
No response to survey

Emerging Gangs:
No response to survey

LaGrange Park Police Department

304 W. Burlington
LaGrange Park, Illinois 60525
(708) 579-2334

Primary Area Gangs:
Latin Kings
Gangster Disciples

Emerging Gangs:
None

LaGrange Police Department

304 W. Burlington Avenue
LaGrange, Illinois 60535
(708) 579-2334

Primary Area Gangs:
Gangster Disciples
Latin Kings
Simon City Royals
Two Six Nation
Two-Two boys
Vice Lords

Emerging Gangs:
Cerano 13

Lake Forest Police Department

255 W. Deerpath
Lake Forest, Illinois 60045
(847) 234 – 2601

Primary Area Gangs:
None

Emerging Gangs:
None

* Lake In the Hills Police Department

1115 Crystal Lake Roads
Woods, Illinois 60102
(847) 658-5676

Primary Area Gangs:
No response to survey

Emerging Gangs:
No response to survey

* Lake Zurich Police Department

61 W. Main Street
Lake Zurich, Illinois 60047
(847) 438-2349

Primary Area Gangs:
No response to survey

Emerging Gangs:
No response to survey

Lansing Police Department

2710 170th Street
Lansing, Illinois 60438
(708) 895-7150

Primary Area Gangs:
Latin Counts
Gangster Disciples
Latin Kings
Vice Lords
Latin Dragons

Emerging Gangs:
None

Lemont Police Department

416 Main Street
Lemont, Illinois 60439
(630) 257 – 2228

Primary Area Gangs:
Disciples

Emerging Gangs:
Lithuanian Group
(Unknown Name)

* Libertyville Police Department

200 E. Cook Avenue
Libertyville, Illinois 60048
(847) 362-8310

Primary Area Gangs:
No response to survey

Emerging Gangs:
No response to survey

Lincolnshire Police Department

One Old Half-Day Road
Lincolnshire, Illinois 60069
(847) 883-9900

Primary Area Gangs:
Latin Kings
Gangster
AD Hoc Russian Gangsters

Emerging Gangs:
AD Hoc Russian

* Lincolnwood Police Department

6900 North Lincoln Avenue
Lincolnwood, Illinois 60646
(847) 673-2167

Primary Area Gangs:
No response to survey

Emerging Gangs:
No response to survey

*Lisle Police Department
1040 Burlington Avenue
Lisle, Illinois 60532
(630) 271-4200

Primary Area Gangs:
No response to survey

Emerging Gangs:
No response to survey

Lockport Police Department
1212 S. Farrel Road
Lockport, Illinois 60441
(815) 838-2132

Primary Area Gangs:
Gangster Disciples
Latin Kings
Four Corner Hustlers
Vice Lords
Two-Sixers

Emerging Gangs:
14th Street Posse
4 Corner Hustlers
True Players
Lockport Thugs

*Lombard Police Department
235 E. Wilson Avenue
Lombard, Illinois 60148
(630) 620-5955

Primary Area Gangs:
No response to survey

Emerging Gangs:
No response to survey

Lynwood Police Department
21460 Lincoln Highway
Lynwood, Illinois 60411
(708) 758-4744

Primary Area Gangs:
Goon Squad
Gangster Disciples
Black Peace Stones
Vice Lords

Emerging Gangs:
Goon Squad

Lyons Police Department
7801 W. Ogden Avenue
Lyons, Illinois 60534
(708) 780-5293

Primary Area Gangs:
Latin Counts
Latin Disciples
12th Street Players
Two-Six Boys
Two-Two Boys
Black Gangster Disciples
Vice Lords
Simon City Royals

Emerging Gangs:
None

Marengo Police Department
142 E. Prarie Street
Marengo, Illinois 60152
(815) 568-7231

Primary Area Gangs:
Fourteens
Latin Disciples
Gangster Disciples
Sureno 13
Latin Kings
Imperial Gangsters
Outlaws
Latin Eagles
Skin Heads
Vice Lords
Brother Motor Cycle
Sureno Locos Treces-Mexican Mafia
World Church of the Creator

Emerging Gangs:
14's
Sureno 13

*Matteson Police Department
20500 Cicero
Matteson, Illinois 60443
(708) 748-5931

Primary Area Gangs:
No response to survey

Emerging Gangs:
No response to survey

Mc Cook Police Department
5000 S. Glencoe Ave.
McCook Illinois 60525
(708) 447-1234

Primary Area Gangs:
None

Emerging Gangs:
None

*McHenry Police Department
1111 North Green Street
McHenry, Illinois 60050
(815) 363-2200

Primary Area Gangs:
No response to survey

Emerging Gangs:
No response to survey

Melrose Park Police Department
1 N. Broadway
Melrose Park, Illinois 60160
(708) 344-8409

Primary Area Gangs:
Latin Kings
Imperial Gangsters
Maniac Latin Disciples
Latin Counts
Four Corner Hustlers
Vice Lords
Gangster Disciples
Black Gangster Disciples
Satan Disciples
Ambrose

Emerging Gangs:
18th Street
Sureno 13

* Metra Police Department
547 W. Jackson Blvd
Chicago, Illinois 60661
(312) 322-2800

Primary Area Gangs:
No response to survey

Emerging Gangs:
No response to survey

* Midlothian Police Department
11004 Carpenter
Mokena, Illinois 60448
(708) 385-2534

Primary Area Gangs:
No response to survey

Emerging Gangs:
No response to survey

* Mokena Police Department
11004 Carpenter
Mokena, Illinois 60448
(708) 479-3912

Primary Area Gangs:
No response to survey

Emerging Gangs:
No response to survey

* Monee Police Department
5130 W. Court Street
Monee, Illinois 60449
(708) 534-8541

Primary Area Gangs:
No response to survey

Emerging Gangs:
No response to survey

Montgomery Police Department
10 Civic Center Ave.
Montgomery, Illinois 60538
(630) 897-8707

Primary Area Gangs:
Latin Kings
Black Gangster Disciples
Vice Lords
Ambrose
Insane Disciples
Sureno 13

Emerging Gangs:
Sureno 13

Morton Grove Police Department
6101 Capulina
Morton Grove, Illinois 60053
(847) 470-5208

Primary Area Gangs:
Gangster Disciples
Latin Kings
Aeros
Black Peace Stones
Simon City Royals

Emerging Gangs:
None

Mount Prospect Police Department
112 E. Northwest Highway
Mount Prospect, Illinois 60056
(847) 818-5247

Primary Area Gangs:
Sureno 13
Latin Kings
Satan Disciples
Cobras
Gangster Disciples
Black Gangster Disciples
Vice Lords
Imperial Gangsters
Four Corner Hustlers
Boxwood Boys

Emerging Gangs:
Boxwood Boys

Mundelein Police Department
221 N. Lake Street
Mundelein, Illinois 60060
(847) 968-4600

Primary Area Gangs:
Latin Kings
Sureno 13
Vampires
Latin Disciples

Emerging Gangs:
Vampiros

Naperville Police Department
1350 Aurora Avenue
Naperville, Illinois 60540
(630) 305 -6224

Primary Area Gangs:
Latin Counts
Sin City Boys
Sureno 13
Latin Kings
Gangster Disciples
Satan Disciples

Emerging Gangs:
Latin Counts
Sin City Boys

* New Lenox Police Department
701 W. haven Avenue
New Lenox, Illinois 60451
(815) 485-2500

Primary Area Gangs:
No response to survey

Emerging Gangs:
No response to survey

* Niles Police Department
7200 North Milwaukee Avenue
Nile, Illinois 60714
(847) 588-6500

Primary Area Gangs:
No response to survey

Emerging Gangs:
No response to survey

* Norridge Police Department
4020 N Olcott Avenue
Norridge, Illinois 60634
(708) 453-4770

Primary Area Gangs:
No response to survey

Emerging Gangs:
No response to survey

* North Aurora Police Department
25 East State Street
Aurora, Illinois 60542
(630) 897-8705

Primary Area Gangs:
No response to survey

Emerging Gangs:
No response to survey

* North Chicago Police Department
1820 North Lewis Avenue
North Chicago, Illinois 60064
(847) 596-8700

Primary Area Gangs:
No response to survey

Emerging Gangs:
No response to survey

* North Riverside Police Department
2359 S. Des Plaines Avenue
North Riverside, Illinois 60546
(708) 447-9191

Primary Area Gangs:
No response to survey

Emerging Gangs:
No response to survey

Northbrook Police Department
1401 Landwehr Road
Northbrook, Illinois 60062
(847) 564-2060

Primary Area Gangs:
Gangster Disciples
Latin Kings
Spanish Gangster Disciples

Emerging Gangs:
None

* Northfield Police Department
350 Walnut
Northfield, Illinois 60093
(847) 446-2131

Primary Area Gangs:
No response to survey

Emerging Gangs:
No response to survey

Northlake Police Department
55 E. North Avenue
Northlake, Illinois 60164
(708) 531-5752

Primary Area Gangs:
Latin Kings
Imperial Gangsters
Gangster Disciples
Vice Lords
Two-Two Boys

Emerging Gangs:
None

* Oak Brook Police Department
1200 Oak Brook Road
Oak Brook, Illinois 2255
(630) 990-3030

Primary Area Gangs:
No response to survey

Emerging Gangs:
No response to survey

* Oak Forest Police Department
15440 S. Central Avenue
Oak Forest, Illinois 60452
(708) 687-1376

Primary Area Gangs:
No response to survey

Emerging Gangs:
No response to survey

Oak Lawn Police Department
9446 S. Raymond Avenue
Oak Lawn, Illinois 60453
(708) 499-7880

Primary Area Gangs:
Satan Disciples
Two-Sixers
Latin Kings
Ambrose
La Raza
Sureno 13
TAP

Emerging Gangs:
Satan Disciples

* Oak Park Police Department
1 Village Hall Plaza
Oak Park, Illinois 60302
(708) 386-3800

Primary Area Gangs:
No response to survey

Emerging Gangs:
No response to survey

* Oakbrook Terrance Police Department
17 W. 275 Butterfield Road
Terrance, Illinois 600181
(630) 941-8320

Primary Area Gangs:
No response to survey

Emerging Gangs:
No response to survey

Orland Park Police Department
14600 S. Ravinia
Orland Park, Illinois 60462
(708) 349-4111

Primary Area Gangs:
Gangster Disciples

Emerging Gangs:
None

Palatine Police Department
200 E. Wood Street
Palatine, Illinois 60067
(847) 359-9001

Primary Area Gangs:
Latin Kings
Sureno 13
Spanish Gangster Disciples
Latin Counts
Vice Lords
Gangster Disciples

Emerging Gangs:
None

* Palos Heights Police Department
7607 W. College Drive
Palos Heights, Illinois 60463
(708) 448-5060

Primary Area Gangs:
No response to survey

Emerging Gangs:
No response to survey

* Palos Hills Police Department
8555 W. 193rd Street
Palos Hills, Illinois 60465
(708) 598-2992

Primary Area Gangs:
No response to survey

Emerging Gangs:
No response to survey

Palos Park Police Department
8999 W. 123rd Street
Palos Park, Illinois 60464
(708) 671-3770

Primary Area Gangs:
TAP
Two-Sixers
Aryan Brotherhood

Emerging Gangs:
None

Park Forest Police Department
200 Lakewood Boulevard
Park Forest, Illinois 60466
(708) 748-4700

Primary Area Gangs:
Gangster Disciples
Four Corner Hustlers
Vice Lords

Emerging Gangs:
None

Park Ridge Police Department
200 S. Vine
Park Ridge, Illinois 60068
(847) 318-5252

Primary Area Gangs:
Latin Kings
Sureno 13

Emerging Gangs:
None

* Plainfield Police Department
1400 North Division street
Plainfield, Illinois 60544
(815) 436-6544

Primary Area Gangs:
No response to survey

Emerging Gangs:
No response to survey

* Posen Police Department
2440 W. Walter Zimmy Drive
Posen, Illinois 60469
(708) 385-0277

Primary Area Gangs:
No response to survey

Emerging Gangs:
No response to survey

* Prospect Heights Police Department
1 N Elmhurst Road
Heights, Illinois 60070
(847) 398-5511

Primary Area Gangs:
No response to survey

Emerging Gangs:
No response to survey

Richton Park Police Department
4455 W. Sauk Trail
Richton Park, Illinois 60471
(708) 481-8956

Primary Area Gangs:
Gangster Disciples
Vice Lords
Four Corner Hustlers
Black Peace Stones
Right Arm CVL
Left Arm CVL

Emerging Gangs:
None

* River Forest Police Department
7810 W. Central
River Forest, Illinois 60305
(708) 366-7125

Primary Area Gangs:
No response to survey

Emerging Gangs:
No response to survey

* River Grove Police Department
2621 N Thatcher Avenue
River Grove, Illinois 60171
(708) 453-9422

Primary Area Gangs:
No response to survey

Emerging Gangs:
No response to survey

* Riverdale Police Department
14140 Tracy
Riverdale, Illinois 60627
(708) 841-2203

Primary Area Gangs:
No response to survey

Emerging Gangs:
No response to survey

Riverside Police Department
31 Riverside Road
Riverside, Illinois 60546
(708) 447-2127

Primary Area Gangs:
Latin Kings
Latin Counts
Maniac Latin Disciples
MS 13

Emerging Gangs:
MS 13

* **Robbins Police Department**
3323 W. 137th Street
Robbins, Illinois 60472
(708) 385-3121

Primary Area Gangs:
No response to survey

Emerging Gangs:
No response to survey

* **Rockdale Police Department**
79 Moen Avenue
Rockdale, Illinois 60436
(815) 725-0360

Primary Area Gangs:
No response to survey

Emerging Gangs:
No response to survey

* **Rolling Meadows Police Department**
3600 Kirchoff Road
Meadows, Illinois 60008
(847) 255-2416

Primary Area Gangs:
No response to survey

Emerging Gangs:
No response to survey

* **Romeoville Police Department**
10 Montrose Drive
Romeoville, Illinois 60441
(815) 886-7219

Primary Area Gangs:
No response to survey

Emerging Gangs:
No response to survey

* **Roselle Police Department**
103 S. Prospect
Roselle, Illinois 60172
(630) 980-2025

Primary Area Gangs:
No response to survey

Emerging Gangs:
No response to survey

* **Round Lake Beach Police Department**
916 W. Rollins Road
Beach, Illinois 60073
(847) 270-9111

Primary Area Gangs:
No response to survey

Emerging Gangs:
No response to survey

Sauk Village Police Department
21701 Torrence Avenue
Sauk Village, Illinois 60411
(708) 758-1331

Primary Area Gangs:
Vice Lords
Insane Vice Lords
Latin Kings
Four Corner Hustlers
Latin Counts
Mickey Cobras

Emerging Gangs:
Mickey Cobras
Insane Vice Lords

* **Schaumburg Police Department**
1000 W. Schaumburg Road
Schaumburg, Illinois 60194
(847) 882-3586

Primary Area Gangs:
No response to survey

Emerging Gangs:
No response to survey

* **Schiller Park Police Department**
9526 Irving Park Road
Schiller Park, Illinois 60176
(847) 678-4794

Primary Area Gangs:
None

Emerging Gangs:
None

Shorewood Police Department
903 W. Jefferson Street
Shorewood, Illinois 60435
(815) 725-1460

Primary Area Gangs:
Two-Sixers
Gangster Disciples
Vice Lords
Latin Kings

Emerging Gangs:
None

* **Skokie Police Department**
8350 Laramie Avenue
Skokie, Illinois 60077
(847) 982-5900

Primary Area Gangs:
No response to survey

Emerging Gangs:
No response to survey

* **South Barrington Police Department**
30 S. Barrington Road
Barrington, Illinois 60010
(847) 381-7511

Primary Area Gangs:
No response to survey

Emerging Gangs:
No response to survey

* South Elgin Police Department
111 West Spring Street
South Elgin, Illinos 60177
(847) 741-2151

Primary Area Gangs:
No response to survey

Emerging Gangs:
No response to survey

* South Holland Police Department
16220 Wausau Avenue
South Holland, Illinois 60473
(708) 331-3131

Primary Area Gangs:
No response to survey

Emerging Gangs:
No response to survey

* St. Charles Police Department
2 E. State Avenue
St. Charles, Illinois 60174
(630) 377-4435

Primary Area Gangs:
No response to survey

Emerging Gangs:
No response to survey

* Steger Park Police Department
35 W. 34th Street
Steger Park, Illinois 60475
(708) 754-8121

Primary Area Gangs:
No response to survey

Emerging Gangs:
No response to survey

Stickney Police Department
6533 W. Pershing Road
Stickney, Illinois 60402
(708) 788-2131

Primary Area Gangs:
Latin Counts
Two-Two Boys
Latin Kings
Two-Sixers
Insane Clown Posse
Gangster Disciples
12th Street Players
Sureno 13

Emerging Gangs:
Sureno 13

Stone Park Police Department
1629 N. Mannheim Road
Stone Park, Illinois 60165
(708) 450-3215

Primary Area Gangs:
Latin Kings
Imperial Gangsters

Emerging Gangs:
None

Streamwood Police Department
401 E. Irving Park Road
Streamwood, Illinois 60107
(630) 837-0953

Primary Area Gangs:
La Raza
Sureno 13
Latin Kings
Two-Sixers
2 - 1 Boys
Future Stones
Gangster Disciples

Emerging Gangs:
La Raza

* Summit Police Department
5810 S. Archer Road
Summit, Illinois 60501
(708) 563-4830

Primary Area Gangs:
No response to survey

Emerging Gangs:
No response to survey

* Tinley Park Police Department
17355 S. 68th Court
Tinley Park, Illinois 60477
(708) 532-9111

Primary Area Gangs:
No response to survey

Emerging Gangs:
No response to survey

* Triton College Police Department
2000 N 5th Avenue
River Grove, Illinois 60171
(708) 456-6911

Primary Area Gangs:
No response to survey

Emerging Gangs:
No response to survey

* University Park Police Department
698 Burnham Drive
University Park, Illinois 60466
(708) 534-0914

Primary Area Gangs:
No response to survey

Emerging Gangs:
No response to survey

* Vernon Hills Police Department
754 Lakeview Parkway
Vernon Hill, Illinois 60061
(847) 362-4449

Primary Area Gangs:
No response to survey

Emerging Gangs:
No response to survey

* Villa Park Police Department
11 West Home Avenue
Villa Park, Illinois 60181
(630) 834-7447

Primary Area Gangs:
No response to survey

Emerging Gangs:
No response to survey

Warrenville Police Department
3S245 Warren Avenue
Warrenville, Illinois 60555
(630) 393-2131

Primary Area Gangs:
None

Emerging Gangs:
None

Waukegan Police Department
13 N. Genesee Street
Waukegan, Illinois 60085
(847) 599-2827

Primary Area Gangs:
Latin Kings
Satan Disciples
Insane Unknowns
Renegade Disciples
Sureno 13
Maniac Latin Disciples
Vice Lords
Gangster Disciples
Four Corner Hustlers
Latin Lovers
Orchestra Albany

Emerging Gangs:
Sureno 13
Renegade Disciples

***Wayne Police Department**
5 N. 430 Rail Street
Wayne, Illinois 60184
(630) 584-3031

Primary Area Gangs:
No response to survey

Emerging Gangs:
No response to survey

West Chicago Police Department
325 Spencer Street
West Chicago, Illinois 60185
(630) 293-2222

Primary Area Gangs:
Sureno 13
Latin Counts
18th Street

Emerging Gangs:
None

***West Dundee Police Department**
555 S. Eight Street
West Dundee, Illinois 60118
(847) 428-8784

Primary Area Gangs:
No response to survey

Emerging Gangs:
No response to survey

Westchester Police Department
10300 Roosevelt Road
Westchester, Illinois 60154
(708) 345-0060

Primary Area Gangs:
Insane Popes
Four Corner Hustlers
Messiahs
Latin Kings
4th Generation Messiahs

Emerging Gangs:
Insane Popes
4th Generation

Western Springs Police Department
740 Hill Grove Avenue
Springs, Illinois 60558
(708) 246-8540

Primary Area Gangs:
Lenzi Latin Kings
Ganster Disciples
Latin Counts
Imperial Gangsters
Two-Sixers
4 Corner Hustlers
Insane Popes
ICP
G Unit Girls
Latin Queens

Emerging Gangs:
G Unit Girls
Imperial Gangsters

Westmont Police Department
500 N. Cass Avenue
Westmont, Illinois 60559
(630) 968-2152

Primary Area Gangs:
Latin Kings
Vice Lords
Sureno 13
Black Gangster Disciples

Emerging Gangs:
MS 13

Wheaton Police Department
900 W. Liberty Drive
Wheaton, Illinois 60187
(630) 260-2161

Primary Area Gangs:
Latin Kings
Thirteens
MS-13's
Sin City Boyz
Two-Sixers
18's
Latin Counts
Gangster Disciples
Vice Lords
Fourteens

Emerging Gangs:
MS 13

Wheeling Police Department
255 W. Dundee Road
Wheeling, Illinois 60090
(847) 459-2675

Primary Area Gangs:	Emerging Gangs:
Spanish Gangster Disciples	Latin Counts
Sureno 13	Black Peace Stones
Gangster Disciples	Brazers
Latin Kings	
Boxwood Boys	
Two-Sixers	

* Willow Springs Police Department
8480 S. Archer Avenue
Willow Springs, Illinois 60480
(708) 839-3023

Primary Area Gangs:	Emerging Gangs:
No response to survey	No response to survey

* Willowbrook Police Department
7760 Quincy Street
Willowbrook, Illinois 60521
(630) 325-2808

Primary Area Gangs:	Emerging Gangs:
No response to survey	No response to survey

Wilmette Police Department
710 Ridge Road
Wilmette, Illinois 60091
(847) 256-1200

Primary Area Gangs:	Emerging Gangs:
Four Corner Hustlers	None
Gangster Disciples	
Latin Kings	

Wilmington Police Department
120 N. Main Street
Wilmington, Illinois 60481
(815) 476-2811

Primary Area Gangs:	Emerging Gangs:
Two – Sixers	None

*Winfield Police Department
27 W. 463 Jewell Road
Winfield, Illinois 60190
(630) 933-7160

Primary Area Gangs:	Emerging Gangs:
No response to survey	No response to survey

* Winnetka Police Department
410 Green bay Road
Winnetka, Illinois 60093
(847) 501-6034

Primary Area Gangs:	Emerging Gangs:
No response to survey	No response to survey

Wood Dale Police Department
404 N. Wood Dale Road
Wood Dale, Illinois 60191
(630) 766-2060

Primary Area Gangs:	Emerging Gangs:
No response to survey	No response to survey

Woodridge Police Department
1 Plaza Drive
Woodridge, Illinois 60517
(630) 719-4740

Primary Area Gangs:	Emerging Gangs:
Ganster Disciples	None
Four Corner Hustlers	
Latin Kings	
Vice Lords	

Woodstock Police Department
656 Lake Ave
Woodstock, Illinois 60098
(815) 338-6787

Primary Area Gangs:	Emerging Gangs:
Latin Kings	None
Fourteens	
Sureno 13	
Black Gangster Disciples	

* Worth Police Department
7112 W. 111th Street
Worth, Illinois 60482
(708) 448-3979

Primary Area Gangs:	Emerging Gangs:
No response to survey	No response to survey

Zion Police Department
2101 Salem Blvd.
Zion, Il 60099
(847) 872-8000

Primary Area Gangs:	Emerging Gangs:
Renegade Disciples	None
Black Peace Stones	
Latin Kings	
Gangster Disciples	
Manic Latin Disciples	
Vice Lords	

Section Thirteen

SECTION 14

Supporting The Chicago Crime Commission

ABOUT THE CHICAGO CRIME COMMISSION

The Chicago Crime Commission (CCC) is a non-governmental, not-for-profit, law-abiding force of corporate and civic leaders who work to reduce crime and violence and improve the quality of justice. It was founded in 1919, after a number of well-meaning citizens tried to combat lawlessness throughout the very early 1900s without success. The futility of the attempts was because of the failure to wage a continuous war. And so, there came the incentive to create a non-governmental, non-partisan group that would translate the desires of the law-abiding citizens into terms of practical operation. Thus, the Chicago Association of Commerce recommended that the Chicago Crime Commission be formed. Currently, the CCC consists of a membership of approximately 200 business and professional leaders.

One historical example of our impact is evidenced by the almost instant results the Chicago citizenry enjoyed with the formation of the Commission. In 1920, the Commission found an unacceptable 138 murder cases pending in the criminal court. One hundred and four defendants were at large on bail. One of the cases was eleven years old. At the insistence of the Commission, four judges were assigned to try murder cases only for a period of sixty days. At the end of that time, eighty-nine defendants were sent to the penitentiary for terms ranging from fourteen years to life. The murder rate in Chicago dropped fifty-one percent in the following year.

Our primary role has been to ensure that government and private entities work together, rather than separately, in dealing with guns, gangs, drugs, youth violence and other crime concerns. The Commission believes that no single resource can accomplish the enormous task of making our cities and communities safe.

It is able to act as a credible liaison between top decision makers in the public & private sectors due to its:

- non-partisan, non-governmental status
- long established relationships
- and unquestioned integrity.

It works with:

- law enforcement and criminal justice agencies
- public health
- education systems
- corporate entities
- researchers
- grass roots organizations
- and the general public.

Its fundamental policy is inclusive:

- we first determine the facts from all reliable sources and then develop the essential implementation plan by capitalizing on the judgment of the brightest people that can be assembled.

Government agencies are often, by their very nature, resistant or unable to change. The prominent, powerful voice of the Commission membership can provide the public backing, the resources or the "push" a system needs in order to move forward.

The Chicago Crime Commission often will place a spotlight on critical problems that are little known or often overlooked by other non-profit organizations, for example:

- child exploitation
- crime breeding properties
- early intervention programs for first time juvenile offenders
- human trafficking
- identity theft
- organized crime and corruption
- and street gang activity.

To support the Chicago Crime Commission activities and programs, send tax deductible contributions to:

Chicago Crime Commission
79 West Monroe, Suite 801
Chicago, IL 60603
312-372-0101 (phone)
312-372-6286 (fax)

A contribution form is available on page 267.

You may also make contributions through the CCC's secure website, www.chicagocrimecommission.org.

CHICAGO CRIME COMMISSION CONTRIBUTION FORM

(Please tear out this form on the dotted line and return it with your gift.)

I would like to contribute $_____ to the Chicago Crime Commission in support of the following activities, partnerships and programs:

■ Street gang research and reports

■ Rescue Illinois Kids — combating child exploitation, prostitution and trafficking

■ Project Safe Neighborhoods Community Engagement — a partnership to reduce gun violence

■ Community Youth Program — providing 'best practices' information on early intervention programming for delinquent youth

■ Anonymous Crime Reporting Hotline

■ The Business Assistance Network

■ Investigative Business Advisory Service

The Chicago Crime Commission is a 501(c)3 tax exempt charitable organization.

Name(s):_____

Company: _____

Title: _____

* Address: _____

* City:_____

* State: _____Zip:_____

* Phone: _____ Fax:_____

* E-mail: _____

_____ Check Enclosed   _____Visa   _____ MasterCard   _____ Amex

* Card Number:_____ Exp: _____

* Signature: _____

To make your contribution online, visit us at: www.chicagocrimecommission.org

Please make check payable to **Chicago Crime Commission** and mail to:

Chicago Crime Commission
79 West Monroe Street, Suite 801
Chicago, Illinois 60603

For additional information or to make an in-kind donation, please call 312-372-0101.

Citizens Combating Crime In Metropolitan Chicago Since 1919.

* Information is maintained confidentially and not sold to third parties.

Section Fourteen

Section Fourteen

Section Fourteen

NOTES

Interviewer: *You want to be an example to your little boy?*

Girl Gang Member: *Living in the hood, living as a gang banger, it's no life. I'm true to my gang. I be down for them. I do what I have to do for them but there's a time to chill...but being a gang banger is not easy. I live day by day, walk in the neighborhood with my son, thinking my son is going to get blasted with me.*

Interviewer: *And that's what happens because bullets don't have eyes.*

Girl Gang Member: *Exactly, the bullet has no name. My shorty's (baby) so innocent, he doesn't know he's helpless. I'd be afraid but I got to be a woman and keep on walking. I was a woman to get into the gang, then I got to be a woman to step forward for my son, be real.*

Interviewer: *Is it hard for you to be a Disciple and your brother to be a Latin King?*

Boy Gang Member: *Yep.*

Interviewer: *Do you love your brother or the gang more?*

Boy Gang Member: *I don't know man, it's kind of a hard question.*

Interviewer: *What if your brother came over and did something to one of your boys? Would you want to hurt your brother? That's blood.*

Boy Gang Member: *Naw, I wouldn't want to.*

Interviewer: *But would you?*

Boy Gang Member: *Yeah.*

Interviewer: *Do you know anybody close to you that you loved that was taken out?*

Boy Gang Member #2: *My cousin Oscar.*

Interviewer: *What happened to Oscar?*

Boy Gang Member #2: *Got shot in his neck.*

Interviewer: *How old was he?*

Boy Gang Member #2: *He was like 16.*